PIER 21

PIER 21: A HISTORY

Steven Schwinghamer and Jan Raska

UNIVERSITY OF OTTAWA PRESS

2020

Co-published by the **Canadian Museum of History,** *the* **Canadian Museum of Immigration** *and the* **University of Ottawa Press.**

The University of Ottawa Press gratefully acknowledges the support extended to its publishing list by the Government of Canada, the Canada Council for the Arts, the Ontario Council for the Arts, the Federation for the Humanities and Social Sciences through the Awards to Scholarly Publications Program, and the University of Ottawa.

Copy editing	Robbie McCaw
Proofreading	Susan James
Typesetting	John van der Woude, JVDW Designs
Cover design	Steve Kress
Cover image	SS *France* at the Halifax Ocean Terminals, ca. 1928. Russ Lownds, Collection of Shipsearch Marine, Capt. Hubert Hall; Canadian Museum of Immigration Collection (DI2013.1878.8).
Back cover image	Passengers of the refugee ship MV *Pärnu* pose by a Canadian Immigration sign near Pier 21, 1949. Canadian Museum of Immigration Collection (DI2014.666.12).

Library and Archives Canada Cataloguing in Publication

Title: Pier 21 : a history / Steven Schwinghamer and Jan Raska.
Names: Schwinghamer, Steven, 1976- author. | Raska, Jan, 1980- author.
Series: Mercury series. History.
Description: Series statement: Mercury series. History | Includes bibliographical references and index.
Identifiers: Canadiana (print) 20200180819 | Canadiana (ebook) 20200181092 | ISBN 9780776631363 (softcover) | ISBN 9780776629353 (hardcover) | ISBN 9780776631370 (PDF) | ISBN 9780776631387 (EPUB) | ISBN 9780776631394 (Kindle)
Subjects: LCSH: Ports of entry—Nova Scotia—Halifax—History—20th century. | LCSH: Canada—Emigration and immigration—History—20th century. | LCSH: Immigrants—Canada—History—20th century.
Classification: LCC JV7225 .S39 2020 | DDC 325.71—DC23

La Collection Mercure

Remarquablement canadienne et hautement spécialisée, la *Collection Mercure* réunit des ouvrages portant sur des recherches effectuées au Musée canadien de l'histoire, et elle s'appuie sur le savoir-faire des Presses de l'Université d'Ottawa. Mise sur pied en 1972, la *Collection Mercure* est le principal véhicule qu'utilise le Musée canadien de l'histoire pour publier ses recherches scientifiques. Elle comprend plusieurs contributions remarquables à l'histoire, à l'archéologie, à la culture et à l'ethnologie canadiennes. Les ouvrages de la série sont publiés en français ou en anglais, et ils comportent un résumé dans l'autre langue officielle.

The Mercury Series

Strikingly Canadian and highly specialized, the *Mercury Series* presents research from the Canadian Museum of History and benefits from the publishing expertise of the University of Ottawa Press. Created in 1972, the *Mercury Series* is the Canadian Museum of History's primary vehicle for the publication of academic research, and includes numerous landmark contributions in the disciplines of Canadian history, archaeology, culture and ethnology. Books in the series are published in either English or French, and all include a second-language summary.

How To Order

All trade orders must be directed to the University of Ottawa Press:

Web : www.press.uottawa.ca
Email : puo-uop@uottawa.ca
Phone : 613-562-5246

All other orders may be directed to either the University of Ottawa Press (as above) or to:

Canadian Museum of Immigration
Web: shop.pier21.ca/books
Email: shop@pier21.ca
Phone: 902-425-7770 ext. 227
Mail: Retail Services Canadian Museum of Immigration at Pier 21, 1055 Marginal Rd, Halifax, NS B3H 4P7

Canadian Museum of History
Web: http://www.historymuseum.ca/shop/#publications
Email: publications@historymuseum.ca
Phone: 1-800-5550-5 621 (toll-free) or 819-776-8387 (National Capital Region)
Mail: Mail Order Services Canadian Museum of History 100 Laurier Street Gatineau, QC, K1A 0M8

Pour commander

Les libraires et autres détaillants doivent adresser leurs commandes aux Presses de l'Université d'Ottawa :

Web : www.presses.uottawa.ca
Courriel : puo-uop@uottawa.ca
Téléphone : 613-562-5246

Les particuliers doivent adresser leurs commandes soit aux Presses de l'Université d'Ottawa (voir plus haut) ou :

Musée canadien de l'immigration
Web : magasinez.quai21.ca/books
Courriel : boutique@quai21.ca
Téléphone : 902-425-7770 poste 227
Courrier : Service de détail, Musée canadien de l'immigration, 1055, chemin Marginal, Halifax, N.-É. B3H 4P7

Musée canadien de l'histoire
Web : http://www.museedelhistoire.ca/magasiner/#publications
Courriel : publications@museedelhistoire.ca
Téléphone : 1-800-5550-5 621 (numéro sans frais) –819-776-8387 (région de la capitale nationale)
Poste : Service des commandes postales Musée canadien de l'histoire, 100, rue Laurier Gatineau (Québec) K1A 0M8

CONTENTS

LAND ACKNOWLEDGMENT

Pier 21 is located in Mi'kma'ki, the land of the Mi'kmaq.

The Mi'kmaq are the First People of Nova Scotia. For thousands of years they have lived in Mi'kma'ki, a territory encompassing Nova Scotia, Prince Edward Island, eastern and northern parts of New Brunswick, the Gaspé peninsula of Québec, and communities in Newfoundland and Maine. The Mi'kmaq have shared this unceded homeland with immigrant communities for more than 400 years.

All residents of Canada are part of the historical and legal relationships between Canada and Indigenous Peoples.

LIST OF ILLUSTRATIONS

33. Embarkation Transit Unit arch, with Pier 20 and Pier 21 in the background, 1946. H. B. Jefferson, Nova Scotia Archives (1992-304 no. 43-1-4 250)
34. A German prisoner of war arrives at "an East Coast Port," 1941. National Film Board of Canada, Library and Archives Canada, PA-176616
35. Flora and David Campbell (foreground) wave at personnel returning aboard HMT *Île de France* at Pier 21, 1945. Lieut. Richard Graham Arless, Canada. Department of National Defence, Library and Archives Canada, PA-192969
36. Members of the No. 6 District Military Band, ca. 1944. Canadian Museum of Immigration Collection (D12014.536.1)
37. Trudy Tansey and J. P. LeBlanc on their wedding day, 1944. Canadian Museum of Immigration Collection (D12015.255.101)
38. "Welcome Home to Canada" was the first view of Pier 21 for postwar immigrants, 1950. Canadian Museum of Immigration Collection (D12013.839.32)
39. Arrival of the first group of Polish veterans to Pier 21, aboard SS *Sea Robin*, 1946. Wilfred Doucette, National Film Board of Canada, Library and Archives Canada, PA-111595
40. Arthur J. Vaughan served as a Canadian customs officer at Pier 21 from 1945 to 1965 (n.d.). Canadian Museum of Immigration Collection (D12013.1250.2)
41. Arrival of a group of Jewish refugees and war orphans at Pier 21, 1949. Alex Dworkin Canadian Jewish Archives, Jewish Immigrant Aid Services fonds, PC 2-4-8A-8
42. Two young displaced persons, Moses Znaimer and Nasha Rosenberg, are featured on the front page of the *Standard Review* newspaper, June 26, 1948. Canadian Museum of Immigration Collection (D12014.515.2)
43. Arrival of 347 mostly Baltic refugees aboard SS *Walnut* at Pier 21, December 13, 1948. Photographer: Robert Norwood/*Chronicle Herald*. Republished with permission from the *Chronicle Herald*
44. The 50,000th displaced person to enter Canada, Ausma Levalds (centre), her mother, Karline (left), and sister Rasma (right) in front of Canadian immigration official Geoff Christie at Pier 21, February 23, 1949. Canadian Museum of Immigration Collection (D2013.1912.24)

56. Canadian Immigration Identification Card issued to Hungarian refugee, Tibor Lukács, at Pier 21, 1958. Canadian Museum of Immigration Collection (D12014.459.6)

57. Cuban refugees who defected from a Cubana airliner at Gander, Newfoundland, arrive at Halifax International Airport, November 3, 1964. Photographer: Ferris/*Chronicle Herald*. Republished with permission from the *Chronicle Herald*

58. Sister Salvatrice Liota (second from right) hands out gifts to Cuban refugees during Christmas celebrations, December 25, 1964. Photographer: Ferris/*Chronicle Herald*. Republished with permission from the *Chronicle Herald*

59. Veronika Martenová Charles in Cuba before her defection in Gander, Newfoundland, 1970. Canadian Museum of Immigration Collection (D12017.962.32)

60. View of Pier 21's front door, formerly a loading-bay door, and the ramp, 1990s. Canadian Museum of Immigration Collection (D12013.1231.1)

61. The central office bay at Pier 21, now the main entrance to the Canadian Museum of Immigration, 2015. Canadian Museum of Immigration, Communications

OPPOSITE: A young Italian immigrant resting in the Annex building at Pier 21 after coming to Canada aboard MS *Saturnia*, 1952. Photographer: Ethelbert Wetmore/*Chronicle Herald.*

Source: Republished with permission from the Chronicle Herald

INTRODUCTION

This is, in a sense, hallowed ground. It's a place of beginnings… if you can see on the horizon, on the ocean, just a tiny, tiny, red dot and that's where the sun is coming up, on the horizon, that's what I would see as Halifax, as Pier 21, and then as the sun rises and gives light to the entire spectrum of the land and the sea, then that becomes sort of like the picture of your life… you've got to start somewhere.[1]
—Mike Frederiksen, a Danish immigrant who arrived at Pier 21 aboard SS *Gripsholm* on June 29, 1951.

Halifax's Pier 21 is a place of beginnings. Between 1928 and 1971, nearly one million immigrants entered Canada at the site. This included those who arrived when immigration was restricted during the Great Depression, those who arrived as refugees or displaced persons after the Second World War, and those who arrived in later years of relative economic prosperity in Canada. These people began new chapters in their lives at Pier 21. As a key ocean transportation hub with good connections inland by rail, Pier 21 also served as a place of departure and return for the vast majority of Canadians serving overseas during the Second World War.

In completing the immigration process through Pier 21, immigrants could begin integrating into life in Canada. Most of those admitted arrived with some kind of plan for their new life, though that plan could be as small as just the promise of a job. For many, the day of arrival began the navigation of the often new and unfamiliar aspects of life in Canada: the language, social cues, and work habits that are part of everyday life. Arriving at Pier 21 was an important milestone for many immigrants, but the "Landed Immigrant" stamp obtained at the site rarely proved to be a ticket to a life of instant prosperity. Hard work and sacrifice often marked the initial phase of life in Canada. These experiences are part of the individual and family memories of hundreds of thousands of Canadians.

These personal connections are a point of pride and purpose for the Canadian Museum of Immigration, Canada's sixth national museum, which is responsible for exploring, interpreting, and presenting histories of immigration to Canada and Canadian immigrant experiences. The museum highlights these histories and memories from Pier 21 through the participation of those who lived them—those who passed through its doors on their way to a new life in Canada, the staff members who operated the site, and the many volunteers who provided services for newcomers.

These memories of Pier 21 are wide-ranging: the ship's arrival, the assembly room, the small-baggage check, the confiscated goods, the Canadian food, boarding the train, and the waiting, uncertainty, and anticipation. For Canadian soldiers going to war in Europe, and for the families of those who did not come back, Pier 21 hosts a completely diffferent set of memories. We know of these divergent memories from written testimonials, oral history interviews, and information derived from personal objects. Together they form a key component of this work. We hope to give these memories better context by developing a deeper picture of the history of Pier 21 as a place.

OPPOSITE: The Meijer family arrives at Pier 21 from the Netherlands aboard SS *Waterman*, 1957. *Source: Canadian Museum of Immigration Collection (DI2013.1558.65)*

This book is the first full-length history of Pier 21 produced by museum staff. The first published history of the site was a short work produced by Employment and Immigration Canada, published in 1978, partly as an acknowledgment of the end of the era of ocean immigration. After the site became a museum and acquired designation as a National Historic Site of Canada, other works emerged, including popular histories, books for children, and coffee-table books.[2] Most are based on the personal stories of people with connections to Pier 21. The strength of these personal stories has led to other artistic explorations, including plays, folk and classical music, and the name "Pier 21" appearing on everything from a tavern to a college rock band. The site was even considered one of the "Seven Wonders of Canada" in a Canadian Broadcasting Corporation competition.

Other immigration facilities in Canada have not attracted this kind of attention, largely because the buildings themselves no longer exist. A notable exception is Grosse Île, the former quarantine station in the St. Lawrence River for the port of Quebec. Like Pier 21, Grosse Île looms large in personal and community stories about coming to Canada, and to North America more broadly. Like Pier 21, it is also a National Historic Site of Canada, and commemoration there includes the Irish Memorial to those who perished of contagious diseases, especially during the Irish potato famine of 1845–1849. There are some written works on other sites connected to immigration in Canada, including those at Saint John, Quebec City, Toronto, Winnipeg, Victoria, and William Head—the quarantine station near Victoria—but there are few full-length histories of immigration processing facilities.[3]

The diverse stories people tell about their immigration experiences through Pier 21 sometimes conflict with historical accounts. It may appear as if there were a dozen immigration sheds at Pier 21, with welcomes ranging from sunny, and filled with cheery volunteers and courteous officials, to bleak and inhospitable. Even so, together these stories, with all their complexity and contradiction, form the basis of how we learn about not only this site but also about the initial personal experiences of immigration and adaptation in Canada. We have pieced together these accounts from written submissions or oral histories, complemented by archival documentation and secondary sources, photographs, and objects.

Chapter 1 of this book provides an overall summary of the experience of immigrating to Canada through Pier 21 during the years of its operation, from 1928 to 1971. The subsequent chapters are chronological, beginning in chapter 2 with a short history of the immigration facilities at Pier 2, which was the predecessor of Pier 21, as well as the construction of Pier 21 and the surrounding Ocean Terminals complex. Chapter 3 covers the wartime history of the site, when the major transit shed served as the principal embarkation point for Canada's military efforts. Chapter 4 outlines the massive postwar boom in immigration and the various groups that passed through Pier 21 up to the mid-1950s. Finally, chapter 5 traces the decline of Pier 21, from the mid-1950s through to 1971.

OPPOSITE: Dutch immigrants in the new assembly area at Pier 21, 1928–1930.

Source: Library and Archives Canada, C-036146

1 IMMIGRATING TO CANADA THROUGH PIER 21

1928–1971

My first steps in Canada took place at Pier 21. After surviving labour camps in Russia and refugee camps in Africa, my family made our way to England. Then, with the sponsorship of my brother Wacław (who had started farming in Canada after serving under British Command in the war), we finally had the opportunity to come to Canada. At Pier 21, we were processed by Canadian authorities, were welcomed onto Canadian soil and became Landed Immigrants. Our train pulled into Calgary in the early morning on August 2, 1952. We stepped from the train very weary, very dirty and with only $5.00 amongst the three of us.[1]

—Bronisława Glod (née Kowalewska), a Polish refugee who arrived at Pier 21 aboard SS *Neptunia* on July 27, 1952.

Bronisława Glod's arrival with her family in 1952 speaks to the place of Pier 21 in the memories of so many families: the spot where they took their first steps on Canadian soil, and where they were examined and granted status to enter the country. Most of the immigrants who entered Canada at Pier 21 had been rigorously screened abroad, but Pier 21 officials still had to verify a person and their belongings for admission into Canada. Therefore, the site provided efficient medical, civil, and customs examinations for passengers—being "processed," as Glod puts it. Along with the staff required for these inspections, volunteers stationed at Pier 21 from the Red Cross, Salvation Army, Young Men's/Young Women's Christian Association (YM/YWCA), Canadian Bible Society, Jewish Immigrant Aid Society (JIAS), and churches provided for the welfare of new arrivals. Each of these functions had a specific space assigned within the facility, which included everything from canteens to a small hospital.

The interior spaces at Pier 21 shifted somewhat over time: rooms in the immigration quarters were rearranged after a serious fire in 1944, and the Annex building acquired an addition in the early 1950s. However, the process for entry at Pier 21 remained largely constant given the major policy changes in immigration after the Second World War. Despite this, Pier 21 was not purpose-built for immigration.[2] Commercial interests and transportation companies controlled the ground floors of the sheds and the majority of the Ocean Terminals development around Pier 21. The immigration quarters, for inspecting and processing people—and detaining them if necessary—were located in the second storey of cargo shed 21 (Pier 21).

The immigration facility in shed 21 was around one hundred feet wide and just over five hundred feet long. While large, it was about half the size of the previous Halifax immigration quarters at Pier 2. However, the Canadian National Railway (CNR), as the owner of Pier 2 and the Halifax Ocean Terminals, constructed a smaller single-storey Annex building alongside shed 21 to provide space for customs examination, voluntary organizations, railway service, and passenger access to food. Overhead walkways connected the two buildings so that immigrants and staff could move safely above train sidings.

Inside the second-storey immigration quarters, the space was divided nearly evenly between a waiting and processing area and facilities for detaining people if needed. The mostly open space of the assembly area was a contrast to the complex floor plan of the detention area, which contained everything from secure strong rooms to a small hospital. Across the walkway, in the Annex building, passengers passed through customs processing and could meet there with charitable organizations or purchase food. In between the two buildings, several railway tracks provided space to marshal special trains to carry immigrants, visitors, and returning Canadians west to homes throughout Canada. Shortly after it opened, a covered walkway was built that extended up from the Annex building to the nearby railway hotel and station.

COMING TO CANADA THROUGH PIER 21

As ocean liners entered Halifax Harbour and drew up to Pier 21, many immigrant arrivals saw Canada for the first time. Carmen Wood (née Wright) immigrated to Canada from Malta in 1950 aboard SS *Nea Hellas*. She was nine years old when she arrived at Pier 21 with her family, and found that Halifax consisted of "green trees and the coloured rooftops," which were a striking contrast from the rocky island terrain of her Mediterranean home. Despite calling at Halifax, Wood carried on with her family to New York and entered Canada at Fort Erie, Ontario.[3] Depending on the time of year, some immigrants were less than enthusiastic upon reaching Halifax. Maria Scornaienchi (née Ammirato) arrived from Italy in January 1957 with her husband and daughter to be greeted with two metres of snow on the ground. She could not imagine walking in the wintry conditions, and because of the snow, she did not like her arrival in Canada at all.[4] Still others, like William Waterhouse, who arrived from Wales in 1948, were happy to see land at all after a tumultuous sea voyage: "Pier 21 was a welcome sight and dry land a gift from heaven."[5]

The formal process of entry for a passenger arriving at Pier 21 started with disembarkation from the ship directly into the immigration facility. A light, mobile gangway on the water side of the shed deployed from the second storey. The open space on the pier and the lower floor of the shed stored cargo and large baggage. This separation helped the security and efficiency of unloading the ships, but the gangway was experimental when the facility opened. About a week before the facility opened, steamship companies protested "[the] present plan for [a] working gangway."[6] They worried that if the gangway did not operate properly, it might prolong a ship's call at the port. The concerns were misplaced: after two weeks of operation, the senior immigration agent at Halifax noted that "twelve transatlantic steamers have docked to date with over 3,700 passengers, and so far none have had to land downstairs." This referred to the option to have passengers disembark on the brow of the pier if the gangway did not function properly or if more than one ship called at a time.[7]

In the mid-1920s, the immigration department called for a different location for its quarters in the Ocean Terminals complex precisely to accommodate more than one ship directly alongside the immigration pier. This arrangement would have required using a pier that jutted out into the harbour, and the department recommended using pier A (in the vicinity of the grain elevator, south of Pier 21).[8] Another agency recommended using the top floors of both Pier 21 and Pier 22 for immigration processing. This approach was not viable, as the project for the immigration department was already expensive and it could not justify the increase in construction costs, as well as in ongoing operations and payroll to maintain staff across two reception piers. Neither of these proposals was pursued, and the accommodation at Pier 21 was built, using the single gangway to access the second level. Nevertheless, the department learned to deal with days when multiple ships called on Halifax. Six ships called at once, for example, on April 6, 1930. If more than two ships were in, officers would often board a ship and conduct processing on board rather than disembarking passengers first.[9]

The immigration quarters in Pier 21 included a large assembly area immediately adjacent to the gangway, where passengers waited for inspection after their arrival. The assembly area was split in the middle by washrooms and a counter. The resulting two spaces were quite similar in size, each seating almost five hundred people on about ninety benches.[10] Both were open, airy spaces, with good natural light from the high windows on the roofline. When Pier 21 opened, the assembly area had partitions of chain-link-style fencing. After a fire destroyed the immigration quarters in 1944, the site was rebuilt with wire mesh partitions only in the medical inspection area. These partitions were removed in the 1950s, leaving the baggage cages as the only wire mesh enclosure in the assembly area. Along

View of Pier 21's gangway as passengers board SS *Ryndam*, ca. 1956.
Source: Canadian Museum of Immigration Collection (D12013.1682.14)

with the removal of some wire partitions, after the fire of 1944 the assembly area also reduced in size. Immigration offices were added within the northern section of the space, and washrooms at the southern end. This reduced the capacity for immigrants disembarking from a ship to just over four hundred at a time.[11]

Upon arrival, immigrants gathered in the assembly area, where they underwent medical screening.[12] They formed standing queues, and when the site opened the separations for the lines consisted of basic railings made of pipe fittings.[13] The priority of medical clearance reflected two important aspects of immigration policy and practice from the time of Pier 21's opening: the need to be alert for communicable diseases, and the persistent barriers to immigrants with certain, often chronic, medical conditions. Quarantine was sometimes a result. In the case of the family of twelve-year-old Hans Schlechta from West Germany, however, it was not unwelcome. His brother recalls that Hans had taken ill on board ship. Since they arrived on Christmas Eve, 1951, "it also meant that we had a place to stay over Christmas. I don't know what we would have done otherwise."[14] Once through the medical processing, immigrants proceeded to the civil examination lines. When it opened, Pier 21 was designed to accommodate five interviews at once, but later this expanded to eight or more desks for officers, due to an increase in ocean liner passenger traffic.[15] These were similar to the medical examination lines of standing queues separated by pipe-fitting rails.

The assembly area and examination rooms at Pier 21 reflected shifting Canadian practices in ocean immigration processing during the early twentieth century.[16] Instead of conducting interviews aboard ship before an immigrant was landed, Pier 21 incorporated space and infrastructure designed for this purpose. The examination facilities built on the experiences of the immigration department at Quebec City's Princess Louise Docks, which was the major port of entry at the time, and in Halifax at the previous facility at Pier 2. In these two facilities, several different building layouts, as well as the occasional use of shipboard examination, pointed to the importance of the open, sequenced spaces to help move immigrants through landing with less confusion or delay.

Even though this type of examination ashore was efficient for some ports of entry, it was not adopted as a universal method for all the major Canadian ocean immigration ports. Staff at the ports on the St. Lawrence River practiced shipboard examination, since officers could join ships from Pointe-au-Père, near Rimouski, where ships had to stop anyway in order to pick up their St. Lawrence River pilot. They could then complete much of the examination work before a vessel arrived at port, with the time savings compensating for the inconvenience of processing paperwork in a common area of a ship. This kind of arrangement was not feasible at Halifax.

These efforts to streamline immigration processing at Canadian ocean ports of entry also reflect the pressures from shipping companies to reduce their time waiting for passengers to be disembarked and examined. Standardized examinations could improve efficiency as well as fairness in the immigration process, and so informal manuals and procedures existed at busy ports of entry even before the creation of a formal Canadian immigration manual. When officials finally created that manual, in the 1950s, regulations indicated that examination "shall be conducted forthwith on shipboard, or on train, or at some other place designated for the purpose."[17]

By the mid-1950s, a number of factors influenced the disembarkation and examination of passengers at Halifax: time of arrival, number of ships to be examined, number and composition of passengers, estimated time of unloading of baggage, degree of urgency in departure for United States ports of entry, and the representations of Canadian customs officials. The immigration branch believed that commencing disembarkation and examination of passengers before the completion of baggage unloading was to the benefit of the Department of Citizenship and Immigration, and to the passengers themselves, as they could visit the canteen or restaurant, dispatch a cable, and be assisted by the voluntary service agencies.

To avoid overcrowding in the assembly area, immigration and customs officials agreed to restrict the number of disembarked travellers at any one time to three hundred individuals. Since Canadian citizens and returning residents were given priority in disembarkation and examination, and were less likely to use Pier 21's services, most complaints about the process and promptness of disembarkation came from this group of passengers.[18] Indeed, members of the Danish Johansen family recall a very orderly situation for the over three hundred passengers who joined them in the assembly hall after arrival in June 1957: a wait for their name to be called, an interview assisted by a translator, and a stamp marked "Landed Immigrant." "From the Pier 21 complex, we then walked through an overhead walkway to where a Canadian National Railway (CNR) train was waiting to take us to our promised job in western Canada."[19]

Beginning in 1960, the Department of Citizenship and Immigration provided immigration examinations on a twenty-four-hour basis, and Canadian customs officers followed suit the following year. However, the norm was still to wait for daylight hours, so that officials completed ship and passenger inspections by 1:00 a.m. each day, and ships that arrived after 9:00 p.m. waited until the following morning for customs inspection, due to the amount of time that it took to inspect each vessel. In 1963, the Canadian Council of Churches, which represented Protestant voluntary aid organizations stationed at Pier 21, informed Canadian immigration officials that ships from the General Steam Navigation Company of

Greece (known as the Greek Line) and Italia di Navigazione Società per azioni (the Italian Line) often arrived during the night and were immediately disembarking their passengers rather than waiting for daylight hours. Port workers representing the various Christian churches at Pier 21 reported that the situation caused unnecessary hardship to individuals and families with small children who did not speak English or French, and who had to navigate immigration and customs examinations "in an unfamiliar country under inconvenient and dispiriting circumstances."[20]

In order to prevent further complaints such as those put forward by the Canadian Council of Churches, the immigration branch instructed its officials at Pier 21 to process all passenger ships that arrived late at night the following morning. Ship officials did not always comply, which sometimes led to unpleasant passenger experiences. One February day in 1963, for example, Canadian immigration officials learned that late-night passenger disembarkation was occurring when a ship, behind in its itinerary, arrived at Halifax and needed to leave immediately for New York. MS *Saturnia* docked at Pier 21 at 10:20 p.m. Immigration examinations were completed at 1:15 a.m., followed by customs baggage inspection, and a train departure at 5:15 a.m. This was much to the condemnation of the voluntary service agencies who looked after the care and well-being of newcomers.[21]

MEDICAL SCREENING

Screening at night had long been a concern for quarantine and immigration doctors at Halifax. Due to a case of measles that developed in the immigration detention quarters in December 1937 after a late examination, Department of Pensions and National Health officers supported a ruling by immigration officials that examinations had to be completed by 10:30 p.m. If a passenger liner arrived after this time, it was to be held for processing until the following morning. One immigration medical officer noted to his superiors in Ottawa that "this ruling was made as it was not thought human to keep the children up at unearthly hours."[22] While this was an important consideration, medical officials were more preoccupied with preventing the spread of contagious diseases on land.

While transportation companies opposed anything causing delays to their ships, medical officials disapproved of late-night passenger disembarkation because certain diseases could not be readily detected and diagnosed by artificial light, which was generally not of good quality in the early twentieth century. Under the 1903 International Sanitary Convention, to which Canada was a signatory, the clearing of ships was not to be conducted during the night. The convention provided no exceptions to this rule on the grounds of commercial interest. In addition, during the early years of operation at Pier 21, nightly medical inspections were not feasible because only one quarantine officer was stationed at the port of Halifax, who normally began work between 6:00 a.m. and 7:00 a.m. Therefore, it was not usually possible to call upon the official in the evenings.

Another reason why medical officials preferred not to perform screenings at night was that, in the case of a ship's late arrival, officials ushered many immigrants into a limited number of available rooms in Pier 21's accommodation quarters to await processing the following morning. Medical officials noted that the facility had poor ventilation and bad air quality, especially if the steam heat was operating during the winter season. Medical officials were concerned about the higher probability of an infectious disease breaking out in the rooms, which could lead to greater exposure and months-long detention for all associated passengers.[23]

Medical clearance had the highest priority among the checks of arriving passengers. This remained true throughout Pier 21's years of operation. During the busiest years at the site, immediately after the Second World War, the expansion of points of origin for immigrants to Canada outstripped overseas medical infrastructure, which led to a renewed emphasis on careful medical examination of immigrants at their point of entry in Canada.[24] Reflecting this priority, the medical facility was the only part of the offices at Pier 21 that was regularly improved and expanded after 1954.[25] Indeed it was in 1954 that officials temporarily detained the family of seventeen-year-old Vera Lamm, from West Germany, due to a Canadian doctor aboard having neglected to add to her mother's passport a medical approval stamp for her little sister. "After a bit of a kerfuffle, we were ordered to stay in a big room with many other people, then our mother, Dagi and I were driven by a very nice man in blue uniform... Policeman? Immigration

Officer?... to the Halifax hospital, where Dagi was X-rayed...After Dagi had her X-ray taken, we were returned to the detention centre at Pier 21. At 6 p.m. we were informed that my sister's health was fine."[26]

The importance of medical clearance meant that the first inspection that passengers underwent at Pier 21 was medical screening. Carried out by doctors employed by Immigration Medical Services under the auspices of the Department of Health (rather than Immigration), this was generally only a confirmation of paperwork and current good health. Potential immigrants went through more detailed screening abroad before being allowed to travel to Canada.[27] For example, Albert Bekkers, prior to leaving the Netherlands for Canada in 1952, recalls that his family had

> at least 40 forms which had been filled out for such things as permission to leave Holland, medical examinations, visas, and permission to enter Canada... other papers were required for such things as passports, X-ray reports, and vaccination reports for smallpox. When the time came for the medical examination the whole family had to go to Den Haag to visit the Canadian doctors. There you can get a stamp on your passport "Passed" which means you have passed your medical examination. But you could also get a stamp "3A" which means "high risk."

The Bekkers family passed their medical examinations and were cleared for immigration to Canada.[28] The circumstances of travel sometimes meant that a person could be injured or develop an illness between their medical clearance and arrival in Canada, and in those circumstances, or if other conditions were suspected, a doctor could conduct a more thorough secondary examination in one of the nearby examination rooms.

Pier 21 opened just as radical shifts in public health began to affect immigration practice, which meant that medical examination at the site was most often a formality. There was a strong historical connection between developments in public health practices and medical services for immigrants in Canada. Halifax and Pier 21 offer a good example of this relationship: medical care and expertise around immigration was a lively local political issue, as the city had been affected by cholera outbreaks and scares in the nineteenth century.[29] The formalization of quarantine facilities and the assignment of permanent medical staff to immigration duties reduced the risk of disease in the city. However, the largest change in public health related to immigration was the requirement for thorough pre-screening before a person could obtain a visa to come to Canada as a prospective immigrant. This change was connected with the technical and scientific advances in medicine at the turn of the twentieth century.

These advances, including such significant steps as common vaccination and the ability to identify pathogens using microscopes, substantially altered the need for and role of medical examination at Canada's ports of entry over just a few decades, from 1900 to the 1920s.[30] Indeed, within a few years of Pier 21 opening, Canada set about closing its ocean quarantine sites. Nevertheless, the site had a complete medical suite, including examination rooms, offices, a surgery, and, later, X-ray, quarantine, and laboratory facilities.[31] Although the majority of the medical service rooms were located waterside on the second floor of shed 21, near the assembly area, which served inspection needs, there was a small hospital and an associated surgical ward at the far north end of the immigration quarters in the interior of the building, with windows looking north over Pier 20.[32]

With the restrictions on immigrants with medical ailments, situations arose regularly that required the attention of medical staff. For example, medical emergencies that arose onboard ship were dealt with by the doctors and nurses on site and sometimes entailed transit to a local hospital. If an illness or medical condition was missed during examination abroad but was evident either after the journey by ship or during the examination at Pier 21, the secondary examination rooms could be used by medical branch staff to assess and diagnose the immigrant. Emergent illnesses were not uncommon at Pier 21, as minor communicable diseases could flare up aboard ship. Children were particularly vulnerable, and shipboard outbreaks of diseases like measles show up with some regularity in the early passenger lists of vessels arriving at Pier 21. Despite advances in care, such cases could still lead to tragedy. A five-year-old Polish girl, Stefania Piasta, died of measles in Pier 21's Immigration Hospital on March 24, 1937.[33] She was the youngest in a large family, headed to western Canada, who had arrived at Pier 21 earlier that month.[34]

Chickenpox was another contagious disease that appeared aboard ship or within the immigration facility. Lloyd Hirtle served as medical doctor at Pier 21 between 1949 and 1958. Hirtle witnessed first-hand how a child's medical condition directly affected family members: "I had a little child in this ward… with chickenpox… the father… in spite of using all the interpreters that were available… came into visit his child that day and the next thing we know—there was a door here onto the roof of Pier 20… and he went flying out that door… a fire exit. And then he just turned and down here, flopped—went right off the end of the pier and broke both of his legs on the pier down below… he thought his child who was sick… had a fatal disease. But it was just chickenpox."[35]

If there was a larger problem with infectious disease aboard ship, the medical staff collaborated with the staff at the quarantine facility on Lawlor's Island, in Halifax Harbour, until the closure of the facility in 1936, or the infectious disease hospital in the North End of Halifax. Other, happier medical interventions were also sometimes needed for immigrants upon arrival, including care for newborns. Pregnant women were usually transferred to the Grace Maternity Hospital or to the Halifax Infirmary for delivery of their babies.[36] Medical staff at Pier 21 also addressed prospective immigrants with mental illness and recent arrivals who had received landed immigrant status but became mentally ill shortly after arriving in Canada, as mental illness would place an immigrant in a prohibited category under the Immigration Act. This involved co-operation with other hospitals, including the Nova Scotia Hospital, and generally resulted in deportation.

Besides the work of screening and assessing immigrants in the immigration facility, immigration or customs staff also availed themselves of medical care from the onsite doctor to treat minor ailments while at work, such as strep throat.[37] Some members of the port's medical establishment also served as quarantine or immigration doctors who regularly boarded vessels prior to their docking.[38] They boarded the large passenger ships via a modest rope ladder, often in inclement weather or at night. This form of screening was intended to prevent any communicable disease from reaching the port itself. The procedure of screening immigrants depended on the self-reporting of each ship's captain and raising the yellow quarantine flag, if necessary. There were severe penalties for a captain who docked a ship needing quarantine without signalling it.

Medical officers were expected to effectively screen hundreds of immigrants each day. Occasionally immigrants who appeared healthy but in reality were carrying contagious illnesses led doctors to misdiagnose them upon examination. Such results could lead to public embarrassment and controversy. In late April 1929, Dr. Judson Graham, a quarantine officer stationed at Pier 21, examined a sick immigrant aboard the British steamer SS *City of Hereford* who appeared to have a case of chickenpox. Graham notified Department of Pensions and National Health that he "saw a case of chickenpox on board this vessel... from the character and distribution of the rash I had no hesitation in making a diagnosis of chickenpox."[39] After the ship left Halifax and entered Boston Harbor, an American quarantine officer diagnosed the immigrant with a case of smallpox. Much to the embarrassment of Canadian medical officials, the *Halifax Evening Mail* reported that the SS *City of Hereford* arrived at Halifax and departed later for Boston after Canadian officials had "given a clean bill of health" to the ship's passengers.[40] Graham left the quarantine service and returned to private practice in 1930.[41]

IMMIGRATION INTERVIEW

Once through their medical screening, immigrants had to satisfy immigration officers that they met the requirements of the Immigration Act. Again, potential immigrants prepared for this process before coming to Canada. They made inquiries and arrangements in advance to ensure their economic situation passed muster, as well as to determine their desirability from the point of view of the political and security concerns of the day.

Thus the process at Pier 21 consisted mainly of potential immigrants demonstrating to immigration officials that they had already cleared all the necessary checks abroad. Where possible, officials dealt with an entire family group at once, rather than individually.[42] The preliminary overseas screening made the process quick: it could take as little as two or three minutes for a single immigrant with sound paperwork to pass the civil examination.[43] Immigration regulations required officials to examine incoming passenger traffic, whether onboard ship or upon disembarkation, and immigrants were still vulnerable to refusal at the port of entry. However, the vast majority of travellers first satisfied Canadian authorities abroad of their fitness to enter the country, and had the paperwork to prove it. Therefore, Pier 21 was part of a functional Canadian border that reached across the ocean and took several months to transit.

The practice of rigorous screening overseas meant that the rate of detention or refusal for newly arrived immigrants was generally low: potential immigrants who might be considered undesirable were often refused before they could board a ship to come to Canada. However, minor issues with health or with practical arrangements meant that some immigrants were detained at Pier 21 after their medical and civil examinations. Fred von Ompteda and his family arrived from West Germany in March 1953, only to learn "the news that our papers were not in order… even though my Uncle had very good connections here in Canada… in effect we were literally held behind bars for three days in a very grey holding area of the harbour; so welcome indeed!"[44] Other immigrants had issues with transportation to their final destination. In April 1953, Connie Uyterlinde and her family arrived from the Netherlands. They headed to Prince Edward Island, but Uyterlinde recalls that "we missed the train and were detained for the weekend in the detention facility… I was with my mother while my brothers stayed with my father in separate quarters… during our weekend stay we wandered through the Volunteer Annex where we were given ditty bags… toothpaste, soap, etc. … the following day… Monday… we boarded the train to PEI."[45]

The interview by immigration officers was the critical process at Pier 21, resulting in an immigrant receiving status as a landed immigrant. When Pier 21 opened in 1928, passenger entries into Canada were processed based on a long form of a ship's manifest, prepared by the ship's purser and submitted on arrival in Canada. The immigration officers verified—and sometimes corrected or expanded upon—the information on that page, but it functioned as the official record of entry and was consulted if needed to validate a person's entry later, such as for naturalization in Canada. The passenger manifest highlighted key pieces of information important for admission into Canada—points that would remain significant as the

A Canadian immigration officer interviews an immigrant at Pier 21, 1965. Ship crew members, seen here in white uniforms, sometimes assisted with translation.
Source: Canadian Museum of Immigration Collection (R2013.1362.186)

paperwork changed in the 1950s, to one form per person rather than a large manifest. Passengers generally were prepared for the questions, based on interviews and examinations in order to obtain visas or other permissions, before they departed for Canada.

The arrival paperwork generally covered the details of a person's claim for landing as an immigrant in Canada: their name, age, birthplace, and nationality; if they had been in Canada before; if they were literate; how their passage was paid; their former trade or occupation, and their intended employment in Canada; their destination in Canada; the name and address of their nearest relative in their country of origin; details such as their passport information and the amount of money in their possession; and a medical declaration.

Once passengers arrived at Pier 21, processing was not necessarily alphabetical or by class of transit. One immigration officer, Bill Marks, describes it simply as "first come, first serve," although this was based on how a ship's crew might disembark their passengers.[46] An immigration official matched up the paperwork from the ship with the arriving passenger, and then an immigration officer conducted a brief interview to verify the information. After the Second World War, a separate officer conducted a secondary examination if needed. If an officer had a sense of trouble around a case, they kept their own line moving and sent the immigrant along to another officer for resolution. If the issue was that an immigrant lacked funds, officers had some discretion to release small amounts of money to help the individual make a few necessary purchases. Otherwise, if the papers an immigrant presented were in order, the interview was quite limited.[47]

Sometimes the issues were not resolved immediately. For instance, Ágnes Simó (née Szabó) and her family arrived in Canada as refugees from Hungary in 1957 and were slated by the federal government to be sent to Winnipeg for employment placement. However, her husband knew of an opportunity in Guelph, Ontario. He followed up the opportunity, and then he alone was permitted to proceed to Guelph while the rest of the family remained in detention until the immigration authorities could verify the job and settlement arrangements. After a few days, his employer, General Electric, was in touch with the immigration department, and officials released the rest of the family to join him in Guelph.[48]

James Braiden arrived in April 1949 from Ireland and remembers how difficult it was to collect the necessary documentation in order to immigrate to Canada: "In those days it was so tough… you had to have [a] medical, you had to have an X-ray, you had to have permission from the Priest or a Minister. You had to have a letter from the Garda Síochána, which is the police, and then you had to have… a letter from a school teacher and two letters of reference… I had to have a letter from my father. I still have the letter giving permission to the Cunard Shipping Line that I was allowed to [immigrate]."[49] His arrival processing was not as complex as all the paperwork might suggest: one of the immigration officers was a family friend, and called him through for the interview as one of the first passengers disembarking from the ship. He passed through the site without much wait and remained in Halifax, where his sister was already a resident.[50]

Braiden's letter from the Irish police service points to the growing priority, in the postwar years, for security screening of immigrants arriving into Canada. Although the apparatus for security verification grew into a complex system involving the Royal Canadian Mounted Police (RCMP) and co-operation with other government departments, it was often out of view of the immigrants themselves and did not necessarily bear on their experience at Pier 21. Still, the politics and concerns of the Cold War were important undercurrents in Canada's immigration policies during the busiest years at Pier 21. Siegfried Speck came to Canada in April 1965 from West Germany. Before receiving his visa in West Germany, he was questioned about "East and West relations… because the Cold War was on and we were very close to the east border." Speck was not much interested in politics, and so was cleared for security after answering "a lot of questions."[51]

Despite the security process largely being a function of co-operation with authorities overseas, security measures did occasionally impinge on arriving immigrants, even those who passed their initial screening. The internal security at Pier 21 led Corrado and Filomena Recchiuti, who came to Canada from Italy in 1951, to feel that the immigration building was like a jail, with gates and guards controlling the movements of passengers. They were directed by guards from point to point within the site, and they remember the immigration staff as police, lining them up in spaces with screens and barriers. It left the Italian couple with a bad impression of Pier 21.[52] Other immigrants could be detained upon arrival, say on the pretence of poor health, only to discover later that their security screening had revealed a concern to Canadian officials.

With all the preparation, many immigrants recall that the process was quite swift. Nicholas Sbarra arrived in Canada in June 1951 as an Italian refugee displaced by territorial change when his hometown of Fiume (now Rijeka, Croatia) was annexed by Yugoslavia after the Second World War. He recalls that at Pier 21 passengers were able to move through the site very quickly because everyone had their pre-approvals in order.[53] Once through the civil examination, foreign passengers who were admitted obtained their status as landed immigrants or received temporary visas according to their needs and circumstances. Returning Canadian residents were also examined and readmitted to Canada.

During Pier 21's years of operation, certain barriers remained for potential immigrants and the officials. For example, foreign languages were a substantial challenge at Pier 21. Although the immigration department had some translators for major European languages such as German and Italian, officers would often also solicit the aid of passengers who spoke English or French along with a language in common with their fellow

Immigration staff at Pier 21, ca. 1950.
Source: Canadian Museum of Immigration Collection (DI2014.240.5)

travellers. This was an important but informal support for the interviews conducted at the site.

Interviews, in particular secondary examination and the creation of records for each arriving individual, required the support of a substantial bureaucracy. Pier 21 opened with only a few private staff offices for senior inspectors and a stenographer. The majority of staff work in support of immigration took place in an open office area situated between the assembly and examination areas and the detention quarters on the upper floor of Pier 21.[54] When a fire in 1944 thoroughly destroyed the building, including the office spaces, where typewriters were melted into the remains of desks, it offered some opportunity for changes throughout the structure.[55]

In the office area, for example, the chief and duty guards' rooms became a boardroom where boards of inquiry to determine an immigrant's admissibility or deportation often took place.[56] This expanded on a long-standing practice in the immigration department of having travelling and senior inspectors rotate through ports to ensure front-line workers were up to date and enforcing regulations appropriately.[57] Later in its operation, Pier 21 also hosted immigration operations beyond the day-to-day processing and detention or accommodation of newcomers. The immigration department moved its Atlantic district headquarters into Pier 21 in 1953, coinciding with renovations to the Annex building.[58]

ACCOMMODATION AND DETENTION

The efficiency of overseas screening and thorough preparation by most immigrants meant that they entered Canada through Pier 21 never encountering the immigration facility's detention quarters. Pier 21 operated two levels of detention quarters. One was for people held due to minor but resolvable issues with their immigration, including lack of personal funds upon entry, employment arrangements that fell through, or incomplete documentation. The other level of detention was for people held because officials considered them likely to flee detention, or who posed serious criminal or security risks.

Immigrants who needed to exchange foreign currency could also be detained if their funds could not otherwise be converted to Canadian currency. At Pier 21, the Canadian Pacific Railway (CPR) and the CNR operated a money exchange office. Every four weeks, the railway companies alternated in handling the duties of the office. In September 1933, the CPR and CNR notified immigration officials that they would not be present to handle money exchanges for all ship arrivals. As a result, some immigrants were detained at Pier 21 until their funds could be processed. That same month, Czechoslovak immigrant Apolonie Dinčík arrived at Pier 21. She arrived in Canada seven months pregnant, along with her seven-year-old daughter, Maria. Destined for Jasper, Alberta, where Dinčík's husband, Mike, resided, they had to wait in Halifax with their 500 Czechoslovak crowns because the money exchange office was closed. The CPR, which operated the office that month, advised Canadian immigration officials that they were exchanging only American, French, Italian, and British funds.[59] Despite this temporary setback, the Dinčíks were able to move freely within the facility and eventually headed west to their final destination.

Immigrants who were in the larger detention dormitories were generally free to come and go during the day, but had to respect a nightly curfew. People held closely, on the other hand, were actually in barred cells.[60] The dormitories were later simply called "accommodation" quarters, and this was a good descriptive label. These larger rooms housed groups of immigrants pending the resolution of minor issues or addressing family members' health. The dormitories housed 150 guests. As an assistant matron at Pier 21, Mary Horwill recalls that as a ship arrived, she would ensure that the dormitories were ready, and that women and children generally stayed together while men stayed in a separate dormitory.[61] Although families might be separated by gendered sleeping quarters, the rest of the accommodations space was shared, so that they could take meals as a group or pass time together during the day. When Pier 21 opened, the dormitories were further segregated between British subjects and "foreign" immigrants, a discriminatory separation that both the department and the press supported.[62] This resulted in four detention quarters, with a fifth designated for members of ships' crews detained for immigration matters.

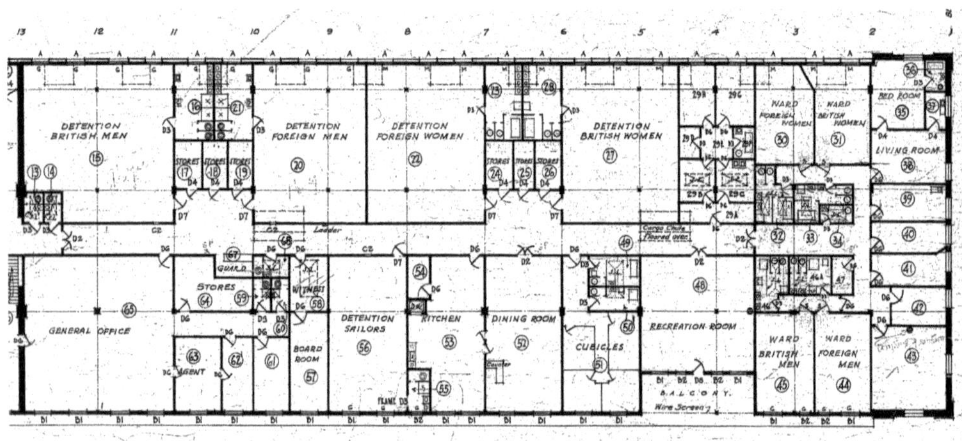

A 1928 floor plan of Pier 21, cropped to show detention quarters. *Source: Halifax Port Authority*

An immigrant family looks out onto Halifax Harbour from the detention quarters' airing gallery, 1951. *Source: York University Libraries, Clara Thomas Archives and Special Collections, Toronto Telegram fonds, ASC01295*

Furnishings in the accommodation dormitories were simple iron bunk beds, and each large room had an adjoining washroom with tubs, later showers. Floor coverings were mastic, to permit flushing with a hose. In the detention rooms, as well as hospital wards and lavatories, steel-barred gratings on the men's windows and heavy iron mesh on the women's windows prevented detainees from escaping.[63] Immigration guards controlled access to and from the space, but, within it, recreation areas, airing galleries, and dining facilities provided some comfort and leisure to the immigrants who had to wait before carrying on to their final destinations.[64] Detainees used the recreation area to stage entertainment if they were there over a holiday, as did the passengers of SS *Walnut* during the Christmas season in 1948.[65] Fourteen-year-old passenger Hans Leppik recalls: "[W]e had Christmas parties. The Salvation Army, I remember, brought presents, and it was good—for a child… other than the Christmas parties and that, everybody was happy that we made it, and looking forward to going on from there, getting jobs."[66] Pier 21's matrons were charged with the welfare of immigrants held in the detention quarters, and one lived on site in a small apartment for most of the immigration facility's years of operation.[67] These matrons were of equivalent rank to immigration officers.

During the Second World War, one of the most common circumstances that led to detention at Pier 21 was a refusal by merchant sailors to accept a shipping assignment. This would land them in detention lasting from a few days to several weeks. Immigration matters around merchant shipping could be particularly complex during wartime. Crews might be comprised of neutrals or sailors born in enemy territory, and so the work of officers in resolving the cases and of guards in maintaining detention for those refusing shipping assignments meant that Pier 21 and the affiliated shipping branch office were just as busy with immigration matters during the war as during the 1930s.

One significant wartime case involved a German-born but British-naturalized seaman who assaulted a guard after a hunger strike, while awaiting a ship. The sailor was brought on charges and transferred to a city jail. Fenton Crosman, an immigration inspector at the time, describes many of the sailors as "frightened neutrals," and notes that "one cannot blame them for wanting to remain on land." The situation led to a mass hunger strike in 1940, wherein seamen incarcerated at the city jail for declining work on ships demanded transfer to the immigration detention quarters, which they perceived as better quality accommodation and more suitable to their predicament. In March 1942, when the number of detainees reached over 170, it appeared that the wish to be held at Pier 21 may have been granted to too many seamen.[68] Although detention in Pier 21 was generally brief, there are several known cases of merchant seamen and immigrants residing in the immigration quarters for several months.[69]

Confinement in the strongrooms was less common, and only occurred when staff was concerned about violence or with people thought to be likely to flee detention, or who posed a significant criminal or, as during the Cold War, security risk. In those cases, staff had access to restraints appropriate for containing a dangerous prisoner.[70] A person being detained passed through a rigorous search of their person and their property, with items down to toiletries being retained and receipted. In later periods, their clothing was exchanged for coveralls. Guards avoided conversation with detainees outside of what was necessary for the completion of their duties.[71]

Kitchen staff at Pier 21, ca. 1950.
Source: Canadian Museum of Immigration Collection (D12014.437.3)

SERVICES AT PIER 21

Prospective immigrants were often in the building at Pier 21 for several hours, even if they were not detained, so meals were a necessity. Passengers also often needed food for their onward journey by train. In the earlier twentieth century, officials viewed food as a requirement for immigrants before they were permitted to carry on from Halifax, but this ceased as more immigrants were able to purchase food during the journey. At Pier 21, the kitchen staff and other staff and religious organizations provided some necessities on a charitable basis. Steamship companies could be billed if they transported someone without sufficient funds to look after themselves. This practice followed from advice given on behalf of the Commissioner of Immigration, in 1920, that detaining someone for a lack of food was more expensive than simply providing it.[72] Often, the reasons for an immigrant's detention were interconnected. If an ocean passenger dispensed their remaining funds in order to pay for their travel, they would be left with no financial resources to purchase food. Upon arriving in Canada, they could be deemed by Canadian officials as likely to become a public charge, which further exacerbated their circumstances.

Food service at Pier 21 included two dining areas. The main dining room operated continuously to serve staff and detained immigrants as part of the immigration quarters on the second floor of Pier 21. There was also a second dining facility in the Annex building, near the waiting areas.[73] Immigrants did not always use this facility, especially in later years when the level of traffic diminished.[74] As early as 1964, the Departments of Public Works and Citizenship and Immigration (DCI) were considering closing the Annex dining area as surplus to needs, and tendering for removal of the kitchen equipment. The National Harbours Board, however, was not interested in reclaiming the space and reducing the rent for the immigration facilities. As a result, no changes occurred to the Annex dining area.[75]

The Annex building did feature one popular and much-used additional food service: the canteen. It offered a modest grocery selection alongside the prepared meals sold in the dining area.[76] Customs officers often confiscated food items intended to sustain immigrants on their journey by train, and so the food available for purchase from the canteen was their only option for sustenance.[77] However, the culture shock at the change in food was often profound. The need to care for children led to another food-related cultural collision at Pier 21: immigrant women often breastfed their infants in the public waiting areas, which was a practice at odds with Canadian social norms at the time.[78]

The dining areas and the exchanges around food were one of the first markers for many immigrants of the differences and unfamiliarity of their new home, but also an opportunity for comfort or reassurance. Milan Gregor arrived from Czechoslovakia in May 1951. He successfully cleared immigration and customs and made his way to the dining hall, where he received his first meal on Canadian soil. Gregor remembers that "many were still seasick and the texture of the nourishment did not help. Compared to European wieners, the hot dogs were tasteless and the mustard too sweet. Along with the hot dog came a slice of white, square pieces of tasteless sponge. All of us, used to European rye bread or white rolls, did not recognize it as… standard Canadian bread. Today I like it, but only as a breakfast toast with jam."[79]

Charitable organizations sometimes distributed snacks to newcomers, whether promotional items like cereal boxes or donated treats for a holiday.[80] Social services were a significant presence at Pier 21, to the extent that they had their own dedicated spaces. This followed the practice in Halifax, as well as at other Canadian ocean ports of entry, of not only permitting but facilitating the work of these voluntary and charitable agencies.

Voluntary service organizations, port chaplains, and churches maintained representatives at Pier 21 throughout its years of operation. These volunteers were stationed in the Annex building, although their location changed with the building renovations of 1953–1954. When the facility opened in 1928, the social services operated out of an open office area on the ground level, between the waiting and dining areas. After the addition to the Annex building, the agencies moved upstairs to a new space, near the entrance into the Annex from the ramp.[81] When the facility was under construction, a number of the voluntary aid organizations wrote to protest the inadequate accommodation. They felt that the open space allocated to them was "so unsuitable that we cannot make use of it" and that the space did not reflect the need for discretion and privacy that was an essential part of the social and religious organizations' support work.[82] The space was changed during the renovations to the immigration and customs quarters in 1953, but it was still not quite the private office arrangements that the organizations had requested.[83] So as Canadian officials were responsible for processing immigrants at Pier 21, the voluntary service agencies had the work of receiving newcomers in inadequate facilities amid changing immigration regulations.

Many immigrants recall charitable workers at Pier 21. Some were happy to encounter a person who spoke a familiar language or who had a newspaper in their native tongue.[84] The work of these organizations could reach beyond the moments of arrival at the Pier, too. Sometimes either the port chaplains or members of another organization supported a detained immigrant as well, either to assist them in the process of immigrating or simply to find some form of solace for them as they waited for their status to be resolved.[85] For Sister of Service Adua Zampese, the experience of immigrating to Canada was personal. In February 1957, Sister Zampese and her brother, Sergio, left Italy for Canada. They arrived at Pier 21 and later met their father in Saskatchewan. Their mother and two sisters followed two years later. In 1968, Sister Zampese was sent to Halifax on a religious mission. She remembers assisting immigrants at Pier 21:

> [W]ith the benefit of having lived eleven years in Canada by then, I understood much more the part the sisters... played in the lives of... immigrants, helping them in whatever way possible, as they stepped from the ship in to Pier 21, through customs, interpreting for them, helping them to stop for the journey ahead... I smiled and understood their surprise when they purchased sliced bread... placing phone calls to relatives in different parts of Canada, for me it was a going back in time to when my brother and I came.[86]

During the immigration facility's years of operation, the religious groups occasionally copied by hand from ships' manifests any information about an immigrant's denomination and intended destination in order to coordinate their arrival with a local parish. As privacy rules changed in the 1970s, this practice stopped.[87]

One banner facility at Pier 21 for the voluntary agencies was the Seaport Nursery, operated by the Canadian Red Cross. By the early twentieth century, several of the Canadian ocean ports of entry featured nurseries staffed by the Red Cross to provide assistance for immigrants upon entry. In Halifax, the Red Cross maintained a nursery and kitchen at Pier 2 in a separate office after the First World War, and their staff moved with the rest of the personnel associated with immigration from Pier 2 to Pier 21 in March 1928.[88] In December 1928, Red Cross personnel reviewed the new quarters for the nursery, and sent a report to their commissioner: "[W]e are very pleased with the splendid place that has been allotted to the Red Cross Nursery...our rooms are spacious, well heated and well lighted, both with window space and artificial lighting."[89]

The Red Cross Seaport Nursery included a rest area, a kitchenette, and a large lavatory, as well as a storage area, and was initially located in the northwest area of the Annex building, close to dining facilities and the religious institutions' shared office area.[90] Immigrants proceeded through the Annex building from the south (customs) to the north (waiting,

A Red Cross volunteer supervises immigrant children in the Seaport Nursery at Pier 21, ca. 1963. *Source: Canadian Museum of Immigration Collection (D12014.222.8)*

dining, and social service areas), so the nursery was in one of the last areas they encountered before departing Pier 21 by train. It was also very convenient to the general waiting area for immigrants. The Red Cross enjoyed substantial success in drawing immigrants, particularly women and children, to their facility for some comfort or care.[91] English war bride Mary Bourgeois, who arrived at Pier 21 in July 1944, recalls how Red Cross volunteers looked after her son, Peter, while she went to find their baggage: "They… changed him and fed him and put him in a little cot… it certainly was a marvelous welcome as I could never have managed if I had to have carried Peter and then they mixed a bottle of food for him for on the train. They used their own nappies and gave me two for on the way and they gave us tea and sandwiches."[92] When an addition was created on the south end of the Annex building, in 1953, the nursery relocated to a newly built area, the second floor of the Annex building, beside where the ramp between Pier 21 and the Annex building exited.[93] It retained distinct rest areas, as well as a kitchenette and a lavatory, and a small office area.

The mission of the nursery remained constant during the immigration facility's years of operation. The volunteers focused on providing for the welfare of mothers and children, but also donated necessities as much as possible to any immigrants passing through, including those being deported. The volunteers, armed with key phrases in common languages for newcomers, as well as coffee, tea, biscuits, and articles of clothing, tried to settle and reassure immigrants and ensure they were prepared for their journey.[94] If immigrants came off a ship with infants or very small children, a representative often invited them to settle their children in the nursery during their wait for processing. Occasionally, the wait might be for some hours: mothers would come and go from the room to feed and change their babies. Services included playpens for toddlers and colouring materials or other activities for older children.[95]

Although the Red Cross and its staff had immediate and practical work at Pier 21, they were also aware of working in a larger ideological context at a Canadian border point. In a "memorandum presented by the social workers at Halifax," prior to the 1928 opening of Pier 21 as an immigration port of entry, concerned churches and welfare organizations, in a submission to the department, asked that immigrants be put in touch with their respective churches and social-welfare organizations upon arriving in Canada. These aid organizations sought to safeguard the moral welfare of newcomers who arrived through the Ocean Terminals, and argued that immigrants should be met as they disembarked from their ships, and looked after at their final destinations.

In addition to the protection and aid such service would provide, the agencies were also concerned with the spread of ideologies they considered harmful to the moral identity of Canadians, and to the newcomers themselves, notably in the wake of the Winnipeg General Strike. In fact, they sought to "counteract the widespread, active and more or less secret communistic propaganda carried on from Halifax to Vancouver." The signatories—many of the major aid organizations stationed at Pier 21—claimed that the Canadian public was "anxious" to prevent "subversive and dangerous doctrines" from being instilled into the hearts and minds of Canadians, newcomers, and their children.[96]

OPPOSITE: A 1954 floor plan of Pier 21's immigration facilities, showing the Annex building with its extension and second-storey addition. *Source: Halifax Port Authority*

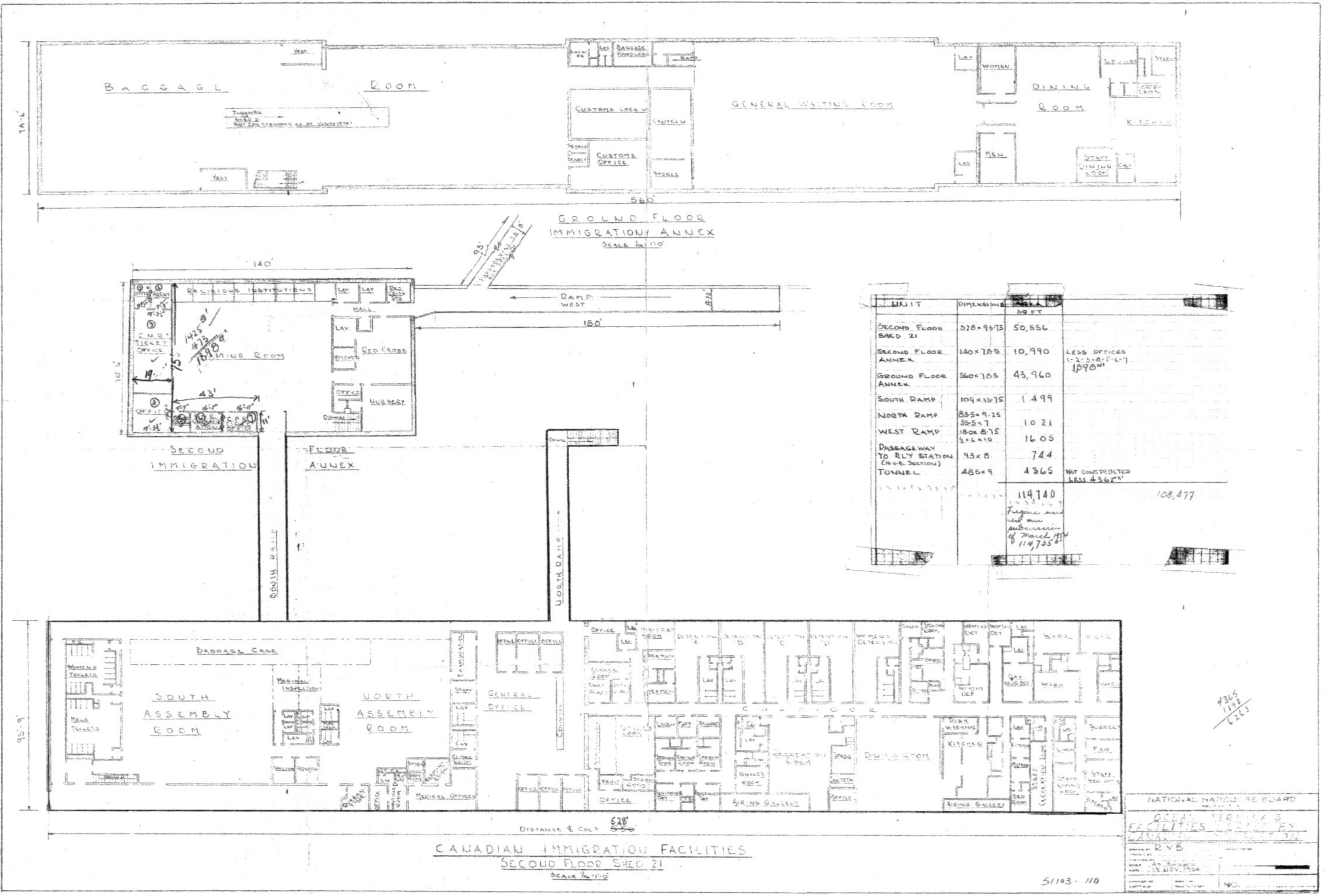

Baggage Room
General Waiting Room
Dining Room
Kitchen
Customs Lock Up
Customs Office
Women
Men
Lav
Staff Dining Room
560'
74'-6"
Ground Floor
Immigration Annex
Scale 1/64"=1'-0"
140'
Religious Institutions
Hall
Red Cross
Nursery
Office
C.N.R. Ticket Office
Ramp West
180'
Second Immigration Floor Annex
South Ramp
North Ramp
South Assembly Room
North Assembly Room
Baggage Cage
Medical Inspection
General Office
Medical Offices
Corridor
Dining Room
Kitchen
Ward
Airing Gallery
Office
Distance ¢ Cols 628'
95'-9"
Canadian Immigration Facilities
Second Floor Shed 21
Scale 1/64"=1'-0"
Unit | Dimensions | Area Sq Ft
Second Floor Shed 21 | 528×95.75 | 50,556
Second Floor Annex | 140×78.5 | 10,990 | Less offices 1-2-3-4-5-6-7 1898
Ground Floor Annex | 560×78.5 | 43,960
South Ramp | 109×13.75 | 1,499
North Ramp | 83.5×9.25 | 1021
West Ramp | 180×8.75 | 1605
Passageway to Rl'y Station (N.H.B. Section) | 93×8 | 744
Tunnel | 485×9 | 4365 | Not constructed less 4365
114,740
108,477
4365
1898
6263
National Har…rs Board
Ocean Terminals
Facilities … by …
R.V.B.
19 Nov. 1954
51103-110

CUSTOMS INSPECTIONS

By 1928, relatives, friends, greeters, and members of the general public were no longer permitted to mingle with disembarking ocean passengers in "an uproarious melee of joyful tears and lost children," as they had been at the earlier facilities at Pier 2.[97] Officials made this regulation change to assist customs officers who had to examine arriving baggage and determine its ownership, while sorting out who the new arrivals were for the immigration agents. At other ports of entry, alongside Canadian immigration officials, customs officers processed immigrants and their luggage aboard an incoming ship or at waterside in transit sheds. Canadian customs officials also processed ship and train passengers' personal baggage and checked luggage before they embarked for their final destination. In the interwar period, Canadian customs officials attempted to reduce the confusion arising from the entry of scores of newcomers by issuing permits to newcomers who were on their way to meet their friends and relatives. As a result, many passengers cleared customs more rapidly than before, except for immigrants who could not effectively communicate their plans, because they could not understand or speak English or French. Volunteers at Pier 21 often served as translators for Canadian officials and immigrants in an effort to help process newcomers through the site.[98]

At Pier 21, immigrants placed their hand baggage in a chain-link cage before they went through immigration processing. After the Second World War, the unit was a single cage, secured by an immigration guard, rather than individual cages or lockers.[99] Once immigrants passed their medical and civil inspections, they took their bags out of the cage and proceeded from the second floor of Pier 21 to the Annex building by way of an overhead walkway called the ramp, so called because of the steep floor angle. Finnish immigrant Tynne Johanna Saarinen, who arrived at Pier 21 in September 1929, recalls that the assembly area had at one end "a series of foreboding wire cages that stretched from floor to ceiling… [and] the baggage was stored under lock and key."[100] The hand baggage immigrants had with them would be checked in the ramp, which had a continuous counter on one side staffed by six to eight customs officers.[101]

Baggage cages in Pier 21's assembly area, 1928–1939. *Source: Halifax Port Authority*

In some cases, interwar and postwar immigrants concealed their valuables for safekeeping and to avoid customs officials. While Canada encouraged immigrants to bring money with them, some home governments outlawed their citizens from leaving with large sums of capital that could weaken their economies. In recalling her immigration to Canada from Poland in October 1938, Gerda Kiel noted that her father "bought a farm 2 ½ miles south of Falun [Alberta] with money he brought from Europe [Poland]. Dad hid money in the sewing machine. He drilled holes in the frame, rolled up large bills stuck them into the holes and covered the holes with wooden plugs. He also hid money in the large loose feather tick. This gave us a good start in Canada."[102] After the Second World War, customs officers also had the use of a few small rooms close to the ramp if they felt it was necessary to conduct a body search.[103] This was an area where female customs officers were often stationed after their introduction into this civil service role, in part to conduct personal searches if needed.

The ramp was a common site for confiscations. Items that were confiscated were held on site in a vault, and then moved to the customs

CUSTOMS

warehouse.[104] The reasons an item were taken could be difficult to explain through an interpreter, and one Department of Agriculture inspector remembers several incidents of otherwise gentle old ladies transforming into "warriors" giving the customs officers "a couple of swift whacks" when they felt an item was being taken wrongfully.[105] Foreign meats, plants, seeds, and soils were incinerated, while some alcohol and cigarettes were discarded, if their respective duties were not paid. This could be an intrusive and even painful process for immigrants, who often arrived in Canada with few belongings. Patricia Leask, daughter of one of the immigration agents, remembers liquor and sausages being taken away, and that the immigrants looked "puzzled and quite scared."[106]

Passengers were reunited with their large baggage once they entered the Annex building. The waiting area in the Annex building included large halls for baggage inspection and a waiting area, as well as a number of secondary examination rooms for customs, and some office space for guards.[107] After the addition of a partial second storey, customs officials gained improved lock-up facilities and more office space. There was also better accommodation for baggage handlers and baggage examination.[108] Larger baggage was usually checked on the ground floor of the Annex building after it was organized alphabetically by stevedores, who also were called to repair and make ready for travel the already-inspected crates and baggage.[109] This was the preferred facility for customs officers, as it was sheltered and close to their offices. Occasionally, baggage was handled in the lower level of Pier 21, a heated space, but with the roll-up doors raised it was often cold.[110] The customs agents took turns working in the open part of the shed and going to a heated office nearby to warm up. In either space, officers marked checked baggage with chalk. Railway officials were also occasionally present in the baggage space, both to check tickets and to process baggage for travel.[111] Once baggage passed through customs and the railway agents, it was ready to load on the train.[112]

The principle regulations of concern for confiscation at Pier 21 were not necessarily customs rules on contraband, but Department of Agriculture

OPPOSITE: Canadian customs officers inspect an immigrant's personal belongings in the ramp, 1965. *Source: Canadian Museum of Immigration Collection (DI2013.1362.6)*

regulations related to items such as plants or homemade meats. The customs officials also regularly confiscated liquor. Although there were occasionally handguns or other weapons concealed in belongings, this was not a common problem. However, immigrants sometimes concealed other minor contraband in innovative ways, such as in olive oil containers with false bottoms.[113] One person tried to sneak in salami, concealed in a bouquet.[114] Occasionally, passengers offered small bribes to try to get their confiscated food returned to them.[115] Customs officer Marguerite Day took one jar of preserved meat from its Italian owner, which dismayed and upset the man. After repeated protests, it came to light that he had packed a fair amount of American currency in a condom inside the jar.[116]

The process of inspection was swift even though a great deal of cargo and baggage moved through the pier. As with the civil examinations, the baggage hall customs screening took only approximately three minutes per individual.[117] Depending on the vessel and the number of passengers, processing all the passengers and their baggage on a ship took about eight hours.[118] This meant that the passengers spent a great deal of time waiting, and so the Annex building provided benches that extended between the steel posts in an open hall. One newcomer aptly described the long, rounded benches as "sausage-shaped."[119]

After inspection of paperwork and luggage, immigrants awaited their train departure on the ground floor of the Annex building. If they had not already done so, they returned to the Red Cross Seaport Nursery to collect their children, who spent time there while their parents sought out information, sent a telegraph, mailed a letter, secured train tickets or purchased food for the journey to their final destination across Canada. Between the nursery on the second floor of the Annex building and the baggage hall below, travellers passed representatives of the voluntary service agencies who handed out various samples including cereal, coffee, and tobacco products. Mary Caravaggio (née Leonetti) arrived with her mother and sister from Italy in July 1955. She remembers receiving a small box of corn flakes while she awaited the departure of her train: "I started

OPPOSITE: Baggage hall located on the ground floor of the Annex building at Pier 21, 1965. *Source: Canadian Museum of Immigration Collection (R2013.1362.7)*

opening the carton not knowing what was in it... and took a few Corn Flakes to taste them... it didn't taste very good. It had very little flavour and it was an odd texture. We had never eaten anything like this before... looking around, children and adults alike were making faces to express their dislike... the adults were putting the boxes down but the children began tossing the rest at each other and in no time the flakes were covering the floor."[120] In the baggage hall, some travellers had to visit a kiosk to get a confirmation stamp of their train seat assignments, if their seats were not previously reserved.[121]

After leaving Pier 21, immigrants departed by train en route for Montréal, where they changed trains if they were heading farther west. From Halifax, the train was a CNR train that many found uncomfortable due to its hard benches and lack of heat. Celia Beemster arrived with her family from the Netherlands in June 1953. She recalls the six-day journey aboard the train from Halifax to Vancouver:

> During the day it was very hot and... the evenings were often quite cold and we didn't have any blankets or pillows. Every morning we would awaken with coal dust covering our bodies... to get to the washing car you had to dig your way through lines of diapers hanging on make-shift lines strewn from one end of the car to the other. There were no dining cars so... we usually had enough time to run to a corner store for a loaf of bread, butter, some milk and a can of beef. We kept our food cold in the top of a water dispenser and we were lucky enough to have an old stove at the end of our car... It was quite futile though, the swaying of the train promptly spilled all the water out and the stove never really got hot enough to boil the water. Our efforts didn't produce the best meals but it did pass the time for us.[122]

Immigrants often did not get much rest due to the train's multiple stops, long waits, and boisterous passengers.[123] Many were in old colonist cars, which some called "cattle cars" due to their lack of comfort and crowding.[124]

OPPOSITE: A father and two children sleep aboard a train before its departure from Pier 21, 1965. *Source: Canadian Museum of Immigration Collection (R2013.1362.224)*

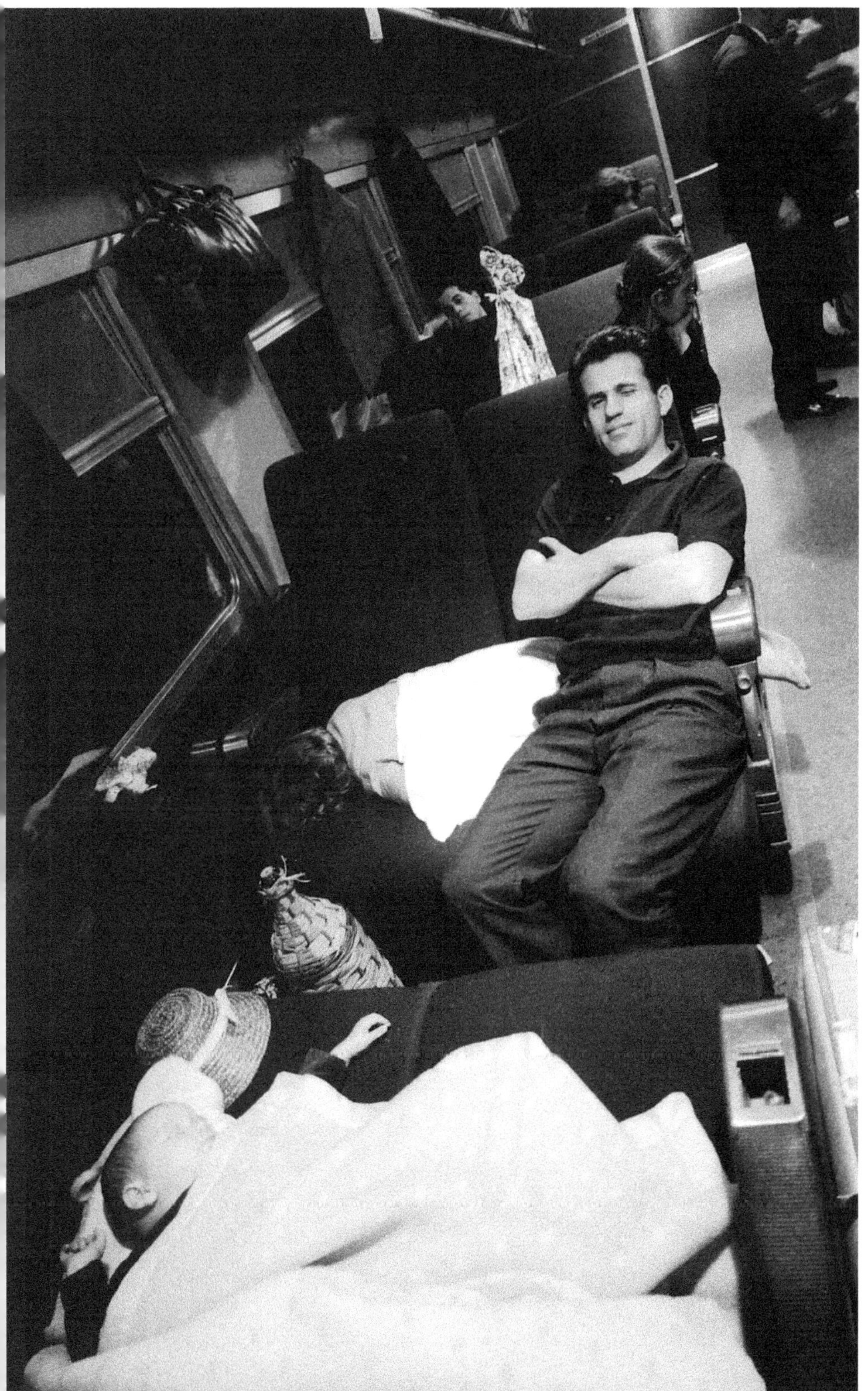

These were minimally equipped passenger cars, often with wooden seats and a simple stove in the car to prepare meals, designed for inexpensive long-distance travel. Nevertheless, for other newcomers, the train departing Halifax was a welcome contrast from the transportation available in their homeland, with more space and amenities than they expected.[125]

For most newcomers to Canada who passed through Pier 21, boarding the train was the first substantive step on the journey to settle in their new homeland, and the last they saw of the Pier. Yet back in 1928 Pier 21 was the final iteration of ocean immigration facilities in Halifax, literally building on the lessons of experience accumulated since the late 1800s. The design and location of the immigration quarters at Pier 21, however, relied a great deal on influences beyond the immigration department. An exploration of the history of immigration buildings in the city really begins before the construction of Pier 21, and illustrates why and how it was built in the South End of Halifax.

OPPOSITE: Deep Water Terminus, with Pier 2 at extreme right, 1900.

Source: Notman Studio, Nova Scotia Archives (1983-310 no. 100026)

2 Pier 2 and the Early Years of Pier 21

1890–1939

> *The whole plant is really a Canadian National Railway enterprise. True the Immigration Department had considerable say with regard to the lay out of the purely immigration quarters, but the Department had first to get the space in the great freight shed assigned to them—or rented to them—if the case may be—from the Canadian National whose property the building is.*
>
> —*Halifax Chronicle*, March 3, 1928

THE SYSTEMATIC PROCESS IN PLACE FOR IMMIGRANTS AT Pier 21 suggests that the purpose of the building was for immigration. With passenger examination handled in the second-storey immigration quarters of shed 21, and customs examination in the Annex building, people certainly could move smoothly through the site. The history of Canadian immigration facilities in Halifax, however, shows that Pier 21 was more tightly linked to transportation and commercial interests. The involvement of transportation companies in Canadian immigration facilities overall was a matter of legislation: the 1910 Immigration Act required transportation companies "to provide, equip, and maintain suitable buildings for the examination and detention of passengers for any purpose under this Act."[1] Pier 21 was, as the quote above states, primarily a railway enterprise.

PIER 2

The creation of the first dedicated Canadian immigration shed in Halifax followed shortly after the advent of the inland rail link to Montreal in the late 1870s. With its inauguration, Halifax became a viable port for passengers and cargo bound for the rest of Canada. At the time, major transportation companies controlled the development and operation of immigration facilities on the waterfront, and this had a profound effect on the city. In particular, the North End of Halifax grew and changed in response to projects from the railways, such as the creation of the North End rail depot in 1877 and the associated piers in 1880.[2] The piers, which were intended to handle both cargo and passengers, were together called the Deep Water Terminus.

One of these piers, Pier 2, in conjunction with several other buildings used by the immigration branch, the railways, and the steamship companies, operated as the significant passenger service pier until the 1928 opening of Pier 21. Pier 2 was located just downhill and a bit north from the Halifax Citadel, at an accessible, central location in Halifax. One of its valuable qualities was that the Intercolonial Railway (ICR) lines had a direct connection to it, as the ICR owned and operated the pier and its buildings. This was convenient for ship passengers and permitted efficient handling of baggage.

While the location was suitable for passenger arrivals, the early facilities were not. In 1889, almost a decade after the completion of the inland rail link, passengers still arrived in a cargo shed. The shed did provide a waiting area and washrooms for immigrants, as well as space to handle baggage and ticketing.[3] However, the passenger waiting area was not large

OPPOSITE: Peninsular Halifax, with the Deep Water Terminus at bottom centre, 1910. *Source: Halifax Municipal Archives, 102-5A-26*

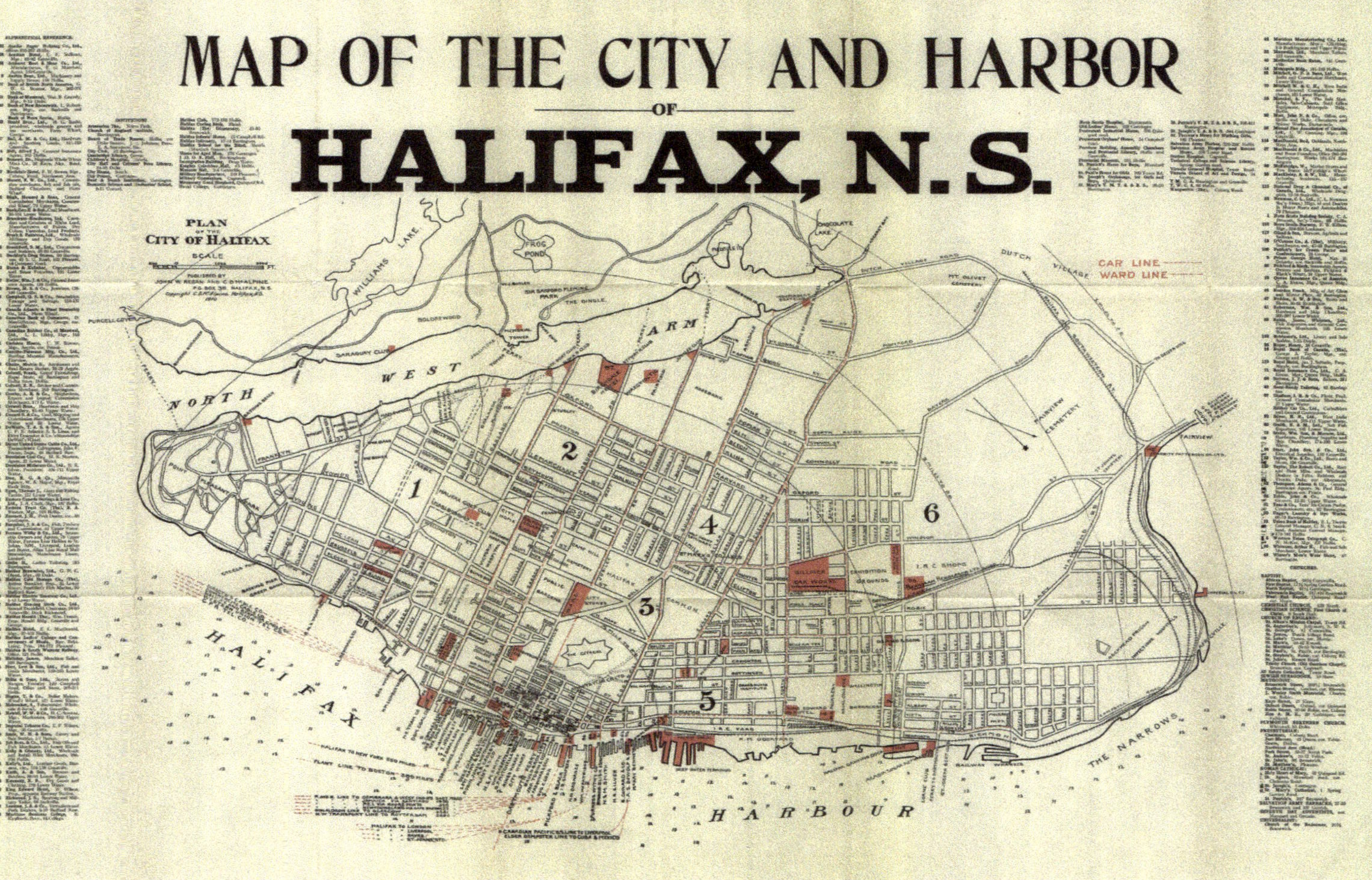

MAP OF THE CITY AND HARBOR
OF
HALIFAX, N.S.
PLAN OF THE CITY OF HALIFAX
SCALE
CAR LINE
WARD LINE
NORTH WEST ARM
HALIFAX HARBOUR
THE NARROWS
WILLIAMS LAKE
FROG POND
CHOCOLATE LAKE
DUTCH VILLAGE ROAD
MT. OLIVET CEMETERY
FAIRVIEW CEMETERY
FAIRVIEW
THE DINGLE
EXHIBITION GROUNDS
I.R.C. SHOPS
THE CITADEL
HALIFAX COMMON
1
2
3
4
5
6

enough for the number of arrivals, and there was often a wait of several hours before immigrants could board their trains. Further, Halifax was not yet a busy port for passenger arrival, and its principal traffic was in winter, so passengers waited in the chill and damp of a wintry waterfront. John Lowe, the deputy minister responsible for immigration, argued the conditions should be improved, "serious sickness having in some cases been caused to delicate children."[4]

Lowe made a pitch for the first dedicated immigration building in Halifax. At the Deep Water Terminus, the space between the curving railway tracks to the docks and the carriage track running along the length of the waterfront left a triangle of open ground. Lowe co-operated with the local agents of the ICR to plan the construction of an immigration shed, about two hundred feet long, to occupy this otherwise unused piece of land. This was to be supported by a "cottage" building, with a kitchen, dining rooms, and sleeping accommodations. The new shed, based on this design, opened in the winter of 1890.[5]

Although having a dedicated shed improved the examination of immigrants at Halifax, the arrangement had a few issues. First, handling of passenger traffic at the port required the immigration agent to work both at the waterfront shed and at the railway station. Second, the raised walkway from the freight shed, where passengers arrived, to the immigration building was difficult to navigate with baggage. It was also a risk to passengers, as in May 1891, when six passengers fell from the raised platforms and injured themselves.[6] Finally, the building itself was not well constructed, and after just a few years, parts of the exterior shingling were gone and gaps had opened up in the floors and interior partitions.

The cottage building to the west of the shed also deteriorated rapidly and needed shingling shortly after opening.[7] An inspector with the Department of the Interior pointed out that there was little space for baggage in the main building, so the bags took up space meant for passengers. Even when there was room, there were only a few benches, so many passengers had to stand while waiting to board their trains. Also, like the freight shed, the large doors of the building were mostly kept open as people and baggage moved about, which made the shed cold and uncomfortable during Halifax's peak migration time in the winter.[8]

The complaints about this first building were resolved in an unfortunate manner on February 27, 1895, when a fire consumed much of the Deep Water Terminus, including the immigration shed and cottage.[9] In the wake of the fire, passengers arrived at the Cunard Line's wharf and were processed at the railway station.[10] By the end of March, the railway was developing plans to rebuild the infrastructure damaged or lost to fire in the area of Pier 2, including the immigration facilities.[11] The effort to arrange permanent accommodation took on further urgency in May of the same year, when the railway suffered another fire. This time, a blaze took the Richmond pier and buildings in the North End, which were occasionally used to clear immigrants after the February fire.

The replacement immigration building opened in February 1897. Despite the year spent on construction, it was poorly built. It rested on pilings, and even before it opened for use, the shed settled so significantly that the plaster was cracking and doors and windows were not usable. More than five years later, the problems remained unaddressed: the floor was uneven and immigration officials were still dealing with sticking or inoperable windows and doors. To exacerbate matters, within a decade of construction the wharf and the front part of the foundation required urgent repairs.[12]

Almost immediately, the Allan Line reported other difficulties with docking at the new facility. The new immigration building was located on a wharf that was both at an angle to adjoining wharves and too short to have passengers disembark directly alongside the immigration building. Instead, passengers often had to use Pier 3, the wharf to the north of the immigration building, and walk across railway tracks and freight handling areas between the piers.[13] Further, the small size of the 1897 building meant that officers in Halifax had no room to detain immigrants found to be inadmissible. One officer was instructed to place detainees in the facility's ordinary bedrooms, which were not secured against escape.

That the building was accessible to the general public compounded the security issues. One immigration agent complained shortly after the building opened that "idlers and loafers" were creating a considerable nuisance for the staff at the site, as they had access to the entire wharf and were peering in the windows. The problem apparently became acute during ship arrivals, when one immigration agent claimed "crowds of people surround the building."[14] Besides the curious members of the public interested in the spectacle of steamship arrivals, hotels sent runners to attract weary travellers, and various transportation companies solicited passengers for their business. The inadequacy of the structure was so clear that within six years of its opening, immigration officials were making sustained complaints.[15] Eventually these deficiencies drove the immigration branch to seek improvements.[16]

Over the next decade, from 1905 to 1915, the facilities at Pier 2 underwent substantial renovation and expansion, and in late 1915, "New Pier 2," as it was called, was completely finished.[17] With its passenger and immigration accommodation on the second floor, and baggage and cargo handling on the ground level, the new Pier 2 building prefigured important elements of the later design of Pier 21. It was designed to serve passengers from two ships at a time, and to have safe access to several train tracks inside and beside the shed. The building also offered space for many others besides the immigration department, including representatives of provincial governments; a caterer; a United States immigration office; and railway, steamship, and telegraph agents.[18] There were also designated rooms, though modest, for volunteer and church agencies, including the Salvation Army.[19] This followed the inclusion of social service spaces at other ports, including Quebec City, and was a precedent for the planning of the new immigration quarters in Halifax at Pier 21. This new building opened during the First World War, an event that disrupted regular operations due to military appropriation and the need for embarking service personnel. Pier 2 remained busy with military transits through the end of the war, and into 1920.

Even as the new Pier 2 was under construction, however, the end of its service for immigration was in view, and the future site for Pier 21 in South End Halifax was receiving a great deal of publicity in the city. Marking the significance of the South End project, in 1915 Prime Minister Robert Borden and Governor General Prince Arthur were on hand for a ceremonial opening of the works. Indeed, the visible work of the filling and levelling of the massive waterfront area in the South End was already well underway.[20] The plan included an artificial seawall some two thousand feet

New Pier 2 immigration assembly room, 1915.
Source: Library and Archives Canada, e011308939

long, several new piers, and accompanying freight and passenger sheds. The terminals needed substantial new railway infrastructure to serve passengers and cargo, including a huge rail cut circumnavigating the Halifax peninsula and a new union rail station. The terminals would sit in large part on an extensive new area of land reclaimed from the harbour. But the project also extended onto the surrounding lands, requiring the destruction of an existing neighbourhood and disrupting properties all around the Halifax peninsula. All this resulted in the immigration branch and transportation companies taking a short-term view of the arrangements at Pier 2, including reducing the quality of materials and scale of the immigration quarters on the second storey of the new Pier 2 shed.[21]

Amid the wartime boom of military and merchant traffic at the port, the construction of Halifax's South End Ocean Terminals proceeded. The new terminals promised to be a major improvement for the capacity of the city to handle commercial and passenger traffic, but in wartime the

TOP: Troop trains at Pier 2, 1916.
Source: Helen Creighton, Nova Scotia Archives (Album 11 no. 32)

BOTTOM: Chinese labourers, returning from war work in Europe during the First World War, disembark at Pier 2, 1919.
Source: Helen Creighton, Nova Scotia Archives (Album 12 no. 233)

terminals could also improve the port's efficiency in lading and replenishing ships engaged to carry war materiel or personnel. The availability of this shipping space at the incomplete terminals was particularly important in Halifax after the Halifax Explosion devastated the North End, including significant damage to transportation infrastructure. The explosion resulted from the collision of the SS *Imo* and SS *Mont-Blanc*, a munitions ship, in Halifax Harbour on December 6, 1917. Two thousand people died in the blast. The explosion damaged windows, doors, interior partitions, the heating systems, and a part of the roof at Pier 2. Nevertheless, less than two weeks later, the immigration facility at Pier 2 was again operational.[22]

In 1925, the Departments of Public Works and Immigration and Colonization, anticipating another five years at the Deep Water Terminus, renewed their lease at Pier 2 with the CNR (successor to the ICR).[23] But pressure was building for the government to complete the Ocean Terminals project, and just one week after the lease was renewed on Pier 2, the CNR invited the immigration department to move to their new quarters at Pier 21. The company anticipated that Pier 21 would open the next year, in 1926.[24]

PLANNING FOR PIER 21

Pier 21, part of the much larger Ocean Terminals, was a massive update to the port of Halifax. Led and championed by transportation company officials, it was part of a national approach to reinvigorate Canada's trade and transport infrastructure. Upgrading the port of Halifax would benefit the Canadian economy by keeping goods and passengers moving on Canadian soil as much as possible. Thus, the Ocean Terminals were designed principally as a commercial project. Passengers, including immigrants, were a secondary consideration.[25]

In 1913, civil engineer Frederick Cowie laid out the case for improving the port of Halifax, and for building new terminals in the South End.[26] Cowie settled on the "Georges Island site," named for its position directly opposite Georges Island in the Halifax Harbour. This area had several key benefits. These included the centrality of the site to the city, the shelter from wind afforded by Georges Island, as well as favourable surveys of

TOP: Ross & Macdonald, a prominent Canadian architectural firm, promoted a grand vision for the Ocean Terminals, ca. 1912. *Source: Nova Scotia Archives Photo Collection*

BOTTOM: Setting the first concrete blocks for the foundation of Pier 21 and the Ocean Terminals, 1915. *Source: Nova Scotia Archives (1986-490 F36)*

the required land near the shoreline and of the harbour area that would be reclaimed. The efficient layout of the long passenger quay would also provide for rapid and efficient transfers of cargo and passengers from ship to shore to rail. Finally, if the Ocean Terminals were built at the Georges Island site, it would have a relatively minor impact on taxation and assessment values in Halifax, compared to the other potential sites.[27] Since the project required land expropriations, the city stood to lose value in the destruction of city-built utilities and services, a possible reduction in property values near parts of the construction, and the ongoing loss of taxable private property to the control of another level of government.

The *Morning Chronicle*, a local newspaper hostile to the governing federal Conservatives, forecast the change to the city in dire terms. It would doom West End residents "to be awakened to the stench of the locomotive and the rumbling of freight trains... the peninsula of Halifax is to be girdled with bands of steel."[28] The *Chronicle* evoked city heritage in its arguments, with a poignant complaint that one of the entrances to Point Pleasant Park associated with the meanderings of Nova Scotia hero Joseph Howe would be closed as a result of this construction.

The *Chronicle*'s competitor, the *Halifax Herald*, struck a different note. The *Herald*'s first two pages were devoted to extensive praise for the project, taking careful note of the reputed expense, scale, and impact of the project for the city's businesses. Amid a nostalgic recollection of the changes in fashionable or desirable neighbourhoods since the city's colonial inception, the paper asserted that the project would bring an effective rebirth for the city, as well as a shedding of the city's parochial identity.[29] Situating the project as a marker of an ongoing process of growth and development for the city, the *Herald* carried remarks from the Minister of Railways Frank Cochrane mentioning the Bulkhead Passenger Landing Quay, where "ocean greyhounds"—the elegant and fast passenger liners of the era—would arrive. Cochrane noted that the quay would feature immigration buildings—but those two words alone mark the full extent of the official announcement of the immigration facility at Pier 21 in 1912. The commercial emphasis, and the narrative of "progress" associated with the site, signalled some of the controversies that dogged the Ocean Terminals and Pier 21 throughout construction.

One aspect of the controversy was the question of aesthetics. The feel of "old Halifax," and in particular the jealously guarded pastoral preserves that still existed on the peninsula at that time, had sentimental weight. Furthermore, the people who lived on the peninsular estates were wealthy and politically connected. Cochrane, anticipating the controversy, dealt with the challenge outright in his announcement, pointing out that railways operated in the heart of other cities while the beauty of the environs was preserved.[30] The rustic image of Halifax had advocates even in the national press. An article in the Toronto *Globe* in 1913 concluded: "These and other developments indicate that the traditional calm and leisurely life of the Province will give way… the American spirit of hustle will take possession, and the quiet enjoyment of life around afternoon open-fires give place to rampant wealth-seeking."[31]

By contrast, editors at the *Herald* mocked this concern for leisure and aesthetics, describing city councillors who opposed the development as preferring Halifax to be a picnic ground.[32] One writer reflected that point of view when he wrote in the *Herald* that major European countries—presumably models for Canada—set aside sentiment when a major public work required the use of land.[33] The objections did amount to more than sentiment: Sir Sandford Fleming, a famed innovator and railway engineer, wrote to Halifax city council about the sewage and pollution risks associated with the new rail route on the peninsula, an argument that also found its way to the floor of the House of Commons.[34]

The public debate inspired some colourful expression. This extended even to the question of the role of the site in immigration, as one correspondent to the *Chronicle* objected:

> What [another writer] tells us as to what the new terminals are intended for is even less reassuring. After telling us that the present terminals are to be retained for local traffic and for trade with the United States and West Indies, he goes on to say: "The new terminals are intended to take care of the swarming immigrants coming into

OPPOSITE: Plan for the Ocean Terminals project, showing the neighbourhood destroyed for construction. *Source: Frederick Cowie, Nova Scotia Archives (HE C16 H13)*

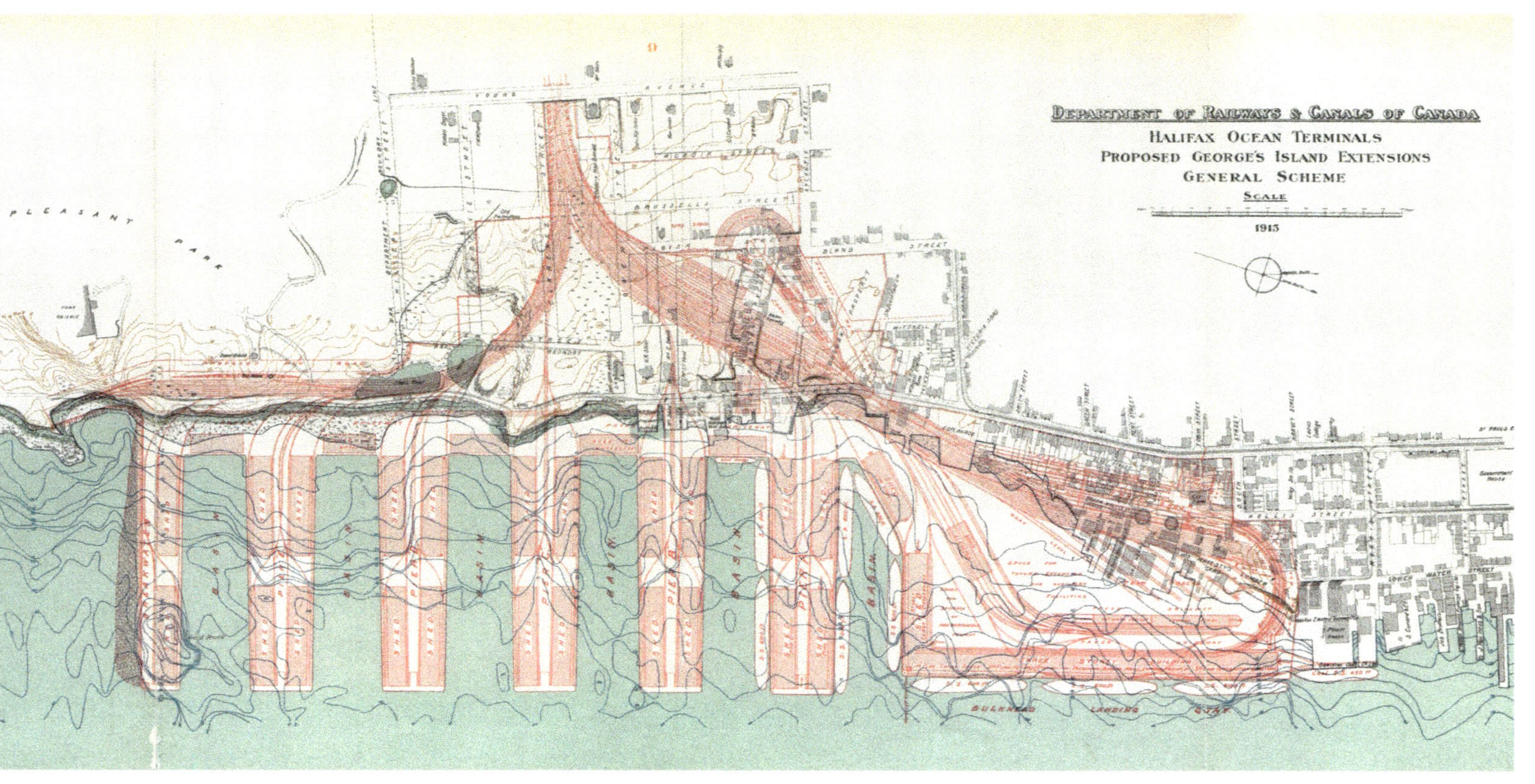
Department of Railways & Canals of Canada
Halifax Ocean Terminals
Proposed George's Island Extensions
General Scheme
Scale
1913
PLEASANT PARK
YOUNG AVENUE
BRUSSELLS STREET
BLAND STREET
MORRIS STREET
HOLLIS STREET
LOWER WATER STREET
BASIN
PIER
BULKHEAD LANDING QUAY

> Canada from Great Britain, Germany, France, Russia, Italy, Austria and other lands." This is what the opponents of the present location have been saying, and its advocates either denying or evading. If this is all we are to get for ripping up our City a good many persons will ask why it should be done.[35]

Contrary to the writer's position, Halifax had received passengers bound for points all over the country since the 1880s. The majority of public attention and debate regarding the site, however, mirroring the project announcement of 1912, focused on commercial opportunities arising from the expansion of Halifax's cargo capacity. The narrative of the port emphasized Halifax as the "Gateway of Canada" for commerce, rather than for people.[36] However, the objection makes evident that the ICR and the Department of Railways and Canals (DRC) had plans for immigration facilities at Pier 21 from the earliest moments of the project. In 1914, the ICR had drawings showing the future shed at Pier 21, with a railway station on the second floor and the immigration quarters on the third floor.[37] The first cargo arrival at the facility was in 1916, and there was already steady shipping traffic at the new piers during the latter stages of the First World War. However, the new Ocean Terminals did not receive regular passenger traffic until the opening of Pier 21 in 1928.[38]

Building new quays and piers along Halifax's waterfront was expensive and complex, not just for the civil engineering involved, but also because the site chosen for the new Ocean Terminals in South End Halifax would require purchasing and altering real estate worth hundreds of thousands of dollars, including residential and business properties.[39] The DRC expropriated land from some property owners, and had to compensate others when blasting or other construction disrupted or damaged their homes. In October 1913, Mr. C. Ochiltree MacDonald, a resident of Young Avenue, wrote to the minister of railways and canals to complain of the hazards to health and property from flying debris, especially from blasting. MacDonald sought paid accommodation at a hotel away from the blasting for himself and his family, as well as caretaking for his property. He was also careful to underscore the high value of his home and its affluent municipal address.[40]

Besides arguments and controversies about the location within Halifax, these improvements at the port of Halifax triggered some political problems on a larger scale. The regional rivalry between the ports of Saint John and Halifax was a weakness in establishing effective advocacy for Maritime regional business: the ports competed for resources from the federal government rather than advancing proposals for improvements together. This undermined larger regional interests and left the ports at a real disadvantage, especially compared to ports in other regions where they would establish common cause in lobbying at the national level. The competition also weakened regional associations for business.[41]

CONSTRUCTION OF PIER 21, 1915–1925

From the moment that construction was announced, the question of when it would be completed lingered over the project. A business leader present at Cochrane's 1912 speech, J. A. MacDonald, offered a prescient critique of the plan, stating that if it were "done now, without the heart-wearying delays we have been so long accustomed to, then Halifax can date its new birth from October 30th 1912."[42] The same optimism carried to the sentiments of Halifax's city councillors. They organized a reception for Captain R. Randall of SS *Sheba* on November 8, 1916, celebrating the first cargo arrival at the new terminals. Invited guests included Cowie, contractors and engineers who had worked on the project, and representatives of the press and railways. The city clerk offered a salutation recognizing the privilege Captain Randall enjoyed as the opening caller to one of the greatest facilities in the world, before noting the potential prosperity that would flow from the operation of the terminals. A phrase in the florid address signalled a problem: the clerk said that the new facility was "prepared in part to fulfil its functions."[43]

One of the functions not yet ready in 1916 was passenger landing. It would be nearly a dozen years between the arrival of *Sheba* and the official opening of Pier 21 for immigration purposes. Even as *Sheba* delivered its first cargo of concrete, the contractor building the Ocean Terminals, Foley Bros., Welch, Stewart & Fauquier, was having severe difficulties with materials and construction. Although the start of work in March 1914

HMT *Olympic* passes the future site of Pier 21, 1916.
Source: Library and Archives Canada, e011308904

unfolded on schedule, trenching for the foundation of the bulkhead passenger landing quay—the two-thousand-foot-long seawall that includes Pier 21—immediately proved difficult. The foundation, resting on uneven bedrock, required extensive underwater work. A year and a half after this work began, the engineers controlling the project, both from the contractor and the ICR, decided that the foundation needed to be ten to twelve feet deeper. The need for reconsidering the stability of the works was made plain through a tragedy: late in 1916, the uncertain foundations caused a crane to overbalance into water, and a worker drowned.[44]

Finally, the wartime role for Halifax as a port impinged on construction, causing further delays. War transports damaged the contractor's buoys, causing thousands of dollars in losses. The contractor occasionally had to divert cranes to assist in moving and removing heavy guns from ships to support the war effort. Finally, the berths completed at the works were frequently required for active shipping after 1916. This ship traffic interfered with the floating plant for construction: the contractor used cranes, dredges, cement mixers, and other apparatus on barges to work on the project. Even a rough accounting for those interruptions ran more than a dozen pages. Indeed, the traffic was such that one of the Ocean Terminals basins was available for construction work for less than a third of the time during the entirety of 1917. After the Halifax Explosion, the need to accommodate increased traffic at the Ocean Terminals due to the damage throughout the harbour was a further obstacle to completing the project on time.[45]

Wartime labour conditions in Halifax also affected rank-and-file workers at the site. The contractor suffered a mass poaching of workers in mid-1916, when a recruiter went around the works promising better employment terms for another project. Sixty-five labourers left in a single day, leaving the contractor substantially short of manpower and dealing with unrest among the remaining workers. Wartime labour demands also drove up wages, increasing the costs for the contractor by more than $1 million.[46]

One way the contractor dealt with these labour difficulties was to seek aid from Major-General Sir William Otter, the officer commanding internment operations during the First World War. During the summer of 1915, the contractors had used a number of internees successfully while the internees were under military supervision. In 1916, the Canadian Government Railways sought to renew the arrangement, and inquired about employing a hundred interned prisoners from a prisoner of war camp in Amherst, Nova Scotia, to overcome the problems in securing labour.[47]

The contractor and the railway argued over the delays and compensation for years. In 1919, two years after the 1917 deadline stipulated in the original contract, the contractor completed their work for the site, having created the piers, but not the associated roads and sheds. In 1921, the contractor sought additional compensation from the DRC of over $500,000 for expenses due to delays. The contractor cited as principal causes the First World War and the Halifax Explosion, both of which led to the heavy use of the Ocean Terminals site before the contracted work was complete. Despite these circumstances, the federal government rejected the claim for compensation.[48]

The initial construction contract had specified only the building of the quay walls, reclaiming land within the walls, dredging where needed, and foundations for buildings and associated utilities. The contractor finally finished those tasks over the summer of 1919, and the Dominion Bridge

Company installed the steelwork framing for the transit sheds at the passenger landing quay in the fall of the same year. Although the original plans had featured larger sheds and more graceful architecture for the sheds along the long seawall, including at Pier 21, that construction was not possible. The representative for the Dominion Bridge Company on the project stated that wartime constraints on steel production and the imperative for infrastructure in Halifax following the Explosion dictated the much simpler construction style of the transit sheds, in contrast to the elegant initial design. The railway and contractor had to use steel and designs that had initially only been intended for the plain sheds of the freight and cargo areas.[49]

After this final effort, the project languished for several years. The sheds put in place at the Ocean Terminals during the First World War were only temporary wooden structures, not suitable for the handling of passengers or mail. Once the plain steelwork for more permanent sheds was in place, Hayes made it clear that the funding for completion of the construction was uncertain, and his doubts about resources were well founded. Contracting for further work collapsed in 1919. No contract was awarded and no construction followed.[50]

This austerity reflected a broad curtailing of government spending after the First World War, and a general economic slowdown. Ocean traffic at the port fell away. Stiff competition from American ports, including New York and Portland, Maine, meant that until the mid-1920s Halifax was a marginal port for trade. A significant part of this decline was linked to changes in railway rates and regulations in favour of central Canadian business. In 1922, the CNR proposed that the DRC allocate funds to at last complete the sheds at the Ocean Terminals, but the department did not alter their budget. The only work authorized was cleaning and painting of the exposed steelwork. In 1924, after close to $17 million in expenditures, the still-incomplete terminals had only an $8,000 project planned for the future, to lay flooring in cargo shed 25, while Pier 21 and the adjacent structures remained open steel framework.[51]

This financial abandonment was linked to the larger economic circumstances of the federal government, compounded by a growing disconnect between the departments involved in the project. In 1920, the CNR

TOP: Pier 2 just before immigration and passenger traffic relocated to Pier 21, 1928. *Source: W. R. MacAskill, Nova Scotia Archives (1987-453 no. 2625)*

BOTTOM: Ocean Terminals office bay and shed 22 steel framing, 1925–26. *Source: Canada Science and Technology Museum, 1966-0549-001*

informed the Department of Public Works that there were no plans to have immigration quarters at the new South End facility, and that the existing building at Pier 2 was running to the satisfaction of the American and Canadian immigration authorities.[52] In 1924, Department of Immigration and Colonization officials stated that there were no plans to accommodate increased entries at Halifax, and that the question of completing the Ocean Terminals did not involve their department.[53] In short, from after the First World War through to the mid-1920s, both the eventual landlord (CNR) and tenant (immigration branch) professed ignorance about the branch's future at Pier 21. The Ocean Terminals project was starved of funds and lacked a department or agency to champion it moving forward. A further obstacle was the absence of political goodwill, as the stalled construction provided fodder for recrimination between political opponents in Ottawa.

CONSTRUCTION OF PIER 21, 1925–1928

The lack of political appetite to complete the Ocean Terminals finally was set aside in the mid-1920s. In response to the troubling economic situation in Halifax, and in an effort to improve the prospects for the city as a major port, the project grew to include an updated grain elevator. The elevator and associated commercial rail traffic were connected to a larger political context in the 1920s, as the Maritime Rights movement took hold in eastern Canada. Maritime Rights advocates looked to resolve losses for the Maritime Provinces in political representation, financial subsidies, and transportation infrastructure. They hoped to regain status as full partners, fairly compensated, in Canadian Confederation.[54] The Royal Commission on Maritime Claims, which investigated the complaints associated with Maritime Rights, recommended completing the Ocean Terminal improvements in Halifax.[55] The government of the day agreed, with the idea that the previous government had "left this shed a mere iron frame rearing itself up to the sky. The storms of five or six years beat upon that stark, half-finished structure, and it was only when this government came into office that the shed was put into proper condition."[56]

In 1925, the federal government advised the CNR to make proposals for funding in order to complete the Ocean Terminals.[57] This change happened in the context of a major partnership between the federal government and Canada's two major railways to recruit and settle European immigrants. An announcement of renewed work followed. That year, the vice-president of CNR gave a presentation to the Halifax Board of Trade regarding expanding commerce at the port of Halifax, and stated that the new terminals would be ready to handle winter traffic. He also spoke about passenger and immigrant arrival at the port, claiming that the new terminals would be as good as any others on the Atlantic coast of North America.[58]

Immigration officials saw their potential future at Pier 21 very differently. They believed the Ocean Terminals facility was much less desirable for receiving both passengers and the ocean liners themselves than the relatively new structure at Pier 2. This was based on a scathing dismissal of the fitness of the cargo shed at Pier 21 for immigration purposes by an immigration inspector who had visited the shed and described it as "altogether unsatisfactory... accommodation could never be provided in such sheds suitable for the examination of passengers and immigrants and for civil detention."[59] Since Pier 21 was built parallel to the shore, officials at the immigration department as well as the steamship companies feared that only one ship at a time could disembark passengers, and that the ships might have to shift to another pier to unload cargo. This was quite different from the large and recently built shed at Pier 2, which projected into the water and could receive at least two ships—one on each side of the pier—simultaneously.[60] Opponents to the move also noted that Pier 2 had cost only a fraction of the amount proposed for the new terminal, was still perfectly serviceable, and could accommodate the largest of ocean liners.[61]

The CNR, which was the agency responsible for the development of the Ocean Terminals and Pier 21 at the time, responded partly that the relocation and the use of the waterfront cargo shed at Pier 21 for immigration purposes was merely a stopgap measure. When the CNR officially gave notice to the immigration department to move in late 1925, it warned that all transatlantic shipping would be bound to the new piers, and so the move to Pier 21 was necessary. The railway even offered a few concrete suggestions on how to save funds and supplies during the move, such as transferring office partitions from Pier 2 to Pier 21. The push for economy in the move eventually reached a bit too far, as the immigration department even brought the toilets from Pier 2 to Pier 21, but the fixtures were in such offensive condition after just five years that they had to be replaced.[62]

Satisfied with their existing space and apprehensive of the new building, the immigration department dithered and resisted moving. In October 1926, the CNR nevertheless proceeded with fitting up and moving the immigration quarters from Pier 2 to Pier 21. Despite this, the railway was in a mixed position with regard to leadership and the future of the Ocean Terminals. Even as they pushed the immigration department to move to Pier 21, the railway was in the midst of negotiations to transfer their Halifax port properties to the newly-formed Halifax Harbour Commissioners.[63]

The immigration department, on the other hand, confronted a practical requirement to move to the new shed, as the transportation companies that provided space on the waterfront and arranged passenger movements were in support of using the new South End infrastructure. Immigration officials had sought the use of both floors of shed 21 and the upper floor of shed 22 for their new quarters. However, steamship companies blocked this proposal and the immigration branch had to compromise on their use of the space. As a further example of the relative authority of business interests, the Halifax Board of Trade sought and obtained the right to review plans for the Ocean Terminals, including Pier 21.[64] This fortified the resistance of the immigration department to the move to Pier 21, and they remained reluctant to move throughout the construction process.

Nor did the immigration department have detailed input into the design.[65] This meant that the CNR designed key features of the immigration quarters, including some features that were done hastily. This included the Annex building, which was only contracted for construction in mid-1927, and opened in early 1928. Despite these conflicts and the hurried work, public impressions of the site remained positive, perhaps because a key source of information about it were agencies other than the immigration department. "Halifax will have the finest immigration facilities of any port in the world," claimed one steamship company official after visiting Pier 21's immigration quarters, just days before the opening in March 1928.[66]

In the end, work to complete the Ocean Terminals spanned two decades, due in large part to construction difficulties and economic challenges.

Politics and influence between departments and transportation companies further complicated efforts to finish the Pier 21 passenger facilities. Not least among the problems was the reluctance of the Department of Immigration and Colonization to move into Pier 21 from Pier 2. However, immigration officials were not as influential as the political and commercial players involved in the Ocean Terminals project, and so their interests were often subsumed. Immigration—even during the peak years of arrivals to Canada of the early twentieth century—was not a particularly powerful government department. Similar to the situation at Pier 2, other organizations, and in particular the railways, had significant control over the creation of immigration infrastructure.

The passenger landing facilities and the associated Annex building were physically central in the new Ocean Terminals. However, they were almost the last features built at the terminals, and were constructed reluctantly by an arm's-length agency of the federal government over the objections, and even outright defiance, of the immigration department. The significant public and private influences on the planning and construction at the site emphasize that Canadian immigration authorities played a surprisingly small part in the construction of Pier 21.

OPENING PIER 21

Immigration operations at Pier 21 began on March 8, 1928, when the immigration department and staff moved to Pier 21 from Pier 2. Persons already in detention or awaiting deportation were also moved to the new immigration facility. Following an overnight transition of personnel, Pier 21 opened and the first vessel to call on the building was SS *Nieuw Amsterdam*.[67] The new immigration facility welcomed fifty-one immigrants from this first official arrival.[68]

Within months of opening, the Halifax Harbour Commissioners—now the Halifax Port Authority—took over many of the CNR's waterfront properties in Halifax, including the Ocean Terminals.[69] That same year, the Department of Marine and Fisheries formally advised the DRC that following negotiations with the CNR, they were prepared to begin administering the "harbour terminals in Halifax which were built with public

Aerial view of Pier 20 (single-storey shed) and Pier 21 (two-storey shed with walkway).
Source: Canadian Museum of Immigration Collection (DI2013.1205.1)

funds."[70] The departments concluded their agreement quickly, with an order-in-council directing the transfer of property on August 16, 1928.

The confusion that this overlap of authority could cause was apparent at times during the delays of the building years, and it extended well past the opening date of Pier 21. Public Works officials were left out of negotiating the lease, resulting in immigration officials moving out of a satisfactory space to a smaller one at double the annual cost.[71] Along with failing to arrange the lease properly and allocate money for it, the immigration authorities also did not pay for their utilities until December 1932, almost five years after moving into Pier 21.[72]

Even after they resolved the rent and utility payments, immigration authorities still felt the effects of not having control of their own space at Pier 21. In 1935, they called on the Halifax Harbour Commissioners to finally secure one of the windows in the detention quarters at Pier 21. This repair was left unaddressed for some time, resulting in a detained stowaway fleeing the facility in the middle of the night. When the immigration officials succeeded in arranging such repairs and maintenance through the commissioners, they occasionally were obliged to delay the work themselves to prevent construction from interfering with the daily operation of the immigration facility.[73]

There was no easy resolution for these conflicts. Immigration officials required the support of various federal departments, the railways, and voluntary service agencies in order to operate the site effectively. In turn, these organizations lobbied for space and access, which often led to further conflicts and confusion. For instance, upon opening the immigration facility, immigration authorities allotted available space to these charities and voluntary service organizations. The Canadian Red Cross set up their Seaport Nursery, while the Salvation Army, JIAS, the port chaplains, and others worked in shared spaces in the Annex building. Within the first year, the immigration department had to prohibit the Red Cross from holding fundraisers in the immigration building.[74]

Since ocean liners also carried passenger traffic en route to the United States, immigration officers from that country required space at Pier 21, which they took up in the adjoining office bay.[75] United States immigration officers also used a separate room to conduct their border business, which included meetings with American residents and visitors who only intended to enter the country for a short period of time. This close co-operation between Canadian and American officials was a feature of major ocean ports of entry in Canada and the United States during the early twentieth century.

For instance, in Victoria, British Columbia, Canadian officials borrowed the use of the Americans' detention rooms when needed, and in Quebec City, historically Canada's principal port of ocean entry, the United States maintained an immigration team to clear passengers landing in Canada who were destined for the United States. In Halifax, the connection reached back into the 1890s, when the Canadian immigration agent for the port of Halifax visited the United States' immigration facility at Ellis Island, in New York, to learn, compare, and improve entry processes. The allocation of dedicated space at the Ocean Terminals for an American processing team reflected this standing relationship—although it also later led to cutthroat badminton competitions between the two country's officials.[76] At the same time, Canadian immigration officers were stationed at Ellis Island to examine immigrants destined for Canada.[77]

The jostling for space was also a signal that staff and volunteers were settling into the new immigration facility. After an initial housewarming event on March 29, 1928, the initial operations at Pier 21 were brisk and busy.[78] In each of Pier 21's first two years of operation, approximately 44,000 immigrants entered Canada. However, less than two years after opening, the Great Depression began and the number of immigrants processed through the immigration facility fell drastically. In 1933, for example, only approximately 1,450 newcomers entered the country through the site. Overall, admissions to Canada fell approximately to one-fifth of those in the previous decade.[79]

During the Great Depression, the Canadian government restricted immigration both to prevent further unemployment and to bar individuals thought "likely to become a 'public charge'" after their arrival. The introduction of strict new regulations to limit eligible immigrants curtailed immigration to Canada sharply, and was part of a global trend of restrictive and nativist immigration policies in response to the challenging economic circumstances of the 1930s. In 1932, Harold Fields, then the Executive Director for the National League for American Citizenship, offered a review of immigration restrictions around the world, which he introduced as "the building up of walled-in countries… the doors which once were opened wide are now but slightly ajar."[80]

Canada's restrictive legislation did have a small opening: American citizens and British subjects from the United Kingdom, the Irish Free State, Newfoundland, Australia, New Zealand, and the Union of South Africa with "sufficient means to maintain" themselves until employment was secured were still permitted to enter Canada. Agriculturalists with "sufficient means to farm in Canada" were also admissible, as were their wives, and minor children of Canadian residents. Immigrants from all other categories seeking to immigrate to Canada were inadmissible and prohibited from entering the country.[81] Following this change in immigration policy, less than 3,100 immigrants per year were admitted into Canada through Pier 21 for the remainder of the 1930s.[82]

As fewer immigrants were admissible for entry into Canada, others who had arrived prior to the Great Depression and had later become dismayed by its socioeconomic effects chose to leave Canada through Pier 21 and return to their homelands. While some immigrants willingly left Canada, others were forced to leave. By 1933, nearly one-third of those eligible to work were unemployed, and Canadian officials viewed deportation as an effective measure against the rising number of immigrants who sought social assistance. The basis for such action could be found in the 1919 amendments to the 1910 Immigration Act, which prohibited any immigrant who "has become a professional beggar or a public charge," including immigrants already "on the dole." Such persons faced the threat of imminent deportation back to their country of origin.[83]

Canadian immigration officials were tasked with enforcing regulations that, in general terms, were established to prevent individuals from entering the country. This mechanism also played a role in protecting provincial and local governments, who were responsible for providing most of the social assistance at the time. Meanwhile, provincial governments also advocated that the Canadian government pursue deportation as a policy, and Pier 21 was frequently a site for embarking those ordered deported from across the country.[84] A report from the Red Cross Seaport Nursery in December 1931 remarked that "[f]or the deports who were in the Detention Quarters over Christmas, gifts were provided. For the children, a new pair of stockings, one of which was filled with oranges, apples, candy, mittens, small toys or books, these were hung by their bedside so they might have them early in the morning. Seventeen women were remembered with gifts."[85]

Despite the much-reduced immigration traffic, and the escalation in deportations, Pier 21 and the Ocean Terminals established an important capacity in Halifax to serve the transatlantic shipping network. At the end of the 1930s, the North Atlantic once again was transformed into a theatre of war—and the capacity of Pier 21 to handle massive volumes of passenger traffic became an asset for sending troops overseas, rather than welcoming immigrants to Canada.

OPPOSITE: Arrival of HMT *Pasteur* at Pier 21 with returning Canadian soldiers.

Source: Canada. Department of National Defence, Library and Archives Canada, e010786543

3 PIER 21 AT WAR

1939–1946

Here is a group of quite sincere and conscientious people who recently have been working against great odds in performing the thankless task of attempting to enforce the Immigration laws during wartime. The office may lack system and, as individuals, they may often have wrong ideas in relation to the work, but on the whole they are doing a good job. I have been sharing their difficulties during the past month, and it has been a rich experience with many anxious and perplexing moments, but not without a few good laughs.[1]
—Fenton Crosman, Immigration Officer, March 31, 1941

HALIFAX'S IMMIGRATION FACILITIES, DESIGNED TO HANDLE the incoming traffic of passengers from large ocean liners, could accommodate a similar scale of outbound traffic if needed, as in times of war. Pier 2, the main immigration shed in Halifax prior to Pier 21 opening in 1928, offered a historical precedent for this use of immigration facilities for war purposes. It was used for military transit during the First World War and on a smaller scale before that, during the Boer War. With the outbreak of the Second World War, the Halifax Ocean Terminals complex in South End Halifax, including Pier 21, was put to similar use by the Canadian military.

Canada declared war on Germany on September 10, 1939. The reality of the new conflict came home to the port of Halifax only a few days later. On September 13, more than two hundred survivors of the torpedoed SS *Athenia* arrived at Pier 21.[2] As with the First World War, Canada's personnel and war materiel needed to cross the Atlantic Ocean. The commercial and economic advantages of the port of Halifax—a deep, ice-free harbour, close to efficient shipping routes to Europe—once again became valuable to military planners. Within a month of the start of the Second World War, military transport units had supplanted immigration operations in large parts of Pier 21.[3]

Pier 21 was the principal embarkation point for Canada during the Second World War. Military personnel stationed at the Halifax Ocean Terminals were mainly concerned with moving soldiers and supplies across the Atlantic. The piers also received arriving Allied military members, enemy aliens, and prisoners of war coming to Canada for internment. Military medical personnel complemented the existing Department of National Health and Welfare staff, working in the new medical inspection room and dispensary. Military units also co-operated with transportation companies, including railways and steamship lines, to move valuable and sometimes sensitive or classified cargoes through the Halifax Ocean Terminals. These tasks required a range of supporting units, from the ceremonial presence of the military district band to the logistical help offered by local transport units based in the Annex building.[4] The army established barracks in the Annex, and some military units even briefly barracked in the assembly area of the immigration quarters.[5] During wartime, Pier 21 was the critical hub for a wide range of movements in support of the Allied war effort.

CANADIAN IMMIGRATION AT THE START OF THE SECOND WORLD WAR

In contrast with the variety and scope of military traffic at Pier 21, ocean immigration arrivals through the pier during the first five years of the war were negligible. The Second World War erupted at the end of the most restrictive decade in Canadian immigration history. Canadian authorities had introduced stringent and exclusionary immigration policies in response to the Great Depression, which led to an average of about 16,000 immigrants entering Canada per year during the 1930s. Only a fraction of these immigrants arrived at Pier 21. This was an enormous drop from an annual average of about 126,000 immigrants to Canada during the 1920s. These numbers did not decline a great deal further during the Second World War, as Canada continued to welcome an average of almost 13,000 immigrants per year during the conflict.[6] Canada's strict immigration criteria meant that the overwhelming majority of these arrivals originated from the United Kingdom or from the United States.

The restrictions in force at the time had been set up in response to the Great Depression. The regulations limited admissibility to agriculturalists with the capital to set up a farm and sustain themselves, or American and British subjects with suitable employment or enough money to assure officers that they would not become public charges. Besides narrow exceptions for the immediate family of Canadian residents, all other immigrants were barred from entry.[7] Immediately after the adoption of that regulation, immigrants arriving from the United States or the United Kingdom comprised approximately 83 per cent of immigrants, and, during the war, these preferred groups made up an even greater share of newcomers to Canada, at over 90 per cent. The main changes in immigration traffic through Pier 21 between its opening in 1928 and operations during the Second World War had their origins in the policies of the 1930s.

In the context of escalating state violence in Europe, the restrictions and exclusions in immigration policy of the Great Depression had a severe humanitarian impact. The Canadian government refused any policy change that might open the door to refugees, including Jews and others driven out of Nazi Germany and the occupied regions of Europe. Canada did accept more than 13,000 Jewish immigrants during the 1930s, but only in accordance with the restrictive general immigration policy of the day.[8] Influential officials within the Canadian civil service opposed the admission of refugees, and particularly Jewish refugees, to Canada. For instance, in 1938, High Commissioner for Canada in Great Britain Vincent Massey, encoded a telegram to Prime Minister William Lyon Mackenzie King, advocating for the admission of a generous number of Sudeten German refugees in order to forestall later claims from "non-Aryans."[9] This reflected a calculation of the desirability of the two groups. Massey viewed Sudeten Germans, displaced from Czechoslovakia by Nazi Germany's seizure of territory, as desirable settlers. By contrast, he and other Canadian officials, including Director of Immigration Frederick C. Blair, viewed Jewish refugees and immigrants as unlikely to integrate in Canada, and therefore viewed them as undesirable.

Perhaps the best-known example of refugee exclusion in the 1930s is the story of the voyage of MS *St. Louis* in May and June 1939. The ship carried more than nine hundred Jewish passengers, who were denied entry to Cuba and turned away from the United States, before making a direct return to Europe. Although the Canadian government did not have direct contact with the passengers or the ship, a group of prominent Canadians petitioned Prime Minister King to grant them sanctuary. At the time, King was travelling as part of the 1939 royal visit to Canada and the United States, so he passed the request to his subordinates. King asked Oscar Skelton, the undersecretary of state for External Affairs, to consult the acting prime minister, Ernest Lapointe, and Blair, to advise how the government could meet the request.[10]

Blair stated in response that an order-in-council would suffice to admit legally the passengers of MS *St. Louis*. However, he went on to list the various dangers of admission, ranging from the worry that the refugees would cross illegally into the United States to the idea that Canada would be implicitly supporting Germany in ridding itself of unwanted refugees. Finally, he argued that admitting the refugees aboard MS *St. Louis* would result in "a demand for a closed door on all others." Blair claimed that the existing assistance Canada was offering refugees would be imperilled by public outcry if MS *St. Louis* was accepted at a Canadian port. He suggested that their existing admissions program—lists of immigrants admitted by special permission every few weeks—would be endangered by a backlash. This advice apparently accorded with Skelton's positions. Based on the views of these civil servants, Canada made no offer of sanctuary to the passengers aboard MS *St. Louis*. The ship was forced to return to Europe, and although the passengers initially found safety in Britain, France, Belgium, and the Netherlands, 254 were killed in the Holocaust.[11]

The discussion regarding MS *St. Louis* and its passengers points to a small but noteworthy stream of immigrant entries that persisted in wartime. As Blair stated in describing how MS *St. Louis* passengers might be admitted, Canadian immigration processes included the regular entry of a small number of immigrants who were not ordinarily admissible, but whose admission was specifically allowed by an order-in-council. During the Second World War, this practice continued, and although the orders-in-council reflected only basic information about the immigrants, including their names, ages, origins, residence, and employment, they did illustrate who was seeking to immigrate to Canada. For example, one of the thirty-four entries approved on November 13, 1940, was for "David Binen Ochs, aged 36 years; wife Mirel, aged 34 years, and three children, Susi, Markus Evi and Judity, aged 9, 7 and 2 years, respectively, citizens of Poland, presently residing in London, England; intended occupation of first named—Rabbi."[12]

A large proportion of those admitted by order-in-council during the Second World War were Jewish immigrants who were able to arrange employment or family sponsorship in Canada and so were not arriving under humanitarian terms. Others admitted by ministerial permit included skilled workers, investors, domestics, and those with immediate family in Canada. The orders-in-council are peppered with notes that indicate an applicant's desirability and undesirability to immigration authorities at the time, such as "Hebrew," "of Asiatic race," "of Armenian race," and "divorced." Finally, a notable number of those admitted in this way were already resident in Canada as non-immigrants.[13]

Overall, from the outbreak of war in September 1939 to the end of the conflict in August 1945, just over 16,000 immigrants entered Canada via Halifax. The vast majority of these arrived after October 1944, as the movement of soldier dependents increased. Between 1940 and 1944, an average of 465 immigrants landed at Halifax each year.[14] The modest number of conventional immigrant arrivals did not tax the resources of the immigration officials at Pier 21. Wartime conditions at the port of Halifax, however, placed new demands on immigration officers, such as monitoring the arrival of thousands of foreign merchant mariners and civilians aboard the massive convoy traffic through Halifax.

MERCHANT MARINERS

The transportation of goods and personnel across the Atlantic Ocean was a crucial link for the Allies in the Second World War, managed through convoys of merchant vessels shepherded across the ocean by warships. Halifax was a key port in the convoy system and hosted huge numbers of foreign merchant ships. The foreign sailors arriving at the port would often disembark. Consequently, demand for the immigration processing of sailors at Halifax expanded dramatically. Immigration officers needed to process entries while guards detained arrivals who breached immigration or wartime merchant shipping regulations.

Processing arrivals was a particularly complex task in wartime. Sailors might disembark legally or "jump ship," as they would in peacetime, but wartime added the problems of sailors potentially being from neutral or enemy countries. Others arrived after surviving a German U-boat attack. All arrivals at Pier 21 had to pass through an inspection. Further, the peril of wartime shipping assignments weighed heavily on the crews and affected their decisions about where and when to accept work. Some of the merchant mariners did not want to go back to sea after experiencing a wartime sinking, or would refuse or resist assignments to ships sailing in war zones. So-called "recalcitrant sailors" could be jailed for three months under Canada's Merchant Seaman Order of 1941.[15]

A system of manning pools was created to organize and track sailors. This ensured a reserve of ready crews for urgent wartime crossings, although historian William Naftel described this system as nearing conscription for British subjects, with others "encouraged" to participate.[16] Officials from the immigration branch had to collaborate with representatives of

Convoy assembling in Bedford Basin.
Source: Canada. Department of National Defence, Library and Archives Canada, e010777293

the director of merchant seamen, as sailors bound for the manning pools passed through Canadian immigration screening as temporary visitors to the country. Once in Canada, the sailors were still subject to immigration requirements and regulations, including deportation for severe infractions.

Immigration officials also worked to arrange temporary employment ashore in Canadian war industries for foreign sailors in the manning pools—many sailors were skilled labourers in valuable trades. In Halifax, the RCMP initially stepped in to revoke the sailors' registration cards, as there was some confusion about who was eligible to work in the program. After this problem was resolved, the registry program—coordinated for foreign sailors by immigration staff on both coasts and at the ports along the St. Lawrence River—provided some support for war industries in Canada. This promotion of entry for those who could contribute to war labour matched the discretionary loosening of immigration restrictions during the war. The tight controls on entry imposed in the early 1930s governed immigration during the conflict. However, by 1941, immigration officers were applying exceptions to the stringent immigration controls based on skills needed to support the war. This surprising leniency reflected Canada's acute wartime labour situation and highlighted the persistent connections between immigration and labour regulations.[17]

In September 1940, officers with the immigration branch submitted reports concerning more than one hundred foreign sailors detained at the Atlantic immigration stations, mostly held because they were not eligible to enter Canada under existing immigration regulations. Immigration officials joined colleagues from the Department of National Defence (DND), the RCMP, and the Department of Transport to hold boards of inquiry to review these sailors' cases. The boards of inquiry could order a sailor's release, assignment to a ship or manning pool, or detention. The sailors began a series of sit-down strikes, along with refusing sailings, to protest the forced work. Since ship traffic was essential to the Allied war effort, the Canadian government passed Order-in-Council P.C. 4751-1940, citing the threat to Canada's security and welfare created by the reluctance of the sailors, and authorized detaining those who refused work at sea.[18]

In Halifax, only a portion of detainees were held for refusing to sail: One immigration official reported that only six of more than 140 men detained in the winter of 1940–41 were recalcitrant sailors. Most could not comply with immigration regulations for entering Canada as visitors. Pier 21's accommodation and detention area remained busy throughout the war with foreign merchant seamen, although rarely was it as crowded as in March 1942, when more than 160 were detained. Wartime accommodation and detention also sometimes exceeded what was lawful, as when two distressed British seamen suspected of sabotage in the British West Indies were held at Pier 21, "not in accordance with the law, but as a matter of safety and convenience."[19]

These requirements for screening, detaining, and reviewing the cases of merchant mariners were a substantial burden on immigration officers and guards in Halifax. The sheer scale of work led an administrator to claim to Immigration Officer Fenton Crosman that the Pier 21 office handled 40 per cent more files early in the war than the average in peacetime. Crosman describes the immigration office at Pier 21 in 1940 as busy almost to the point of disorganization, but mainly with the foreign crews from freighters, as there were few regular passenger ships or incoming passengers.

There were so many it was a challenge to control them, let alone "the large number of deserting seamen."[20] Immigration Secretary Alison Trapnell confirms that the work of the immigration team at Pier 21 expanded dramatically in wartime. Trapnell recalls that "when the war broke out, they started taking on staff—it got busier. Before you knew it, there were seven or eight girls working there instead of me doing everything."[21]

Confusion around the new and changing immigration tasks arose shortly after the war started. For example, in mid-October 1939, a crewman arrived in Halifax who was a citizen of Danzig, an independent city state within Polish territory that had since fallen in the German invasion. Immigration authorities failed to reach a decision on how to process him, and the RCMP arrived the next day and placed him under arrest. Then the arrest was cancelled and the man was released to return to his ship. At the same time, immigration officials tried to persuade the shipping company to accept another detained sailor as crew, too. Even as this case unfolded, the minister responsible for immigration entered into a contract with the City of Halifax to use the city's prisons to detain foreign crew members. Within the immigration branch, Halifax officers also accepted transfers of sailors detained at Montreal, responding to a pressing need as the Laurentian port closed during the winter.[22]

The circumstances at Halifax were not necessarily better for mariners. In 1941, foreign mariners held in Halifax at Rockhead Prison under the supervision of immigration officers were continually reporting sick. The level of claimed illness may have been related to the daily routine at Rockhead, which included roughly eight hours of breaking stone in the prison yard, cleaning the prison facility, or working in the kitchens. Conditions there led the detained seamen to hold a hunger strike. They demanded to be moved to the immigration quarters at Pier 21 instead. Crosman believed the strike was incited by a foreign diplomat with pro-Nazi sympathies. The Immigration Medical Services doctor at Pier 21 accordingly declined to provide a medical opinion on the mariners, a position supported by his superiors in the Department of National Health. This left immigration authorities nurturing the suspicion that the sailors were malingering in refusing labour at the prison, and the tension over their detention conditions was prolonged.[23]

Dealing with so many foreign sailors created other pressures for the immigration staff. Although some of the immigration officers spoke several languages, the immigration branch needed additional interpreters to overcome language barriers. The staff at Pier 21 also added a dedicated administrative employee, responsible solely for paperwork related to the merchant mariner cases. Eventually, the demand on the Halifax immigration staff was such that the immigration department had to establish a separate branch office for handling matters related to merchant shipping and foreign sailors.[24]

EVACUATED CIVILIANS

Amid the surge in merchant shipping, some passenger ships still made regular calls at Pier 21. A wide range of transatlantic ocean liners came into the port during the war as troopships, including many famous ships that did not usually call in Halifax, such as Cunard's celebrated HMT *Queen Elizabeth* and HMT *Queen Mary*, and the French liner HMT *Île de France*. Locally, the best-known of these wartime callers might have been HMT *Aquitania*, one of the few true four-funnel ocean liners ever built. During the Second World War, Haligonians referred to HMT *Aquitania* as "the Ferry" thanks to its frequent calls. Besides these grand and storied ocean liners, the demands of the war meant that the smallest and least elegant vessels were also pressed into service. All were stripped to minimal comforts for their service. While overwhelmingly used to carry personnel, some passenger ships also carried a notable type of non-immigrant civilian traffic. In wartime, Pier 21 received evacuated civilians from abroad, including the guest children sent to safety in Canada from the United Kingdom.

Across the country, Canadian families agreed to care for British children during the Second World War. Early in the conflict, parents and officials in the Britain feared the risks to children from aerial bombardment, which led to urban evacuations to rural areas. These damaging aerial attacks failed to materialize in the early stages of the conflict—the "Phoney War"—and the evacuation effort lost urgency. However, as the war progressed and the public in Britain perceived an invasion threat—especially after the fall of France in June 1940—the removal of vulnerable children from Britain to safety became a priority again. The plans included both public and private efforts to send children to overseas sanctuaries, including Canada, Australia, and New Zealand.[25]

The Children's Overseas Reception Board (CORB) sent Adrienne Downs (née Derue) to Canada as a nine-year-old evacuee in 1940. She recalls that she "was so excited over this big adventure which I thought would just be a holiday."[26] Behind this adventure, however, was a fear of strategic bombing of civilian centres. In September 1939, almost 1.5 million civilians were displaced within the United Kingdom, evacuating from major cities to rural areas to seek safety, and also overseas to Canada, Australia, and other relative safe havens.[27] The British government funded CORB; other schemes for evacuating children and civilians made use of relationships between private companies or universities, and some evacuees resorted to family sponsorship to cross the Atlantic.

The Canadian public's response to the evacuated civilians was generally favourable, couched as it was in terms of the historic and imperial relationship with the United Kingdom. However, there was also resistance to the movement. Frederick C. Blair, Canada's director of immigration—a crucial authority over any migration plan—nurtured an abiding skepticism toward the admission of children without their parents, whether as orphans or as a measure of family separation. In the United Kingdom, it was a matter of public resentment that many of the children whose safety was obtained privately did so through privileged networks of wealth and power.[28] British Prime Minister Winston Churchill thought evacuating the vulnerable was an undesirable and defeatist movement, and so a potential embarrassment.[29]

The public program, however, suffered much worse than embarrassment before it was brought to a close. German U-boats torpedoed two ships carrying evacuees in the summer of 1940. One, SS *Volendam*, was not seriously damaged, but the second, SS *City of Benares*, went down, killing almost eighty children. Although the roughly 1,500 publicly funded children are the group most readily remembered from the evacuees, 5,951 privately and publicly funded children, 117 adult men, and 1,847 adult women were sent out to Canada for safety in the first eighteen months of the war. Public funding for ocean evacuation with CORB was terminated in 1940, but many thousands of privately evacuated children were sent to safety in Canada during the war.[30]

For the first stages of their journey, the evacuee children required assistance from voluntary organizations, as well as temporary accommodations at schools or other gathering points. The information given to the children could be confusing or incomplete: Patricia and Pamela Pyle remember being advised to prepare for a two-week holiday, rather than for evacuation across the ocean. Another evacuee child recalls being asked if she wanted a holiday in Canada. She and her sister prepared for the trip, and on the day of their departure, boarded a bus. Only then were they told their parents would not be travelling with them.[31]

Aside from the dangers of bombing and torpedoing, the voyage across the North Atlantic could be stormy and nauseating, and the process of joining the ship and observing the routine aboard could be bewildering. The food aboard the ships impressed some of the children even as the various safety drills provoked both nervousness and excitement. This tension was captured by Catherine Read (née MacKinnon), a Scottish evacuee, who writes: "On August 16th, we sailed down the Firth of Clyde on the SS *Bayano*. My sister recorded that she was optimistic and happy, as she regarded this as an adventure. However, as I stood on deck watching the gigantic waves, I became aware of the vast distance separating our family, as well as the danger of being at sea during the war."[32]

Once in Canada, the children were placed with a host family, and the adjustment for both hosts and young people could be difficult. Some child evacuees have glowing recollections of their hosts, such as R. Stanley Goat, who praises the couple that took him in, describing them as loving and extremely generous. One pair of sisters integrated into their Canadian host family so strongly that they did not wish to leave, and the hosts tried to adopt them. The parents went through the British consul to intervene and have them returned to England. Others had experiences like Daphne Levy (née Nardell), who was compelled to move regularly between hosts, some carefree and others strict. Levy states, after the many moves, she came to the end of the evacuation as a nervous teenager with little personal confidence.[33]

The alienation some children experienced from their parents points to a significant aspect of the movement: returning to the United Kingdom

Photograph of Catherine MacKinnon and other evacuee children on the deck of SS *Bayano*, 1940. *Source: Canadian Museum of Immigration Collection (DI2014.233.17)*

was a difficult "homecoming" for the children. Expecting a separation of a few months, many were in Canada for their formative years as teenaged students. Levy recalls embarking for her return to the United Kingdom as a proud Canadian patriot, and Peter Clarke recalled that his Canadian accent and clothes singled him out for taunts when he returned to school in England in September 1945. Sometimes parents and children scarcely recognized each other. The Canadian influences on the children had a notable and enduring impact, such that some of the children evacuated to Canada during the war later returned as immigrants. In his written account of his immigration, Donald Stephen Chandler notes passing through Pier 21 in 1940 and 1945 as an evacuee, and in 1948 as an immigrant. A small group of the evacuees never returned to the United Kingdom. The annual report of the immigration branch of 1946/47 noted some seventy British children brought forward under the program were still in Canada in March 1947, with a substantial number granted status as landed immigrants in Canada.[34]

SENT FOR SAFEKEEPING IN CANADA

Besides the evacuated children, the dangers in Europe also compelled several governments to take steps to send others to Canada for safekeeping. Courtesies were also extended in July 1940 to staff and family members from the Polish government-in-exile, who entered Canada via Halifax on diplomatic or service passports. They were accompanied by classified wireless equipment and an operator, intended to help coordinate the diplomacy of the Polish government-in-exile. They arrived thanks to negotiations between the consul general of Poland in Canada and the Department of External Affairs.[35] Collaboration between Canada and the Allies extended to hosting conferences to coordinate the war, and in August 1943 Winston Churchill arrived at Pier 21 aboard HMT *Queen Mary* to attend a conference at Quebec City.[36] A well-known example that still touches public culture is the sanctuary granted to Princess Juliana of the Netherlands and her children in Canada via Halifax.[37]

Alongside the arrival of diplomats and royalty, European state assets—including significant amounts of gold bullion—were also sent to Canada, beginning almost immediately after the war broke out. Only a portion of the gold that arrived in Canada came to Halifax: the tremendous weight of the shipments led to some of the heavily laden rail cars jumping the curved sidings at the Halifax Ocean Terminals.[38] Shipments of gold also went directly to Quebec City and Montreal. Other treasures arrived as well, with one remarkable example being the Polish Wawel Treasures, which arrived at Pier 21 in Halifax in July 1940.

Days after Germany invaded Poland, staff at Wawel Royal Castle in Krakow, Poland, began moving a selection of irreplaceable state treasures. The selected items included Szczerbiec, the coronation sword of Poland used between the fourteenth and eighteenth centuries, and original manuscripts of Frédéric Chopin's compositions. The curators moved the artifacts by river barges and peasant carts, as well as by truck, reaching the Romanian border in about two weeks.[39] From the border they carried on with their cargo to the Polish embassy in Bucharest, considered their options for safety and preservation of the artifacts on continental Europe, and at last chose to seek refuge for themselves and the cultural treasures in

France. In early 1940, they reached a converted factory in Aubusson that was used to store the French state's art collection.[40]

In May 1940, Germany invaded France, and the collection and its curators were again forced to move. This time, the curators headed to England en route to Canada. On July 4, 1940, the Free Polish ship MS *Batory* departed the United Kingdom for Canada, carrying the Polish cultural treasures and staff. MS *Batory* was in convoy with ships carrying British evacuee children, half a billion dollars in gold and securities, and diplomats and wireless equipment for representatives of the Polish government-in-exile in Canada. The collection arrived at Pier 21 on July 12, 1940, before departing for Ottawa, where the Wawel treasures were housed in a records-storage facility of the National Archives of Canada, located on the grounds of the city's Experimental Farm. The collection remained there until 1945, with some additions from the cultural artifacts used in the Polish display at the 1939 World's Fair in New York.[41] When Poland was occupied and subsumed into the Soviet bloc at the end of the Second World War, Cold War sensibilities and prejudices contributed to Canada's refusal to repatriate the artifacts. The full collection did not return to Poland until 1961, more than twenty years after its arrival at Pier 21.

The Halifax Ocean Terminals area remained an active transit facility for ordinary cargo as well as for these types of remarkable shipments occasioned by the war. One distinctive feature of the Pier 21 environs after the Second World War was a large wooden ramp, built for convenient access to the second floor of shed 22. The CNR constructed it in 1942; despite its wartime construction, its purpose was prosaic. With the sheds at the port of Halifax being quite busy, more space was needed for export goods, especially grain and flour. The sturdy timber ramp opened up the spacious second floor of shed 22 for these trade goods.[42]

MILITARY USE OF PIER 21

While the variety of civilian traffic at Halifax during the Second World War reflects the range and complexity of the War itself, the diverse military uses of the pier reflect the changing roles Canada had in the conflict and its aftermath. The scope of Canada's commitment to the war meant that Canadian military personnel were by far the largest group to pass through Pier 21 during the war years. However, Canadian troop movements occurred alongside a number of other important military movements through Halifax.

The central role of Halifax—the un-named "East Coast Port" in wartime press releases—during the Second World War became evident to the public on December 10, 1939, when the 1st Canadian Infantry Division departed for Europe. Some 7,400 soldiers set off for duty overseas aboard the troopships HMT *Aquitania*, HMT *Duchess of Bedford*, HMT *Empress of Britain*, HMT *Empress of Australia*, and HMT *Monarch of Bermuda*.[43] This departure affords some insight into operations at Pier 21 and Halifax Ocean Terminals broadly, and particularly one of the continuous threads of wartime operations at the port: secrecy and security. This was a large movement of well-known passenger ships, guarded in convoy by an impressive military escort. Although specific details of the convoy were sensitive, there was no way to conceal the scope and nature of the transit from even the most casual of observers in Halifax. Nevertheless, the local press did not report on the event until the convoy had arrived safely in the United Kingdom.

More than a week after its departure from Halifax, headlines began to appear trumpeting the First Division's arrival on December 19, 1939. Journalists hearkened back to the initial deployments of the First World War and called the news that the Canadian contingent had arrived "the most welcome and heartening news" for Britain.[44] The departures are commemorated in part by the iconic photographs of soldiers marching through the streets of Halifax to the waterfront sheds, including Pier 21, and filing across gangways into the troopships used to carry them across the Atlantic Ocean.

PIER 21'S CRITICAL WARTIME ROLE: EMBARKATION

Amid the variety of other traffic associated with the war, the departure of Canadians was the most visible and critical role of the pier in wartime. Celebrities such as the English singer Gracie Fields participated in events at the pier or aboard ship. Bands played to bid farewell or to welcome personnel home. The majority of Canada's 425,000 soldiers sent overseas went by way of Pier 21. In 1942, over the course of three months, almost 60,000 soldiers embarked at the Halifax Ocean Terminals for service overseas. In this role, Pier 21 was often the site of the last steps in Canada for the people going to war. Regarding recruitment and accepting service overseas, Kenneth MacLaren reflects on and nuances the familiar narrative of duty and service for country with the place of peer relationships and pressure: "I guess some of them had relatives in the army, as I did, and we were endeavouring to—as they say in England, [we] expect every man to do his duty. We were endeavouring to do that which we thought was right for our country and our families. Standing up for right and, I guess, most of the soldiers had friends like I did."[45]

Harold Hayward echoes MacLaren's comment on peers. Hayward joined the army shortly after the war broke out, and he remembers that he was not pressured to join in any way but that his friends were going and it was because of their enlistment that he wanted to go. James Gregg shares that sentiment, commenting that he went along with a crowd to enlist as all the young men he knew were joining up. Social pressures took other forms, too: a Halifax stevedore, whose work exempted him from military service, nevertheless joined up early in the war. His reason: "I got tangled up with a married woman… I said, I have to get out of this mess."[46]

Work and employment loomed large in soldiers' enlistment decisions. Gaston Audy remarks that most of the men in his unit had been unemployed before the war, and "one way to find something to eat was to join the army, you know… they were quite happy to move overseas."[47] One Halifax resident recalls joining the militia in 1937 as a teenager. He was part of a military family, but laughed at the idea of fighting for country; his family had been so poor in Halifax that he had gone days without eating, and even passed out in school from hunger: "[F]ight for their country—I mean, what for?" He was automatically mobilized at the start of the war, and went from a situation of poverty to making $50 a month in Depression-era Halifax, on top of having meals and accommodation provided.[48] Reginald Crowe had a good job as a machinist at Canada Car & Foundry in Fort William (now Thunder Bay), Ontario. However, he was constantly harassed by his foreman for his Indigenous heritage, and

Soldiers leaving their train to board a troopship at Pier 21 (n.d.).
Source: Canada Science and Technology Museum, CN005772

eventually punched the man, knocking him out. The supervisor fired Crowe, who walked by an enlistment centre the next day and decided to sign up. Within hours he was on his way to Winnipeg for service in the military as an engineer.[49]

Once service members were ordered overseas, the actual process of moving through Pier 21 was usually quite efficient. Soldiers could march right into the shed from a train arriving directly outside, or they could move to the site from other military accommodations in Halifax. In either case, they usually passed straight through the building and headed up gangways onto their ship from either the ground level or the second storey of the pier—depending on the size of the troopship. The same streamlined movement that made the site useful for handling arriving passengers was suitable for transferring thousands of personnel in the other direction, to board ships bound for the war in Europe.

Veterans who passed through Pier 21 on their way to serve overseas have various recollections of the way that departure was marked and acknowledged. Donald H. MacKenzie recalls that some events were formal. MacKenzie's contingent aboard HMT *Orion* received a farewell address by Colonel James L. Ralston, the minister of national defence, in July 1941. William Barker, on the other hand, describes a much less formal send-off. Members of the public met his train from Petawawa in Halifax, presenting the soldiers with Black Horse beer and rum that they drank by sticking their fingers in the bottle and licking it, chasing it with their tears. Reginald Crowe was sent off with coffee and doughnuts from Red Cross volunteers working at Pier 21. Claude Cowan describes feeling like walking up the ramp to the ship seemed to take forever, but he had a surprise once he reached the top. His father had arranged to send him money as a gift, and a cheque was waiting as Cowan stepped aboard the ship.[50]

Others remarked on the entire absence of ceremony. This was the case for Dorothy Chartrand, who deployed with the Canadian Women's Army Corps. Chartrand remembers arriving at "the dark dingy sheds at Pier 21 before the sun rose," with only train and dock workers in sight. She recalls that her contingent had already made their farewells with loved ones, so "[t]here would not be any tears visibly shed on this occasion." Chartrand boarded HMT *Andes*, painted in a dull wartime scheme and with the name blotted over, and the ship slipped out of the harbour in the dead of night.[51]

For a very few veterans stuck in service with units stationed in Canada, the opportunity to serve overseas did not come soon enough from the military, and so they attempted to stow away on merchant vessels to make their own way to the war, avoiding the orderly embarkation at Pier 21 entirely. Discovered by members of the crew before departure, they were sentenced to twenty-eight days of confinement. One member, a coastal artillery gunner, tried again with the help of a sympathetic merchant mariner—himself an army deserter—and actually made the crossing to England from Newfoundland manning a deck gun on a merchant ship. He served another twenty-eight days in custody after his arrival, and then was released to serve in an anti-tank unit.[52]

No matter how they left for their service overseas, the requirement for security of information limited what soldiers were supposed to share with

Members of the Toronto Scottish Regiment board HMT *Empress of Australia* at Pier 21, 1939.
Source: Canada. Department of National Defence, Library and Archives Canada, PA-137186

their families about their travel, although they could find ways to bend the rules. Douglas Power, an army stretcher-bearer, contradicts himself when asked whether he had informed family about his departure for Europe: "No. No. Well, accidentally. My father was working here on the station, and I had an uncle, and when we were coming into Halifax, I saw my uncle, and I hollered to him, and I said, 'Tell Dad that I'm going to be down here.' So he came down on one of the shuttle trains and I had about five minutes to talk to him."[53]

One member of the Canadian Women's Army Corps, Della Johansen (née Holmes), states that her unit had no information about where they were going at all after being ordered overseas, even as they boarded the ship. As she embarked at Pier 21, she recognized one of the security personnel was a relative, a veteran of the First World War. He whispered to her that the ship she was boarding was bound for the United Kingdom. After five days at sea passed, they received their first concrete information: an announcement that the ship was bound for Europe. Johansen had actually volunteered to go overseas for service in the Pacific and Japan, so the destination was a surprise, but she reflects that she had signed up for service wherever needed. After arrival, Johansen was still kept from communicating her location to her parents for a time.[54]

The need for security struck some as excessive: there was no way to conceal the major movements of ships in the harbour from anyone who wanted to observe them. The danger to shipping was quite real, however, and occasionally delayed departures, as was the case for Everett MacLeod. MacLeod boarded HMT *Duchess of Atholl* in June 1940 but waited for two days before being allowed to sail due to the threat of German submarine activity. There were also internal security matters that affected embarkation and crossings. For instance, the military needed to segregate personnel working on sensitive technology, like radar, from other passengers crossing on the same troopship.[55]

This arrangement for security reflects the fact that, once aboard ship, personnel movements were often controlled strictly. On larger vessels, personnel were often only free to move around within certain areas on the ship. This was in part for safety, as well as for control and discipline. Douglas Power points out that that the sheer numbers of personnel aboard the larger troopships could have created a stability problem if they all crowded to one side at once. He escaped from this movement control as a member of a medical detail supporting a forward gun position, and so enjoyed freedom to travel all over the vessel. His berth, however, was in a cramped space quite far forward and below decks. The soldiers in that room were briefed that they would have to clear out quickly if there was an alarm, as automatic hatches would close. With that news, one of the other soldiers simply refused to stay there, and had to be allowed to spend most of his time on deck. Although no emergency arose, Power recounts a German propaganda broadcast received on their second day at sea, claiming HMT *Queen Mary* had been sunk. This was relayed to the troops as an ironic notice that "in case you don't know, you've just been sunk."[56]

Military personnel often had duties assigned to them related to the crossing, whether during embarkation or while at sea. Robert Linden was

Embarkation Transit Unit arch, with Pier 20 and Pier 21 in the background, 1946.
Source: H. B. Jefferson, Nova Scotia Archives (1992-304 no. 43-1-4 250)

an officer with the Royal Canadian Air Force who left Canada for service overseas in 1942 aboard HMT *Queen Elizabeth*. During the loading of the vessel at Pier 21, he and a small cadre of other Air Force officers were tasked with bringing cartons of cigarettes from shore, up a gangway and to ships' stores. As Linden explains, through a series of diversions, each of the officers involved arrived in England with five thousand cigarettes. He also made the most of assigned duties during the crossing, as he and his cohort were tasked with serving meals aboard ship. Most personnel on the ship got two meals per day, and there were four sittings for each meal. Linden would have an early meal, serve meals, and then have a late meal—and then do the same three hours later for the second round of dining. Linden sums up his work on the ship: "[W]e ended up fat and happy with all of the cigarettes."[57]

For some veterans, the voyage across the ocean was not new. Johan Frederick Havinga arrived at Pier 21 as a ten-year-old child emigrating from the Netherlands in 1930, and went out from the pier in December 1940 for service overseas. The cook, recognizing a fellow Dutchman, provided Havinga with a bucket of kippered herring, which he says "did not do much to improve the condition of my seasick mates, or my popularity."[58] For others, the pier would acquire further personal significance after the war, as the wives they had met and married abroad in the course of their service arrived in Canada as war brides, at Pier 21.[59]

Moving personnel from inland onto the ships required local coordination, which was provided by a military movements staff known for much of the war as the Embarkation Transit Unit. That unit took over most of the immigration quarters at Pier 21 immediately after the outbreak of war, and by late September the immigration staff had been squeezed into a section of their former offices. Military staff moved into both the larger offices and the detention area. The immigration hospital was used for immigration detention, and other similar cases were sent on to jail in Quebec City.[60] With military tasks consuming the pier, tight security was the rule in wartime. Joyce Woodford (née Penney) enlisted in the Canadian Women's Army Corps and worked in the Embarkation Transit Unit at Pier 21 from 1943 to 1946. She states that "[we] had to pass through a guard gate when we'd come. Now, if there wasn't what we used to call a move, when the people came—if there wasn't a move on, we could come there, and we'd say hello to the RCMP and everything else. But once the move came up, if we didn't have our card to get in, we didn't get in, even though he knew us. That was very, very strict."[61]

Embarkation and troop transport had support from social services in Canada, even during the crossings. One of the major organizations providing assistance to the military was the YMCA, through their War Services branch. The YMCA coordinated with ships' officers aboard troop transports in order to obtain a berth and some work space for their representatives. Once placed aboard ship, YMCA War Services workers would share magazines, books, games, and cards, among other items, with military personnel. The regional supervisor for these services visited Pier 21 with his staff, and as Woodford mentions above, was subject to strict security controls for access to the site and the ships during wartime.[62]

Although embarkation for Canadians was the central role of the site, Allied—and sometimes enemy—service personnel also arrived in Canada at Pier 21. One of the major Canadian contributions to the Allied war effort was its participation in the British Commonwealth Air Training Plan, a project with more than one hundred affiliated training facilities across Canada. Over the duration of the conflict, almost 60,000 foreign personnel trained in the country through this program, representing the air forces of the United Kingdom, United States, New Zealand, and Australia. Among these were Polish, Norwegian, Belgian, Dutch, Czechoslovak, and Free French allies serving in the Royal Air Force. The program was seen to be of such importance that President Franklin Roosevelt termed Canada "the aerodrome of democracy."[63] The core of the associated teaching personnel, a total of about three hundred expert instructors from the Royal Air Force, arrived via Pier 21. Halifax continued to serve the air training plan as its only significant ocean embarkation depot throughout the duration of the scheme. A few of the servicemen brought to Canada as part of this plan courted or married Canadian women during their training and returned to Canada upon their demobilization from service, usually after the war.[64]

INTERNEES AND PRISONERS OF WAR

At the same time as the embarkation unit was investing its efforts in transferring Allied personnel out of Canada, Pier 21 also received a significant number of arriving enemy prisoners of war for internment at camps in the Canadian interior. Canada had taken steps as soon as the war started to intern designated enemies. There were twenty-five permanent internment camps across the country, which eventually housed 34,000 German prisoners of war. A host of peripheral labour camps supported these principal camps. The early operations of these camps also witnessed civilian internment, generally of Canadian residents or citizens, which historian Martin Auger calls "incarceration."

These civilians were assessed not to be a threat as the war progressed, but as programs for their release proceeded in 1942 and 1943, new inmates began to arrive at the camps. These arrivals were German military personnel

OPPOSITE: A German prisoner of war arrives at "an East Coast Port," 1941. *Source: National Film Board of Canada, Library and Archives Canada, PA-176616*

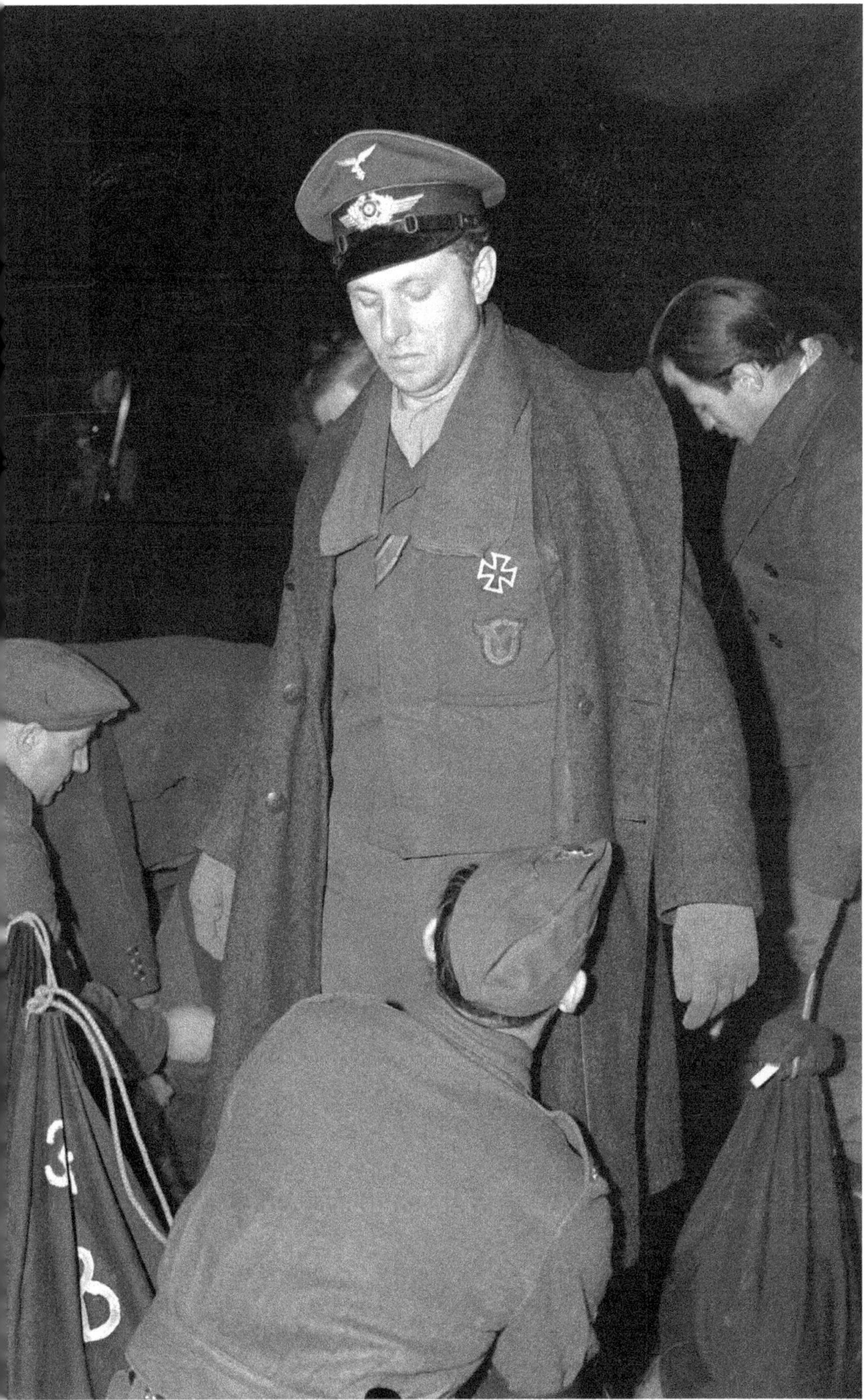

captured as military operations escalated.[65] In 1942, three thousand German prisoners of war arrived at Halifax aboard *Scythia*, including Gotthard John Schönfelder. Schönfelder was a German merchant mariner whose work included supplying U-Boats and ferrying German military personnel to Norway. He was captured by the British after one year of service, and spent almost a year in camps in the United Kingdom. Schönfelder thought, as he arrived in Canada, that he was safe and that his war was over. He and his fellow prisoners arrived on April 20, 1942, Hitler's birthday and a major German holiday at the time. Schönfelder moved through a series of camps and work placements in Canada, finishing at a major dairy farm near Ottawa. He reluctantly left Canada in November 1946, but five years later returned as an immigrant, sponsored by the same Ottawa-area dairy farmers, sailing aboard *Scythia* once more.[66]

The prisoner of war arrivals, after some initial lapses that allowed two prisoners to escape briefly into the city of Halifax, were handled with very high security. The prisoners joined trains immediately to go to detention camps farther inland, with the nearest camp located in New Brunswick. Many of the prisoners provided valuable labour in Canada, such that at the end of the war, a movement of veterans of service in Polish forces was put in place to replace them. The politics of replacing enemy prisoner labour with Allied veterans was delicate, and so the public messaging was quickly reframed by the immigration branch. This movement of Polish veterans was a critical experiment in Canada's postwar acceptance of displaced persons and refugees via bulk labour arrangements.[67]

The prisoners initially sent from the United Kingdom included an unexpected group: German refugees intermingled with prisoners of war. Canada did take in a total of approximately 34,000 prisoners of war, but also about 4,000 German civilians, many of whom had fled to the United Kingdom to escape persecution in Germany. The initial group sent from the United Kingdom was particularly problematic, as it was composed about equally of German prisoners and civilians. Upon their arrival, Canadians began to realize that there was a problem, as, in the words of one of the interned civilians, Eric Koch, "[t]he overwhelming presence among the new arrivals of high school boys, students, professors, priests and rabbis was not what London had promised to deliver"—that is, a group of military prisoners of war.[68] Despite this issue, all of those sent from the United Kingdom in this group were placed in internment camps. These included more than twenty installations in New Brunswick, Quebec, Ontario, and Alberta.

Anti-Nazi civilians and refugees in the group benefited from a substantial change in their living conditions in Canada in 1941, including camp reassignments that placed internees from similar circumstances together. The change, which was forced on the camp system, was made despite the resistance of Canadian immigration authorities, who held that the release of the interned refugees would effectively allow them to avoid normal immigration processes and restrictions. Nevertheless, in June 1941, the refugees among the interned Germans were granted status under Order-in-Council P.C. 4568. About one thousand of these civilians accepted naturalization in Canada after the war, and Koch alludes to the group's deserved reputation as one of the most successful groups of immigrants that Canada has ever admitted. Nevertheless, historian Paula J. Draper quotes one of the interned Jewish refugees complaining that "the injustice of the whole thing still rankles."[69]

The enemy prisoners, on the other hand, created some issues within Canada. There were some acts of resistance at the camps, including a full-scale riot at the Bowmanville camp, when Canadian guards shackled the German prisoners during a set of diplomatic reprisals for similar treatment of Allied prisoners.[70] Outside the camps, occasionally the internees crossed paths with soldiers bound for service. Canadian soldier Edward J. Weaver entered infantry training late in the war at Farnham, Quebec, which was also the location for one of the internment camps for prisoners of war. Weaver states:

> I was on my way to town, following a well-beaten path through the snow, when all of a sudden I came face to face with an officer in a grey uniform. I quickly realized he was a German army officer. But what in the name of Hades was a German officer doing here, on the loose, no less. He resumed his way towards the camp, and I went to town. On inquiring, I was told German war prisoners were kept here, and some had privileges to go to town for instance. That didn't sit right with me, because their type had killed my brother.[71]

THE 1944 FIRE

Amid this varied ocean traffic, the busy Embarkation Transit Unit witnessed a significant accident at the site. On March 5, 1944, fire swept through Pier 21, gutting the immigration quarters and causing an estimated $250,000 in damage. The facility had added many new functions to accommodate the demands of the war, and these helped cause the fire, which was traced to fumigation equipment in Pier 22. The equipment was used by the military embarkation staff to clean ships' bedding. Though the main construction of the shed at Pier 21 was concrete and steel, the building had numerous wooden partitions and walls, and the wooden attic grain galleries provided an excellent channel for the blaze to move quickly. By the time firefighters arrived, the entire five-hundred-foot shed was ablaze. Fortunately, immigration guards successfully evacuated seventeen detained mariners, and the matron had taken the weekend with family elsewhere in the city.[72]

The displaced immigration staff took up residence in the Annex building and in temporary wooden sheds nearby while shed 21 was repaired. They also made use of a shipping agent's offices briefly after the fire. Alison Trapnell returned with Hugh Grant, the senior immigration officer, to view the space after the fire. They found that the fire had destroyed many active files and reports, and the heat had melted typewriters into the desks beneath them. This was a difficult setback for the immigration staff, exacerbated by the crowded, verminous conditions of the temporary quarters north of the Annex. Even simple immigration tasks were much more difficult when the office's records, forms, stamps, and other supplies had been destroyed.[73]

Although Army personnel had immediately undertaken the task of clearing loose debris, the damage was profound: the National Harbours Board described the second storey of the shed as "almost entirely destroyed" and sought contracts for its complete demolition as the first step in repairs. Pier 21's second-storey immigration quarters did not reopen until December 1946. The Embarkation Transit Unit continued to operate from temporary buildings near the Annex, from the Annex itself, and out of the waterfront sheds until early in 1947.[74]

REPATRIATION

Pier 21 was therefore in poor condition for the return of thousands of soldiers after the end of the Second World War. The military staff and immigration authorities made do through the peak of postwar traffic in 1946. Pier 21 was the principal point of return for the 403,197 Army and Air Force personnel who were repatriated to Canada following service overseas between September 1939 and the end of January 1947.[75] The returning soldiers were greeted with bands and—after the cessation of hostilities—with exuberant press. Sometimes children in the city would run down to meet the ships, although their motives were not always patriotic or sentimental. John Connolly remembers counting the stacks on the ships coming in, and if it was a large vessel, he and his friends would go to the brow of the piers at the Halifax Ocean Terminals, "[n]ot so much to welcome the troops back, but to say, 'Throw us some money,' and they would throw the English coins overboard, or over the ship, which would land on the cement dock and bounce all over. Whichever kid was the fastest, the toughest, the roughest, we'd get the most coins by pushing the others out of the way."[76]

Service personnel had varied experiences of returning to Pier 21. Walter Adlam remembers his return to Halifax including a number of ceremonial touches, including an escort from a Royal Canadian Navy warship, flags and bunting on Pier 21, a band playing popular music, and receptions for the troops in Halifax, in Truro, Nova Scotia, and in Moncton, New Brunswick. For Colin Hunt, a veteran of service in the Forestry Corps, his return to Pier 21 was marked not by a large ceremony but by the presence of a lone civilian on the wharf. His wife had asked for the privilege, and was on the brow of the pier to greet him as he arrived back in Canada after serving overseas.[77]

Simply getting off the ship was a relief for some, as for Nick Wiebe, whose return voyage to Canada had been treacherous. So much ice accumulated on the decks that Wiebe would secure himself to fittings with his web gear to avoid slipping overboard. After enduring a series of storms, there was some damage to the ship, and the captain briefly held course for New York rather than Halifax due to the weather and the damage. Once

they arrived, Wiebe dashed through the pier to the train, eager to have a good seat and be on his way home.[78]

The relief of returning home safely from war resonates in many veterans' accounts, including that of Keith Craig. Craig says, "you never saw so many smiling faces as were on that boat" as the soldiers hung over the side, taking in their first close-up view of Canada again as their ship came in at Pier 21.[79] Alfred Cassidy, a radar technician, returned with HMT *Île de France* and, as they entered Halifax Harbour, so many people rushed to the port side that the ship took on a list. Once the ship's crew was able to restore order, they docked. Cassidy's brother-in-law, a naval officer, was posted at the pier, and they were able to celebrate with a few drinks at a nearby hotel before Cassidy had to join his train heading west.[80]

The return for many Canadian service personnel was more sombre: the embarkation staff at Pier 21 also served hospital ships that repatriated wounded Canadians. Victor Gray, a bandsman and stretcher-bearer who regularly worked at the Embarkation Transit Unit, saw "a young lieutenant being taken off by two other soldiers, him in the middle, and them with his arms around their shoulders, holding on to him, and dragging his feet, right out of it completely with shell shock."[81] Joyce Woodford echoes the gravity of that homecoming, saying "the saddest thing was we went down one time to see the people coming off the hospital ships, and we were just—we had a busy spell—a spell, and so we went down. Oh, it was so sad. Some were coming off in baskets. Oh, it was awful sad."[82]

Hospital ships called at Pier 21 and would disembark wounded returning military personnel for transportation back to their home military districts. Regular troopships also occasionally carried a small number of stretcher-borne wounded, and some ambulatory cases, although those ships were much more cramped and unsuited to moving the wounded. Those returning with serious injuries would usually be moved aboard one of the Canadian military's specialized hospital train cars upon arrival.

OPPOSITE: Flora and David Campbell (foreground) wave at personnel returning aboard HMT *Île de France* at Pier 21, 1945. *Source: Lieut. Richard Graham Arless, Canada. Department of National Defence, Library and Archives Canada, PA-192969*

Members of the No. 6 District Military Band, ca. 1944.
Source: Canadian Museum of Immigration Collection (DI2014.536.1)

About twenty rail cars, from the CNR and CPR, were converted to include accommodations for the wounded during the Second World War. Since the cars could be brought up beside the waterfront shed, Pier 21 was little more than a transitional passageway for these returning soldiers, from the gangway of the ship to the ramp onto the train cars. Although wounded soldiers might pass through the care of several hospitals overseas in the course of being returned to Canada, they did not receive treatment at Pier 21's medical facilities.[83]

Floyd De Nicola passed through the pier as a wounded American soldier, and recalled assistance from the American Red Cross before embarking on a train for injured personnel returning to the United States. He remembers a "grey lady"—a term for Red Cross volunteers—giving him a bottle of Coca-Cola as he joined the train. While he was partly glad to have the drink, he had arrived in February and the drink was half frozen: "I may not sound grateful, but… a cup of something hot would have been a lot better!"[84]

Perhaps the dry observation of a Canadian veteran best encapsulates a part of the sentiment around repatriation. William Barker notes that "Pier 21 was a very nice place going overseas, but a more enjoyable Pier coming back."[85]

WAR BRIDES

About 10 per cent of the military personnel returning to Canada after service in the Second World War had met and married their spouse while overseas. This group, known as soldier dependents to the immigration branch, is better known as the "war brides." There were approximately 48,000 marriages of Canadian service personnel during and just after the Second World War. The majority, nearly 45,000, were to British women, followed by almost 2,000 to Dutch women. These represent areas in Europe where the Canadian military—especially the Canadian Army, which accounted for about 80 per cent of the marriages—was stationed for longer periods of time and in conditions of local peace.[86]

The ways Canadian military personnel met their future spouses were as varied as can be imagined. Iris Bartlett's future husband, Anthony Vincent Shortell, had the good fortune to crash his bicycle just where he might be picked up and dusted off by a pair of British nursing students.[87] Paul Dumaine and his bicycle had a rather gentler introduction to his future wife: as a francophone Canadian, he had to struggle with English to ask to leave his bike in the yard of a house so that he could go to a movie. The daughter of the house, Joan Waller, came out, and Dumaine says of that moment, "I just looked at her and I couldn't see anymore." He gathered his courage—and a few more bits of English—to ask her to come to the cinema with him.[88] Others tell stories of dances: Florence Frantsi (née Meldrum) jokes that she was attracted to her husband, a radar technician, because he was a good dancer, though "he wasn't the type to look it or anything." Many met through chance encounters as their wartime duties overlapped. Romance was clearly in the air for Dorothy Bescraft, a nurse, who met her husband Bert Scott, an injured airman, through the process of cajoling him to take two needles in his buttocks. Others recall meeting during the fighting to liberate Western Europe, or during the period of occupation by Allied forces.[89]

As courtships became serious, however, there were many potential barriers to marriage, including requirements for permission from family—for younger brides—and from the military for many Canadian servicemen. Jean Slater (née Vardon) got her soon-to-be husband to write her father for permission, and recalls being on tenterhooks when the letter was due, waiting for the conversation with her parents. Slater remembers being intimidated by the prospect of getting her father's permission to marry, but he was agreeable to the marriage proposal. Religious differences could also prevent a wedding. Iris Shortell, a Baptist, converted to Catholicism in order to marry. Sylvia Schuster elected to become a ward of the court in order to proceed with her marriage to Doug Power, circumventing religious issues and her parents' disapproval.[90] Doreen Daley (née Tugwood) handled the challenge in a different manner. Asked why none of her immediate family was at her wedding, Daley laughs: "Oh my, well of course I couldn't have told them; they wouldn't have let me get married!"[91] Permission to marry often included a medical clearance for brides, much like for regular immigrants. This process could include screening for venereal disease.[92] War bride Veronica Mitenko (née Hardcastle) was horrified when this requirement was explained to her, and recalls unleashing her very best British "I beg your pardon" in protest. She complied with the blood test, however, and proceeded through the process.[93]

The wedding itself could be difficult to arrange in wartime. The rationing of clothes meant that many war brides simply borrowed dresses. Jean Slater borrowed her own dress, but as a dressmaker, made her bridesmaids' dresses. Petronella VanderDonk's fiancé, Emmanuel Amirault, asked his family in Canada for a wedding gown, veil, and shoes. He also had to trade a thousand cigarettes for some wine for the reception after their ceremony. Even undergarments suitable for the dress could be difficult to acquire in wartime.[94]

Timing the wedding around the work of both spouses during wartime could also be a challenge. Hugh Asher was to be posted to the Pacific early in 1945, so he took leave in February to marry his fiancée, Marjorie Petty. They spent his leave time together, and then he resumed his duties, preparing to return to Canada for Pacific duty. Like others who volunteered for that service, the war ended prior to Asher reaching the conflict in the west, and he was able to make settlement arrangements to sponsor his wife to join him in Canada. Dorothy Scott's husband asked her to marry him in

OPPOSITE: Trudy Tansey and J. P. LeBlanc on their wedding day, 1944.
Source: Canadian Museum of Immigration Collection (DI2015.255.101)

December 1945, but he was almost immediately posted away. Her mother was appalled by the prospect of this marriage, and so when her daughter's suitor managed to get leave to come back to her home and get married, her mother told him that Dorothy was not there. He was leaving the property—and since he was on embarkation leave, it was not long before he would be sent back to Canada, likely ending their relationship—but fortunately Dorothy heard the exchange and raced to catch him. He had a paper from his unit padre giving him permission to marry, so they went straight to a church and were married immediately.[95]

Once married, other problems arose before a war bride could join her husband in Canada. An employer strike compelled one soldier to postpone his wife's travel, as he could not yet provide a home. Another wrote that his wife was not welcome in Canada, that he would not accept responsibility for her, and that he was proceeding immediately with a divorce. Still another soldier telegraphed his superiors that he refused to accept his wife in Canada and that he had started divorce proceedings—but he still sought travel arrangements for his son from the marriage. This strife sometimes existed after a bride's arrival, as well, and perhaps as many as 10 per cent returned to their country of origin. The Department of National Defence's Directorate of Repatriation also acknowledged that there were a notable number of marriages that were unreported and for which only private arrangements were made in terms of support and transportation.[96]

Despite the precedent from the experiences of military and immigration authorities during the First World War, the system for support and transit of the war brides was not well-established until late in the war. At the outbreak of the war, there existed no clear plan to assist or facilitate the immigration of new military spouses, despite the previous experience of transportation for soldier dependents from the First World War. Proposals for providing minimum passage costs for dependents provoked opposition from Blair, who argued that only those married in Canada who had followed servicemen overseas should be receiving assistance. Canadian Military Headquarters joined the debate on transport with an objection regarding the number of irresponsible marriages taking place. Despite bureaucratic opponents, and possibly in light of the Allied forces' repatriation policies, in January 1942, a single minimum-cost plan for transportation of war brides was adopted by cabinet. This plan, administered under the immigration branch, remained in place until August 1944, when the military took over organization of the movement. This decision proceeded from the fact that the Canadian Army had been deducting pay in the amount of $200 for some time to cover costs for the repatriation of the war brides, and had also arranged dependent allowances. This combination of factors was thought to create a "moral responsibility on the Services as to the type and method of transportation of the dependents."[97]

The services met this responsibility by collaborating with the Canadian Red Cross and setting up an internal unit, the Canadian Wives Bureau (CWB). This unit was created within the Directorate of Repatriation, reporting to the Special Assistant to the Adjutant General. Operating alongside the clubs set up by war brides waiting for transport to Canada, the CWB distributed information on Canada and the provinces, followed up on pay allocations, coordinated distribution of charitable gifts from organizations like the Red Cross, assisted the Salvation Army in delivering film presentations on Canada, and collaborated with the clubs in delivering courses on subjects like cooking and child care. Private and charitable organizations bolstered the preparations of the brides with other information and supports, ranging from a cookbook to financial advice. The result of this attention to organization and support for dependents travelling under military auspices was generally positive. Veronica Mitenko describes an exceptionally well-organized transit, with the only risk being overeating on the boat. The organization helped smooth the way for the war brides, but Mitenko said that the emotional burden of the journey hit home for many brides when their call came to depart for hostels prior to departure, and that many wives were "absolutely in floods of tears" as they wondered if they would see their families again.[98]

Similarly, being well-organized in wartime did not guarantee comfort. Although war bride Joyce Andersen (née Harrison) received a very complete set of instructions on her voyage, luggage entitlements, and so on, when asked about the passage itself, she calls it "wartime first class"—that is, troop accommodation.[99] Further, she only had ten days' notice to travel. Mitenko travelled on HMT *Queen Mary*, one of the most luxurious and famous ocean liners in peacetime. For the war brides, however, the vessel was trimmed as a troopship. Even the ship's beautiful swimming pool had been converted for utility, into a laundry for the women and children.[100]

The timing for a war bride's crossing to Canada occasionally seemed mysterious at the time, but it was determined by a series of factors. First, the CWB and the Directorate of Repatriation considered issues that prevented transit to Canada outright, including a lack of settlement arrangements, reluctance to proceed on the part of the bride, evidence that the marriage was bigamous, and the poor health or death of the bride. Second, priority for transit was determined based on the husband's health, service status, and whether or not he had returned to Canada; as well as pregnancy of the wife or other compassionate grounds.[101]

The accommodations and assistance granted to the dependents extended beyond their passage arrangements to Canada. For example, in 1947, female British subjects married to natural-born Canadian citizens were made citizens as part of the adoption of the Canadian Citizenship Act, as were all children born in Canada or abroad to a Canadian parent. Other regulations confirmed the citizenship rights of a Canadian soldier's children. The modified citizenship rights were either temporary or required some action to confirm—information that was not clear to many of the dependents. This resulted in many of this group, hailed at the time as an exemplary movement of desirable new Canadians, discovering over the years of their residence that they were not officially Canadian. The official facilitation of their entry, involving multiple government departments and much favourable propaganda, led many war brides to believe they were made citizens of Canada. Most had in fact entered Canada as landed immigrants, a status requiring further action before they could become citizens. Media scholar Sidney Eve Matrix describes them as having acquired and exercised cultural citizenship, as distinct from legal citizenship.[102]

As a whole, there were many challenges for both the bride and groom in integrating into life in Canada after the war. However, members of the Canadian public, civic organizations, and the government practically and symbolically embraced the settlement of the war brides after the Second World War. The Ships' Commandant for HMT *Queen Mary* published a note to his war bride passengers in July 1946, stating that "I have every confidence in the type of women we have on board... remember that [Canada] is a land that years ago your pioneering forebears founded."[103]

Pier 21 as a major ocean immigration port of entry was in a significant lull for most of the war. Until larger movements of soldier dependents to Canada began in 1944, the majority of immigrants were presenting themselves at the land boundary rather than arriving by sea. The war brides marked the opening of Pier 21's busiest years. Further, the movement was the largest contiguous group of immigrants to pass through Pier 21—64,446 war brides came to Canada from 1942 through 1948, with the overwhelming majority arriving by way of Pier 21.[104]

Halifax was the principal strategic port for migration and military movements to and from Canada during and just after the Second World War. The Halifax Ocean Terminals facility, including Pier 21, hosted much of the associated traffic through the port, providing a smooth transition from ships to trains. Despite the military presence and the scale of military traffic, Pier 21 also continued to operate as an immigration facility during the Second World War. Although the annual rate of immigration was very low during the war, the immigration authorities dealt with many other kinds of cases, including evacuated civilians, refugees, foreign military personnel, and merchant mariners from all over the world. The Halifax Ocean Terminals also welcomed diverse and valuable cargoes during the Second World War, and, in particular, cultural treasures and financial reserves from endangered or occupied European nations. As the war drew to a close, the war brides led the way in opening the postwar immigration boom to Canada. In part due to the early postwar movements and their influence in shifting Canada's policies toward the millions of migrants seeking refuge or new opportunities in the wake of the war, the decade after the Second World War would be the busiest years of Pier 21's operations.

OPPOSITE: "Welcome Home to Canada" was the first view of Pier 21 for postwar immigrants, 1950.

Source: Canadian Museum of Immigration Collection (DI2013.839.32)

4 HEIGHT OF POSTWAR IMMIGRATION AT PIER 21

1946–1955

My visual memory of that day begins with entering a huge hall... children were running around the food pile in the centre, Girls were fetching little ones who were lost, Mothers tried to calm down crying children, while holding babies in their arms. Men were carrying and pushing luggage, calling to each other across the hall. All these men gesticulated with both hands, trying to make themselves understood by the officials. Finally all immigrants were seated and all was quiet. An immigration officer greeted and welcomed us to Canada. My English was not good enough to understand the exact wording. But the atmosphere of that moment will always be in my mind.[1]

—Ilse Koerner, a German immigrant who arrived at Pier 21 aboard SS *Conte Biancamano* on June 22, 1954

IN THE DECADE AFTER THE SECOND WORLD WAR, HUNDREDS OF thousands of immigrants entered Canada, many through an ocean port of entry, without any knowledge of English or French. Nevertheless, they navigated the immigration process with the help of Canadian immigration officials, voluntary service organizations, and their fellow travellers.

After the Second World War, immigration increased substantially, from a wartime low of 7,500 immigrants in 1942 to 125,000 newcomers by 1948.[2] From 1946 to 1955, over a million immigrants entered Canada. Most were of European origin.[3] The Canadian government encouraged postwar arrivals to come to Canada through government-supported contract or bulk labour schemes, immigrant sponsorship, and family reunification. As part of this large movement of postwar immigration, more than 400,000 individuals arrived at Pier 21.[4] During this period, Pier 21 was an important site of disembarkation for returning Canadian servicemen and a busy port of entry for tens of thousands of persons displaced by the Second World War, as well as political refugees who fled the emergence of communism in their homelands. This large migration of individuals and families was followed by a significant movement of postwar immigrants in search of a new life in Canada.[5]

No port of entry in Canada was more active than Pier 21. The processes within and uses of the site provide important contexts for some of the most significant immigration events of the Second World War and postwar period. This began from the arrival of soldiers' dependents and Polish veterans to the tens of thousands of displaced persons and political refugees who left their homes devastated by six years of war or who fled the Soviet invasion of their homelands. Pier 21 also reflects shifts in policy and practice by the federal departments responsible for the immigration, health, and customs portfolios during the postwar boom in immigration to Canada.

POSTWAR IMMIGRATION POLICY

After the Second World War, Canada's doors to immigrants were slow to open, as a restrictive immigration policy remained in place. Canada's postwar economy continued to grow and Canadian workers moved into better-paying employment, which caused a labour shortage in several industries, including agriculture, forestry, and mining. As a result, big business, ethnocultural organizations, church groups, and voluntary aid organizations lobbied federal officials to increase immigration to Canada.

In early 1946, a federal cabinet subcommittee was formed to consider the issue of postwar immigration to Canada. Soon thereafter, an interdepartmental committee was established with representatives from the Departments of External Affairs, Mines and Resources (then responsible for immigration), Labour, and Health and Welfare.

Following the interdepartmental committee's deliberations, the Canadian government agreed to bring Europeans displaced by the Second World War, including political refugees fleeing repatriation back across the Iron Curtain, to Canada.[6] Meanwhile, federal officials permitted the entry of visitors to Canada who possessed a valid passport and were in good health. If a visa to travel to Canada could not be obtained from a Canadian representative in Europe, British officials were permitted to issue travel documents on behalf of the Canadian government. Visitors to Canada would later have their papers examined at a Canadian port of entry. Many Canadians used temporary travel regulations to bring their family members to Canada for stays lasting from a few weeks to several months. In May 1946, the Canadian government issued Order-in-Council P.C. 2071, which permitted Canadian citizens to sponsor their close relatives, including parents, siblings, and orphaned nieces and nephews. However, most displaced persons residing in Western Europe were forced to wait as federal immigration regulations remained firm. Soon, heightened public pressure forced federal officials to respond to the international refugee crisis in Europe by opening Canada's doors to immigration.

Although various organizations continued to lobby Ottawa to increase immigration levels, an opinion poll conducted in 1946 found that only 37 per cent of respondents were willing to consider Northern European immigrants and an overwhelming majority opposed Eastern and Southern European immigrants.[7] The movement of some 44,000 war brides and their 21,000 children represented the single largest contiguous migration of people to Canada, specifically through Pier 21. With Canadian immigration officials initially lukewarm to the idea of bringing the war brides and their children to Canada, the impetus behind the resettlement scheme was due in large part to the DND and Canadian military authorities. Soon thereafter, the Canadian military co-operated with the immigration branch to bring the first significant movement of postwar immigrants to

Canada: Polish veterans residing in the United Kingdom, who had previously fought on the Italian front, and who refused to be repatriated to their homeland after it was liberated by Soviet forces.

POLISH VETERANS

In late 1946, the movement of war brides began to slow down. At that time, British officials lobbied Canada to accept Polish army veterans into the country. The removal from Canada of German prisoners of war left a noticeable shortage of agricultural labourers—one that was difficult to fill and was politically sensitive due to the fact that whoever filled the jobs would be taking the place of an enemy prisoner.[8] Further, demobilized Canadians were not returning to farm work in pre-war numbers.[9] As ardent anti-communists, the Polish veterans refused to be repatriated from Britain to their Soviet-occupied homeland.[10] Without a federal postwar immigration policy in place and following the resettlement of the war brides and their children, the Polish veterans became the first significant movement of postwar immigrants to Canada.

These former soldiers represented an important experiment in the evolution of Canadian immigration policy. Ultimately, their resettlement, integration, and social acceptance would determine how many other displaced persons and political refugees would be accepted by the Canadian government in the early postwar period.[11] In a telegram to the Department of External Affairs, Canada's acting high commissioner in London, Norman Alexander Robertson, argued that "these men are young and good material, and loyalty will be carefully checked by Mission if authorized to by Canadian government to give consideration to these men." Robertson noted that if these men were not accepted, the pool of qualified immigrants, who had fought on the Italian front, could be less than four thousand.[12]

Polish war veterans were among the first beneficiaries of Canada's loosening of immigration controls. Through Order-in-Council P.C. 3112, signed in July 1946, Canada accepted 4,527 of these veterans as "qualified agricultural workers" between 1946 and 1947. With British authorities paying for their transatlantic resettlement, the ex-servicemen arrived at Pier 21 in five

Arrival of the first group of Polish veterans to Pier 21, aboard SS *Sea Robin*, 1946. *Source: Wilfred Doucette, National Film Board of Canada, Library and Archives Canada, PA-111595*

contingents. The first and largest contingent of veterans arrived aboard SS *Sea Robin* on November 12, 1946, and a second group aboard SS *Sea Snipe* twelve days later.[13] The landings at Pier 21 occurred without incident; however, disembarkation was initially put on hold due to irregularities discovered by Canadian officials in the identification papers of three veterans. An investigation revealed that the three men had lied about the date they had joined the Polish 2nd Corps. The Canadian government only permitted entry to Polish veterans who never served in the German forces and who joined the Polish 2nd Corps prior to the cessation of operations against the German military. Subsequently, the RCMP took the three individuals into custody pending their return to Europe.[14] The remaining Polish veterans were granted entry into the country.

The *Globe and Mail* captured the arrival of SS *Sea Robin* at Pier 21, declaring that the Polish war veterans who arrived in Halifax would be dispatched across the country to work as agricultural labourers. The paper noted that the men were pleased to be given Canadian funds upon disembarking from their ship.[15] The Polish veterans received a clothing allowance, as well as spending money for the trip inland, a ration allowance and a war gratuity, all of which was charged back to the British Army through their staff office in Washington.[16] This reflected the role of the United Kingdom in accepting a residual responsibility for displaced Polish 2nd Corps veterans, and indeed the agreement to bring the soldiers to Canada was implemented between Canada and the United Kingdom.[17]

To facilitate the movement of Polish veterans to Canada, the federal cabinet appointed an interdepartmental committee, which became responsible for administering the resettlement movement and establishing selection teams—consisting of representatives from the Department of Labour, the immigration branch, and the RCMP.[18] The Canadian selection teams, which were sent to Italy in August 1946 to examine the Polish veterans' military and medical records, found that their agricultural experience could not be ascertained by documentation and depended on the applicant's word. Polish veteran Stanisław Kendzior remembers that Canadian officials in Europe did not know for certain whether the former Polish servicemen were in fact trained as lawyers or farmers. As a result, many Polish officers who knew nothing about farming applied for resettlement in Canada as agricultural labourers. Kendzior asserts that "they gave us a little test where we had to distinguish between a sheaf of wheat and a sheaf of rye. And they asked us whether we could milk cows. I did not know how to do that but said yes. Most of the men did not know either, because even if you came from a farm, women milked cows in Poland. I had to lie because otherwise I probably would not qualify to go to Canada."[19]

Health concerns, including both tuberculosis and minor infectious diseases, were also an important consideration for Canadian officials in connection with this movement. The soldiers were screened for tuberculosis after arrival in Canada. Despite the delay until the Poles were in Canada, Atlantic District Superintendent of Immigration H. U. McCrum, describes the screening as of value as it might identify prohibited cases.[20]

Although seventy-five cases of tuberculosis were identified among the veterans, Canadian representatives approached the idea of declining their entry delicately, as they were accepted following medical examination and returning them—likely to the United Kingdom—would have been an act of poor faith in transferring the burden of care.

Weighed against this was the possibility of negative public perceptions and political pressure.[21] The *Winnipeg Free Press* sought to address the "rumour" of Polish soldiers arriving with tuberculosis with the district superintendent of immigration in Winnipeg, who tried to defuse the matter but also sent an urgent airmail letter to his superiors in Ottawa to forewarn them of the matter.[22] The *Globe and Mail*—presumably based on a spectacular error of basic math—reported the 3 per cent rate of tuberculosis in the movement of four thousand men as resulting in a thousand of them being "kept off farms," an error in coverage that underscores the vulnerability of the settlement project to wary public opinion.[23] Public opinion did run strong on the subject. With reports circulating on the radio indicating that 15 per cent of the Polish veterans had tuberculosis, one correspondent suggested to the minister that he was guilty of treason.[24] Even management of the minor infectious disease cases in the movement was considered important and urgent, although the number of affected soldiers on arrival in Canada was much smaller than reported from overseas. The imperative for action derived in part from the fear of negative public responses to the health risks, particularly as some of the soldiers had venereal diseases.[25]

Besides health, public discussion of the arrival of the Polish veterans also included resistance to the arrival of labour from outside the country while the postwar employment situation for Canadian soldiers was still difficult. The North-West Council of the Labor-Progressive Party sent a protest to the prime minister, arguing that the Polish veterans were fascist and anti-democratic, while calling on the government not to exclude immigrants based on politics or race. They also opposed the movement because of its role in the labour market, claiming that the Polish veterans were "the first contingent of [a] vast army of men intended to take [the] place of prisoners of war and to create cheap surplus labor prepared to carry out strike breaking activities and to… carry through [a] wage cutting campaign."[26] Even after the initial groups of soldiers were already in Canada, government officials were tempering language and expectations around the outcome of the movement out of caution. Government officials urged handling subsequent components of the movement delicately in case the experiment later proved to be a failure and public opinion became strongly opposed to allowing more Polish veterans to resettle in Canada.

Despite its sensitivity to public opinion, the Canadian government required further agricultural and industrial labour and continued to examine applications from Polish ex-servicemen hoping to permanently resettle in Canada. In 1947 a further group of the Polish veterans arrived at Pier 21, aboard HMT *Aquitania* on three separate transatlantic crossings.[27] During the movement of Polish ex-servicemen to Canada, federal officials hoped to sign each veteran to a two-year farm labour contract. However, following opposition from the veterans themselves, officials agreed to one-year contracts, which the Polish newcomers could renew or leave and find better-paying work in Canada's cities. The veterans arrived in Canada as agricultural labourers, and the government did not consider them as landed immigrants until they officially concluded their contracts.[28] The Poles were entitled to apply for and obtain a permanent landing after two years of residence in Canada, and five years after their arrival, were able to apply for Canadian citizenship.[29] Most of the ex-servicemen chose this direction: between 1948 and 1951, just over four thousand Polish veterans received landed status and permanent residency in Canada.[30]

Notwithstanding public criticism, Canadian officials viewed the movement of these veterans to Canada after the Second World War as exceedingly successful. The Poles moved about more than anticipated given their agricultural labour contracts, but this was largely due to exploitation at the hands of Canadian farmers rather than the veterans themselves. The movement of Polish veterans to Canada was an important early postwar experiment in admitting Europeans displaced after the Second World War in order to meet Canadian labour needs.

ADDITIONAL FARMERS WANTED

In an attempt to increase the rural population of Canada and secure additional agricultural labour, the Canadian government signed its first postwar bilateral immigration agreement with the Netherlands to bring families to Canada. Under the resettlement scheme, some 94,000 Dutch immigrants came to Canada between 1947 and 1954. Over 80 per cent of this sizeable movement possessed an agricultural background. Most of these Dutch immigrants chose to resettle on farms in the southern regions of Ontario and Alberta.[31] The success of this resettlement program encouraged more Dutch agriculturalists to immigrate to Canada during the 1950s.

Soon Canadian officials would open the country's gates to diverse groups of immigrants who wished to restart their lives away from the devastation and deprivations caused by war and political upheaval. Yet, opinion polls indicated opposition to Canada further opening its doors to European immigration. Despite this, on November 7, 1946, Prime Minister Mackenzie King issued orders-in-council to bring displaced persons to Canada, and introduced labour programs. First, the bulk labour scheme which allowed Canadian employers to specify the number of labour contracts and workers they required, and second, the individual sponsorship scheme, a close-relative plan which permitted Canadian residents to sponsor family members and individuals who were not relatives if employment and housing were guaranteed for them. Federal officials recruited European displaced persons from camps in Allied-occupied Germany, Austria, and Italy. The selection process was ultimately guided by economic considerations; ethnic prejudices, as Jews were routinely rejected; and political biases, as individuals with left-wing or communist sympathies were labelled as "undesirables." If these limitations were not enough, federal immigration and health officials only sought out individuals who were in good health.[32] Similarly, Canadians wanted young, strong, and willing workers who would be content to stay in their jobs.

INDIVIDUAL SPONSORSHIP AND BULK LABOUR SCHEMES

When Canadian officials began to consider Europe's displaced population as potential immigrants, they also attempted to increase Canada's rural populations in an attempt to help with a lack of available labour in the agricultural sector. In January 1947, the federal government removed

Italians from the category of enemy aliens, which led to a significant rise in immigration from Italy. That same month, a Canadian immigration officer was stationed in occupied Germany, and, two months later, two Canadian immigration teams were interviewing, selecting, and examining prospective displaced persons for immigration to Canada. The Canadian immigration mission was tasked with ensuring "a reasonable division of nationalities."[33] In April 1947, the Canadian government launched the Displaced Person (DP) movement, which brought almost two hundred thousand individuals to Canada over the next six years.[34] In the first year of the program, Department of Labour officials were also sent to occupied Germany to examine and select prospective applicants for immigration to Canada. On April 4, the first group of displaced persons, including relatives of Canadian citizens to be resettled in Canada, sailed aboard HMT *Aquitania.*

As one of the larger vessels to dock at Pier 21, *Aquitania* often carried over 1,800 passengers, which forced Canadian officials to conduct immigration examinations, customs inspections, and railway ticketing aboard the ship, because the immigration facility could not handle such a large volume of passenger traffic. According to a Cunard White Star Line pamphlet about landing arrangements, passengers were instructed to follow an examination procedure adopted by Canadian immigration officials. It prioritized disembarkation as follows: a) returning Canadians in first and tourist class; b) all remaining first-class passengers; c) tourist-class passengers proceeding to the Maritimes; d) tourist-class passengers heading to Port Arthur, Ontario, and points west; and e) remaining passengers.[35]

Most displaced persons travelled in very simple accommodations and so were among the last to be disembarked from their vessel. Since the displaced persons came to Canada either through individual sponsorship or as part of the bulk labour scheme, a variety of officials met them at Pier 21. A representative of the International Refugee Organization (IRO) met individuals sponsored by relatives, and the representative was responsible for seeing them safely aboard their trains and providing funds for their journey. Each newcomer was also given an identity tag and a telegram was sent to their Canadian relatives informing them of their arrival. Displaced persons who signed one-year manual labour agreements for work in forestry, mining, agriculture, construction, or domestic service, were met at Pier 21 by a representative from the Department of Labour, who was responsible for ensuring that they were safely delivered to their final destinations. If a displaced person could not be immediately sent to their employer, they were temporarily housed, for two to four days, in Department of Labour hostels at Saint-Paul-l'Ermite, near Montréal, or at Ajax, near Toronto. Once there, displaced persons were boarded and fed at government expense. Upon reaching their final destinations, these newcomers met with a local representative of the National Employment Service, who was responsible for assisting them in settling into their new jobs in Canada.[36]

In May 1947, in seeking to assuage demands for a liberalized immigration program, King outlined his government's immigration policy before the House of Commons. King declared that his government would slowly increase Canada's population by encouraging immigration. With Europe devastated by six years of war, the Canadian government decided that future immigration should involve the resettlement of individuals with close relatives already in Canada, and the admission of displaced persons and political refugees. Federal officials would continue to carefully select prospective immigrants according to the "absorptive capacity" of Canada's economy. Additionally, King remarked that postwar immigration would have to be specifically related to the social, cultural, political, and economic situation resulting from the Second World War. He famously stated in the House of Commons that immigration should not be allowed to "make a fundamental alteration in the character of our population."[37]

As a result, Asian immigration continued to be restricted, even after the Canadian government had repealed the exclusionary 1923 Chinese Immigration Act, while immigrants from the United States and the British Commonwealth continued to enjoy preferred treatment.[38] King argued that entry into Canada was not a fundamental human right and was subject to the control of Parliament. However, the prime minister did concede that discriminatory provisions within immigration legislation should be removed. This political statement referred to Southern and Eastern European refugees, who were viewed increasingly as prospective immigrants for resettlement, while non-Europeans continued to face barriers to immigration largely due to their ethnoracial identity.

Federal immigration policy also took into consideration the necessity for a humanitarian response to the plight of Europeans displaced and left homeless by the Second World War, and those fleeing repressive regimes behind the Iron Curtain. Although Canada was a member of the United Nations and the IRO, it was not legally obligated to resettle displaced persons and political refugees. However, sensing that public opinion was on the side of a Canadian role in international humanitarianism, King indicated before his colleagues that Canada was morally obligated to join with other countries and international organizations to resettle permanently individuals and families displaced by the Second World War or who fled Soviet-backed totalitarian regimes in Europe.[39]

By the summer of 1947, five Canadian immigration teams in occupied Austria and Germany were selecting individuals for resettlement. In June, the federal cabinet authorized an order-in-council for the entry of an initial movement of 5,000 non-sponsored displaced persons. Subsequent orders, passed between July 1947 and October 1948, permitted over 45,000 displaced persons to enter Canada.[40] Estimates indicate that over 100,000 displaced persons and political refugees entered Canada through Halifax.[41]

The displaced persons and political refugees arrived in Halifax from France, Belgium, Netherlands, Italy, and occupied Austria and Germany, while many political refugees arrived at Pier 21 from communist regimes in Czechoslovakia, Poland, Soviet Union, Yugoslavia, and Hungary. Professionals and labourers from diverse ethnoreligious backgrounds, including Jews, Catholics, and Protestants, boarded ships for Canada. Most of these newcomers who arrived at Pier 21 brought few possessions with them. In many cases, displaced persons arrived in Halifax with just the clothes on their backs. Canadian customs officer Arthur J. Vaughan, who was stationed at Pier 21 from 1945 to 1965, remembers that:

> The arrival of the Displaced Persons brought scenes in stark contrast to those of the cheerful, chattering war brides. It is difficult to comprehend what those desperate souls had endured through man's inhumanity to man. They came with almost no items of value; their few belongings were carried in sacks of various kinds and a few battered

> cardboard suitcases, these people came from many walks in life; farming, industrial trades, merchandising and, in many cases, professional fields. The ravages of war had taken away their homes, their livelihood and, in too many instances, their loved ones. They brought their skills with them and a burning hope for a new life devoid of oppression and deprivation. As may be imagined, there was very little work for the customs staff and we knew that we would be working merely as aides to help them through the required procedures.[42]

Some displaced persons and political refugees accepted under the family reunification and bulk labour schemes secured provisional visas from Canadian representatives overseas and later learned that their manual labour contracts failed to materialize, often because the prospective employer opted out of the agreement, once they arrived at Pier 21 and were interviewed by Canadian immigration officials.[43] Contract labourers were fortunate since federal Labour officials received telegrams giving the number and nationalities of displaced persons for resettlement prior to their departure from occupied Germany. They avoided overnight stays in Pier 21's facilities since their visas and work contracts were cross-referenced before their arrival in Canada. Other displaced persons were less fortunate because Labour officials were only given word about their arrival in Canada as their ships docked at Halifax. Therefore, some displaced persons

Arthur J. Vaughan served as a Canadian customs officer at Pier 21 from 1945 to 1965 (n.d.). *Source: Canadian Museum of Immigration Collection (DI2013.1250.2)*

had to stay at Pier 21 until officers checked their paperwork. A lack of adequate facilities for overnight stays within the immigration shed meant that many displaced persons were divided up into groups as quickly as possible according to their intended destination and put on trains heading westward.[44]

In some cases, displaced persons created more problems for themselves by remaining less than forthcoming during their interview with an immigration official. Deception was a useful life skill in war-torn Europe but could prove dangerous as misrepresentation was an offence under the Immigration Act, which could lead to deportation. Individuals could also be deported for a previous criminal record, "moral turpitude" or behaviour outside of the accepted standard of the community, political background, or for falsifying information. Oftentimes, deception and the falsification of information were used by individuals in an effort to keep their families together. The lack of accurate documentation was also a major source of concern for Canadian immigration officials.

The displaced persons who arrived without any financial means at Pier 21 were assisted by aid agencies. The Sisters of Service had also appealed to the Canadian public for an "immigration fund." The money collected was used to clothe and feed displaced persons.[45] Soon, Catholic voluntary aid organizations, including the Sisters of Service, were preoccupied with the arrival of a group of Polish orphans whose migration from the Soviet Union via East Africa to Canada was fraught with political sensitivities.

POLISH ORPHANS

Back in February 1940, four large groups of Poles had been deported from Soviet-controlled eastern Poland to the Soviet Union. In the spring of 1942, a Polish Army was established from those Poles and prisoners of war who were forced to move eastward. The remaining adults and unaccompanied children were eventually permitted to leave the Soviet Union and made their way to Kazakhstan and Uzbekistan, before reaching Iran. While the newly established Polish Army was sent to the Middle East, many of the children, who were orphaned or separated from their families, were also scattered across the world in refugee camps. By 1948, some of these minors reached the children's orphanage at the Tengeru refugee camp in northern

Tanganyika (Tanzania). Upon hearing of their plight, the archbishop of Montreal decided to sponsor their permanent resettlement in Canada.

Cold War politics soon directly affected the movement of Polish orphans to Canada. Communist authorities in Poland learned of their journey and sparked an international incident when Warsaw publicly attacked Canadian, British, and American authorities, and the IRO, for "kidnapping" the Polish orphans rather than repatriating them to their country of origin. Communist Polish representatives pursued the children from East Africa to Italy and Germany, and eventually to Canada. On September 7, 1949, USAT *General Stuart Heintzelman* docked at Pier 21, carrying 123 Polish Catholic orphans. Several weeks after their arrival, the orphans were followed by another, smaller, group.

Polish communists awaited the arrival of the children at Halifax. With the help of several Catholic priests and nuns, including representatives of the Catholic Immigrant Aid Society, the orphans were safely escorted past the "Soviet Poles" before boarding a train destined for Montreal. Proponents of the Warsaw government unsuccessfully followed the children to Catholic summer camps near Drummondville, Quebec, where they were temporarily housed before reaching their final destinations. A small number of the orphans remained on the train and arrived in Montreal to find Polish communists waiting with sweets. For its part, the Canadian government refused to surrender the orphans to Polish officials. The orphans eventually became Canadians.[46]

JEWISH WAR ORPHANS

As part of the much larger DP movement to Canada, the Polish orphans were not the only significant group of minors to be admitted into the country. In the late 1940s, over a thousand Jewish war orphans arrived in Canada. Earlier, in 1942, the Canadian Jewish Congress had received permission from the Canadian government to resettle up to a thousand Jewish orphans from Vichy France. However, the German occupation of French territory made it nearly impossible to implement the scheme. Coupled with restrictive immigration regulations that prevented Jewish immigration to Canada during the 1930s and 1940s, the plan was shelved

Arrival of a group of Jewish refugees and war orphans at Pier 21, 1949. *Source: Alex Dworkin Canadian Jewish Archives, Jewish Immigrant Aid Services fonds,* PC *2-4-8A-8*

until the end of the war.[47] In 1947, the Canadian government responded to calls for the country's doors to be opened to Europe's war-torn population. That year, Jewish organizations, including the Canadian Jewish Congress and JIAS, were successful in lobbying federal authorities to have visas granted for Jewish refugees. The Canadian government passed Order-in-Council P.C. 1647, which specified that the Jewish community would be fully responsible for the resettlement and care of approximately a thousand Jewish orphans. Between 1947 and 1949, the orphans, under the age of eighteen, arrived in Canada. Only thirty-seven of the young refugees were under the age of ten. Within this group, almost eight hundred had survived the concentration camps, while the remainder had been in hiding during the war. Originally from fifteen different countries, most of these young newcomers arrived at Pier 21. An initial group of twenty Jewish orphans arrived at Halifax aboard HMT *Aquitania* on September 18, 1947.[48]

Many of the orphans who had survived the concentration camps were later forced to move from one displaced persons camp to the next.

Throughout war-ravaged Europe, Jewish orphans waited to be accepted for permanent resettlement by a Western government. While the Canadian Jewish Congress arranged and paid for the young refugees to come to Canada, JIAS received them and helped the newcomers to successfully resettle in their new country. In Halifax, under the leadership of Noa Heinish, a local merchant, JIAS welcomed and offered assistance to the newly arrived Jewish orphans at Pier 21. On behalf of the organization, volunteers were able to welcome the newcomers in their own languages, including German, Polish, Russian, and Yiddish.[49]

On February 14, 1948, Celina Lieberman (née Kolin), a Jewish war orphan from Poland, arrived at Pier 21 aboard USAT *General S.D. Sturgis*. She recalls that the transatlantic voyage did not feel like a big adventure because the orphans, like herself, had seen so much during the war. According to Lieberman, the orphans' big adventure was their survival. She recalls that along with her fellow orphans, they found the hot dogs served aboard ship to be such a novelty that they ate too many of them and became sick. Upon arrival at Pier 21, Lieberman remembers standing in a large hall with other orphans for passport control. While Canadian immigration officials examined the children, Lieberman was frightened by all the authority figures and the fact that many of the orphans did not hold the necessary travel documentation. When it came to her own expectation for resettlement in Canada, she notes that "I do not think that I expected much. I was without a family or a country and very little seemed to matter to me, I felt a certain apathy. I reasoned that since I had already been someone else's child, Helena's, then I could be yet another person's child in Canada. All I was told was that I was going to Regina, Saskatchewan, presumably to a Jewish family but I was not sure." Eventually, Lieberman and her fellow newcomers were put on trains heading westward, across Canada, to their final destinations. For Celina Lieberman, that meant Regina, where she was welcomed by the local Jewish community.[50]

As a Jewish war orphan, Pejsach (Paul) Kagan arrived at Pier 21 aboard SS *Nea Hellas* on March 21, 1948. Born in Wilno, Poland, Kagan survived the Wilno Ghetto and several concentration camps while losing his family and home, only to end up in a displaced persons camp in Italy in 1946. From there, Kagan hoped to leave Europe and find permanent resettlement elsewhere. In late 1947, camp officials informed him that Canada was interested in resettling young people. If Kagan was interested, he would need to register. He subsequently registered without knowing where Canada was on a map. At the time, Kagan only spoke Yiddish and Polish. After his immigration interview and medical examination, the young refugee was admitted to Canada with other Jewish war orphans. Upon arriving in Halifax, a social worker, on behalf of the Canadian Jewish Congress, decided where Kagan would be permanently resettled. While the young orphans were sent to thirty-eight communities across Canada, around eight hundred were resettled in Montreal and Toronto.[51] The young Holocaust survivor was given a train ticket and $10 to travel to Edmonton, Alberta. According to Kagan, "it was a long journey but I was happy that I was in a free country. I met on the boat another survivor, Chaja Blayways, who also ended up with me in Edmonton." After arriving in the city, Kagan found life difficult without family support and struggled to learn English. During the day, he worked in a bakery for $18 a week, and in the evenings attended school, where he learned English. By the 1950s, Kagan began to acculturate fully to his new surroundings and married that fellow ship passenger, Blayways. The couple later had three children.[52]

Jews formed one of the largest groups within the movement of displaced persons and political refugees to Canada after the Second World War. Less than a year after Lieberman and Kagan's arrival, in January 1949, a further seventeen Jewish orphans arrived at Pier 21. They were met with widespread interest from the press and local citizens. Among the group of young arrivals was an eleven-year-old girl from Czechoslovakia, Ruth Miller (Růžena Meuller-Gewuerzman), who was declared the one thousandth Jewish war orphan to enter Canada under the auspices of the Canadian Jewish Congress. Miller was presented with small gifts and had her picture taken by local media, eventually appearing in the *Halifax Mail-Star*. JIAS then brought the orphans to Halifax's Robie Street Synagogue for refreshments before they were permanently settled with foster families in Montreal.[53] Between 1947 and 1952, approximately 34,000 Jews immigrated to Canada, of whom approximately 11,000 were displaced persons.[54]

During this period, Jewish children were among the displaced persons permanently resettled in Canada. Moses Znaimer, born during the Second

World War in Kulob, Tajikistan, to Latvian and Polish parents of Jewish origin who fled the German invasion of the Soviet Union, ended up with his family in a displaced persons camp near the town of Kastel, in the American-occupied zone of Germany. Znaimer recalls that toward the end of the Second World War there were stockpiles of ammunition, large shells, and bullets dumped into a nearby stream. While playing with other children from the camp, he attempted to crush a howitzer-type cartridge onto a rock, but was chased by a frantic adult. Znaimer ran to a nearby bombed out building before jumping from the second floor to get away. He remembers waking up the next day with a serious hernia. The family's admission to Canada as displaced persons hinged on the passing of their medical examinations. In order not to draw attention to his medical situation, he was tied down "to keep me from jumping about, and on-board ship and later on shore, the hernia is suppressed with a truss. My condition was never discovered by the authorities, but even years later, mom still half-expected Immigration to come through the door and say, 'hey, wait a minute.'" On May 24, 1948, Znaimer and his father and mother arrived at Pier 21 aboard SS *Marine Falcon*, before boarding a train for Montreal.[55]

For other Jewish displaced persons, it was the anticipation of arriving in a new country that occupied their thoughts. On June 28, 1948, Ann Kazimirski (née Hanka Ressels), her husband Henry, and their two sons, three-year-old Mark and eight-month-old Seymour, arrived at Pier 21 aboard USAT *General M.B. Stewart*. Along with a group of other Holocaust survivors, the family sailed from Munich on a troopship that was ill-equipped for passenger travel. Aboard the ship, Ann, who knew six languages, acted as an interpreter, while Henry, a dentist, provided his services to other passengers. The family received a few privileges including real milk and eggs instead of powdered products, which helped Ann breastfeed her youngest son. Kazimirski remembers feeling "overwhelmed when we saw a large sign which said Welcome to Canada. Some of us wept and knelt down to kiss the ground. We had arrived at a country which offered us, the Displaced Persons, freedom and a new home." The family was instructed to have their visas stamped by an immigration officer and they then proceeded into the two-storey immigration shed. As they lined up to be processed through immigration, Kazimirski notes that "even now,

I really cannot find words to adequately describe the emptiness and ugliness of that long shed. But who cared? We were in the promised land of freedom, and free of the Nazis. We had left behind an ocean of bloodshed and tears and we were looking forward to a happy, bright future." With their visas stamped, the family felt that their right to a new life was confirmed. The following day, they boarded a train for their final destination of Montreal.[56]

Other displaced persons families were not as lucky getting processed through the immigration facility in Halifax. Eleven-year-old Jackie Eisen (née Solski) arrived at Pier 21 with her parents, sister, and brother aboard USNS *General Langfitt* in March 1950. As Polish Jews, the Solskis left after Germany's invasion of their homeland. The family fled eastward to Uzbekistan and then to Siberia, where Jackie's father was in a work camp. Following the birth of her sister and her mother's illness, Jackie and her younger sibling became wards of the state and were sent to an orphanage. When the Solskis attempted to take their children out of the orphanage, they were prevented from doing so by the local authorities. In the middle of the night, the Solskis broke into the orphanage and removed Jackie and her sister. After the Second World War, the Solskis returned to Poland only to find that many members of their extended family had been murdered in the Holocaust. Due to anti-Semitism, the family decided to seek refuge elsewhere. In Germany, the family lived in a displaced persons camp.

Jackie's aunt immigrated to Canada in 1948 and was able to sponsor them for permanent resettlement. Upon arriving at Pier 21, Canadian immigration officials detained the Solskis for three months because they claimed that Jackie's younger brother had strep throat. In reality, the detention was due to another reason: political affiliation. Jackie's father was a socialist, and her family's sponsors, Jackie's aunt and uncle, were linked to the Communist Party. Her uncle had signed a membership card as a young man, but did not participate in the party. In order to release their relatives from detention, David Lewis, national president of the

OPPOSITE: Two young displaced persons, Moses Znaimer and Nasha Rosenberg, are featured on the front page of the *Standard Review* newspaper, June 26, 1948. *Source: Canadian Museum of Immigration Collection (DI2014.515.2)*

The Standard

REVIEW

MONTREAL, JUNE 26, 1948.

NEWS IN REVIEW — OTTAWA REPORT

WOMEN'S FEATURES — SPORT — RADIO

DPs WITH FUTURE. Russian-born Nasha Rosenberg, aged three, found a playmate from Latvia among passengers of SS Marine Falcon, which brought 800 immigrants from eastern Europe to Halifax. Children are among 20,000 DPs whose entry to Canada is approved. (See p. 4.)

Co-operative Commonwealth Federation, lobbied on the family's behalf, eventually securing their release and subsequent admission into Canada.[57] Aside from ethnocultural origin and political orientation, Canadian immigration officials were also concerned about displaced persons and political refugees without proper travel documentation, as their identities and backgrounds could be difficult to ascertain.

BALTIC REFUGEES AND "VIKING BOATS"

While some immigrants faced social and institutional hurdles due to prejudices and stereotypes regarding their ethnocultural origin and political background, other displaced persons and political refugees were considered "preferred" immigrants based on another set of preconceived ethnocultural categorizations. As early as 1945, Canadian officials in Europe had their preferences. Vincent Massey, the Canadian high commissioner to London, reported from occupied Germany in 1945 that if Canada was going to admit new immigrants from Europe, the Balts—especially the Latvians—might be the best of the lot. The Latvians impressed Massey, who claimed they were "industrious, clean, resourceful, and well mannered." Conversely, Massey was unimpressed by the Poles in the camps, claiming that "one did not want too many of them about."[58] While Canada's representatives overseas were busy assessing the desirability and admissibility of Europeans for possible resettlement in Canada, federal authorities were concerned with how to make a substantial contribution to the international humanitarian crisis in Europe without altering Canada's sociocultural and economic identity. Although Massey considered Polish displaced persons less desirable than the Balts for entry into Canada, they were nevertheless admitted for their labour and ability to integrate into Canadian society.

Besides those refugees who were fortunate enough to be granted admission into Canada through either government or private sponsorship, in the late 1940s some refugees arrived at Pier 21 without money, sponsors, or documentation. They arrived on their own and were completely dependent on the Canadian government, which later functioned as a sponsor. They were irregular arrivals who had sought asylum without first being processed for immigration to Canada in their country of departure. Some of the Balts arrived in small wooden boats, grossly inadequate as a passenger transport. Many were small fishing vessels.

In August 1948, the first of several vessels carrying Estonian, Latvian, Lithuanian, and Ukrainian refugees arrived on the east coast of Canada.[59] Many of the individuals aboard had used their savings to pay for their journey to Canada aboard one of the transport vessels. These vessels were dubbed "Viking Boats" by newspaper reporters due to the refugees' departure from Scandinavia and voyage across the North Atlantic to Canada. The Viking Boats that arrived in Canada included SS *Walnut,* SS *Gladstone,* SS *Sarabande*, SS *Pärnu*, SS *Østervåg*, SS *Goren*, SS *Atlanta*, SS *Astrid*, SS *Amanda*, and SS *Capry*. A former British gunboat, SS *Capry*, sailed into Halifax in August 1948 with twenty-three Latvian and five Estonian refugees aboard.[60]

One of the vessel's passengers was Ernests Kraulis, a Latvian refugee, who recalls the journey: "[I]n the beginning the ocean was comparatively calm. We enjoyed the company of dolphins who swam and jumped playfully ahead of the boat for long periods of time. After about three days we encountered heavy wind with waves as high as the roof of a two-storey building. We couldn't see the horizon, which normally marked the boundary between the water and the sky. It seemed the ocean would swallow our boat and everything in it."[61] The Balts sailed from Sweden, where they were living under threat of forced repatriation to the Soviet Union. They sought resettlement in Canada, but were frustrated by the long delays and barriers in Canadian immigration processing. They were detained on arrival and processed through an ad hoc arrangement. Almost all the Viking Boat refugees were accepted into Canada; however, twelve individuals were deported as security risks.[62]

Of all the Viking Boats to land in Canada, perhaps none garnered as much attention as SS *Walnut.*[63] In 1947, Baltic refugees residing in Sweden were officially registered as Soviet citizens. Coupled with Soviet demands to extradite their citizens, Baltic refugees feared a forced return to Soviet-controlled Estonia, Latvia, and Lithuania. Frightened by Soviet radio broadcasting, which repeatedly claimed that "we shall catch you everywhere you are" and fearful of the very real threat of repatriation to their homelands under Soviet rule, a group of predominantly Baltic refugees residing in Sweden pooled their financial resources in a bid to leave the country for sanctuary elsewhere. The group purchased a former British minesweeper originally equipped for a crew of fourteen and fifty passengers, but later retrofitted for two hundred individuals, and formed an ad hoc ship's company, "Compania Maritima Walnut S.A." They subsequently registered the vessel with the Panamanian consul in Stockholm. On November 13, 1948, *Walnut* left Gothenburg carrying 347 passengers: 123 women, 154 men, and 70 children.

Although the majority of the passengers were over the age of twenty-one and were married, the ship also carried seventy children under the age of sixteen. The youngest passenger was an Estonian girl, Maret Pauts, less than one year old, and the oldest was Anne Maria Kotilainen, aged eighty. The ship passengers were divided among several nationalities: 305 Estonians, ten Latvians, nine Lithuanians, nine Poles, eight Finns, three Austrians, two Americans (claimed), and one Dane. Two weeks after sailing from Sweden, the vessel left Sligo, Ireland, after a brief stopover in order to replenish its bunkers. Although originally destined for the port of Quebec, the vessel instead reached the port of Sydney, Cape Breton, in dire need of coal.[64] Haligonians first learned of the ship's plight on December 11, when the *Halifax Mail* reported that 347 refugees, who had fled the Soviets, were on their way to Halifax.[65]

Upon learning of the ship's arrival and lacking the necessary infrastructure to process all the passengers effectively, Acting Inspector-in-Charge, H. J. Fenton, stationed in Sydney, telephoned his colleagues in Halifax to inform them that *Walnut*'s 347 passengers were in possession of official documents: many carried Swedish passports, but very few had visas for entry into Canada. Fenton was instructed to divert the ship to Halifax and that Canadian immigration and customs officials would refuse clearance if *Walnut* sailed for the port of Quebec. After taking on enough coal, *Walnut* departed Cape Breton and docked at Halifax on December 13, 1948.

Pier 21 Matron of Nursing Florence Waldron recalls the vessel sitting in Halifax Harbour between Georges Island and McNabs Island. The temperature outside was cold and some of the passengers were sleeping on the decks of the vessel due to overcrowding. Medical officers were dispatched

Arrival of 347 mostly Baltic refugees aboard SS *Walnut* at Pier 21, December 13, 1948. Photographer: Robert Norwood/*Chronicle Herald*.
Source: Republished with permission from the Chronicle Herald

to go out and clear the vessel for quarantine.[66] The immigration branch summoned its inspection and stenograph staff from the ports of Quebec, Montreal, and Saint John to Halifax to assist in processing *Walnut*'s passengers and to hold boards of inquiry pertaining to admission, detention, and deportation for individuals who failed their medical examinations or security assessments.[67] Pier 21 Immigration Secretary Alison Trapnell remembers that the refugees who arrived aboard larger ships were processed normally, while those who arrived on the Viking Boats were individually screened and then processed. Trapnell notes that once the Baltic refugees disembarked from their vessels—many of which appeared to be in terrible shape—she began to wonder how they had been able to make the transatlantic journey to Canada. Trapnell, who did not interview the refugees but sat in on their boards of inquiry, recalls that immigration and customs staff initially found it difficult to keep up with the names of the passengers and their individual files.[68]

As one of several Viking Boats of various sizes and conditions with experienced crews of captains, seamen, and mechanics, the passengers from *Walnut* were processed according to existing immigration regulations. Dr. Alfred A. Valdmanis, a Latvian immigrant and instructor at Carleton College in Ottawa, who worked as a translator, interviewed the ship's captain, August Linde, and other group leaders on behalf of Canadian immigration officials. Valdmanis indicated that it was the intention of the entire group of passengers to become good Canadians if they were permitted to remain in Canada.[69] After investigating the backgrounds of the passengers and performing X-ray examinations, the federal government admitted all but two of the ship's passengers, waiving the immigration restrictions of the day by issuing orders-in-council providing entry for each individual.[70] However, Grigori Kattai and Johannes Liivamees's appeals to overturn their denied admission into Canada were rejected by separate boards of inquiry under Order-in-Council P.C. 4849 ("Does not come within the occupational classes described in this section") and Order-in-Council P.C. 4851 ("Passport Regulation"). Kattai was also prohibited entry under section 3(c) of the 1910 Immigration Act for being "physically defective," while Liivamees was excluded under the same section for "likely to become a public charge."[71]

Immigration officials in Halifax informed the Department of Mines and Resources that they could only provide accommodations for 150 of the newcomers at most. The remainder of the refugees were to be housed at Rockhead Hospital in Halifax's North End. In all, ninety-seven passengers were detained within Pier 21's detention quarters, while the remaining 250 individuals were housed at Rockhead.[72] Although the quarantine hospital was not "completely equipped with kitchen utensils," immigration officials in Ottawa requested that their counterparts in Halifax organize the passengers to be housed in the quarantine hospital so that they could cook their own meals, while Canadian officials would be responsible for purchasing the necessary food. Immigration officials in Halifax also received instructions to place guards in the building during the passengers' stay.[73]

In January 1949, the individuals who had arrived in Canada aboard *Walnut* held a farewell party with local Canadian immigration officials before leaving in groups of approximately a hundred for various regions of Canada, where employment had been secured for them.[74] Some Canadians believed that a precedent was set that showed "illegal" displaced persons and political refugees how to enter Canada. The arrival of the Viking Boats demonstrated that the reception of displaced persons would continue to be a pressing issue for Canadian immigration officials.

SHOWCASING THE "IDEAL" POSTWAR IMMIGRANT

In an effort to turn public opinion toward DP resettlement as a means to fill Canada's postwar labour shortage and to provide a humanitarian response to the plight of Europe's displaced and persecuted, Canadian immigration officials chose a young, blonde-haired Baltic girl as Canada's 50,000th displaced person under the IRO's resettlement plan. Their choice was meant to demonstrate to Canadians that their government was resettling young, astute, and physically healthy refugees with an anti-communist disposition, who also fit existing Cold War "norms" in Canada. On February 23, 1949, eight-year-old displaced person Ausma Levalds, from Liepāja, Latvia, arrived at Pier 21 aboard SS *Samaria*. She recalls that the transatlantic voyage was miserable and everyone became ill. As she yearned to be reunited with her father, Levalds was thrust into the public spotlight. Levalds remembers that it was a frightening experience because she did not understand what was happening.

In the end, Levalds was content to be in Canada because she believed that her recently reunited family members were now free to decide their own future.[75] That morning she received a large welcome in which Canadian officials greeted her in the immigration shed, while radio and newspaper outlets gathered and took photos of her reception.[76] Levalds was one of 1,200 displaced persons who departed Europe from Cuxhaven, occupied Germany, for new homes in Canada. The young newcomer was presented with a book about Canadian birds by federal immigration officials, a doll by Halifax Mayor John Ahern, and a locket from his wife.[77] Along with her mother, Karline, and sister, Rasma, Levalds soon departed

The 50,000th displaced person to enter Canada, Ausma Levalds (centre), her mother Karline (left), and sister Rasma (right) in front of Canadian immigration official Geoff Christie at Pier 21, February 23, 1949. *Source: Canadian Museum of Immigration Collection (D2013.1912.24)*

Pier 21 by train to rejoin her father, Janis, who was a farmer's helper in New Hamburg, Ontario.

Baltic displaced persons in search of refuge from threats of repatriation to their Soviet-occupied homelands continued to arrive in Halifax Harbour. On August 19, 1949, the minesweeper *Sarabande* brought a group of 238 Baltic refugees, including sixty children, to Pier 21. Food and water was running low aboard the vessel. The captain and shipping agent were both charged $400 for engaging in the transportation of "illegal" refugees to Canada, which was a violation under the Immigration Act. Several days later, the RCMP towed a converted fish packer, SS *Amanda*, into Halifax Harbour. The tiny *Amanda* was skippered by three Latvians and carried twenty Baltic displaced persons. Many of these individuals did not possess proper documentation and were placed in detention until their papers could be put in order.[78]

A fellow Baltic displaced person, Ilmar Rakfeldt from Estonia, who arrived at Pier 21 aboard RMS *Aquitania* in November 1949, recalls his detention experience: "[W]e were 20–30 men of different nationalities thus separated from our families and locked in. Some men took it very hard and when steam started to leak from the cold radiators, many thought that they were with certainty in a gas-chamber. They started to bang on the door and make a great deal of noise. I don't remember that anybody came to calm them. We, two Estonians, tried to calm them and explain that we were just getting heat in the room, nothing else from the radiators."[79] The large movement of displaced persons continued to capture the attention of Canadian authorities.

RESETTLING DISPLACED PERSONS IN CANADA

As a primary ocean port of entry, Pier 21 played a significant role in welcoming thousands of postwar arrivals, many of whom were European displaced persons. Between 1947 and 1952, over 165,000 displaced persons entered Canada, either through individual sponsorships by their families and ethnocultural communities or by signing labour contracts. In the latter situation, individuals agreed to work as manual labourers for a term of one year in forestry, mining, construction, agriculture, domestic service, and other industries where employers sought contracted labour.[80]

In 1950, the Canadian government issued an order-in-council replacing all previous orders-in-council and amendments pertaining to immigration. The order retained Canada's preference for British, Irish, French, and American immigrants but widened the admissible classes of European immigrants able to gain entry into the country. European immigrants that could now resettle in Canada were to include any healthy applicant of good character who had skills important to the country's economy. That same year, the federal government removed Germans from the category of enemy aliens. With the removal of this legislation, the Canadian government more aggressively recruited skilled workers from abroad. Soon over 400,000 individuals arrived in Canada from Austria, West Germany, and Switzerland in the following two decades.[81] By the early 1950s, Canada witnessed a shift in postwar immigration from displaced persons to a broader definition of immigrants who sought greater economic opportunity and a better quality of life for themselves.

Officials at Pier 21 participated in federal attempts to liberalize immigration policy: the site continued to welcome the largest number of immigrant arrivals in Canada during the late 1940s and early 1950s. In order to effectively process the arrival of tens of thousands of postwar newcomers as immigration regulations evolved, Ottawa established the Department of Citizenship and Immigration in 1950.[82] Less than a year later, Ottawa introduced an interest-free Assisted Passage Loan Scheme to help bring immigrants to Canada. This plan was restricted to European immigrants even though the federal government had signed agreements with India, Pakistan, and Ceylon (Sri Lanka) to permit small numbers of their citizens to resettle in Canada. That same year (1951), the international community adopted the UN Convention Relating to the Status of Refugees. Ottawa did not sign the declaration until 1969 because the RCMP feared that it would restrict Canada's ability to deport and deny entry to individuals it viewed as undesirable, including persons deemed to be security risks. Even though it had not become a signatory to the international agreement, throughout the 1950s and 1960s Canada used the convention as a framework to select and admit refugees.

Canadian immigration officials continued to showcase their views of the "desirable" immigrant through the commemoration of immigration milestones, and took another opportunity to publicly symbolize the ideal postwar immigrant. In May 1951, SS *Nelly* made its maiden voyage to Halifax, bringing approximately 1,300 displaced persons to Canada. One of these newcomers was Leons Ziemanis, who walked down the gangway from the ship to the sounds of "O Canada," escorted by IRO and Canadian immigration officials, and was later greeted by the mayor of Halifax, Gordon Kinley. Canadian immigration officials chose the tall and blond sixteen-year-old Latvian as Canada's 100,000th displaced person to immigrate to Canada under the auspices of the IRO. Ziemanis was to tour the city before boarding a train for his new home in Toronto.[83] While Canadian officials commemorated Ziemanis's arrival, the federal government was in the midst of strengthening its Immigration Act to counter a growing public perception that undesirable individuals were attempting to enter the country, including communist spies and sympathizers, homosexuals, prostitutes, drug users, and drug traffickers.

In 1952, the federal government introduced a new Immigration Act—the first such overhaul in over four decades. The new act streamlined the administration of immigration in view of the increasing numbers of displaced persons entering Canada. It gave wide-ranging powers, including a significant amount of discretionary power, to the minister responsible for immigration. The selection and admission of prospective immigrants were vested in the federal cabinet, which was represented by the minister of immigration. Due to these changes, the federal cabinet could deny entry to any individual on the basis of nationality, geographic origin, ethnicity, occupation, lifestyle—including homosexuality, drug use, and drug trafficking—unsuitability to Canada's climate, perceived inability to be readily assimilable, and ideology or personal belief—in particular, communism.[84] While officials were vigilant in preventing "undesirable" immigrants from entering Canada, they processed most newcomers deemed "desirable" through Pier 21.

WELCOMING NEWCOMERS AT PIER 21

At Pier 21, immigrants could count on the volunteers representing churches and voluntary service organizations to provide them with various forms of assistance and spiritual support. Religious and voluntary service organizations welcomed and assisted incoming immigrants, returning Canadians, and visitors. These groups played an important role in the processing and accommodation of newcomers. They welcomed new arrivals, and assisted them with their immigration documentation if they could not speak or read in English and French. They also provided assistance to immigration and customs officials, who often could not communicate in the language of the newcomer. Volunteers also comforted and reassured distraught, exhausted, and confused travellers, and helped them find their way through the immigration facility. For many immigrants, this period marked their very first steps in Canada. Volunteers also provided support to detainees awaiting admission into Canada or deportation to their former homes.[85]

In the early postwar period, the IRO joined the voluntary service groups at Pier 21 by stationing a representative at Halifax. After the Second World War, John Lugass was sent to Halifax on behalf of the IRO to welcome and assist displaced persons and political refugees resettled by the organization in Canada. Lugass was expected to handle the large number of arrivals on his own, and his work was often arduous and the days were long. The IRO's lone representative offered food and support to countless European displaced persons, who often arrived at Pier 21 hungry, lacking sufficient funds, and without winter clothing. Lugass concluded his duties in Halifax with the arrival of the last chartered refugee transport in December 1951.[86] The postwar arrival of tens of thousands of immigrants, displaced persons and political refugees required volunteers who could speak several European languages.

An organization known for its voluntary service at Pier 21, the Sisters of Service, had previously worked at Pier 2 in Halifax's North End during the 1920s. The community of Roman Catholic religious women was founded in Toronto in 1922 to provide immigrants with spiritual support, and to assist them in integrating into Canadian society. After the Second World War, the sisters who worked at Halifax's immigration facility welcomed thousands of displaced persons and political refugees. When a new sister arrived at the immigration facility, another one usually departed. During Pier 21's years of operation, a total of thirteen sisters served at the immigration facility, including Josephine Dulaska, who spoke Polish, Slovak, and Ukrainian; Florence Kelly, who was referred to affectionately as the "German sister," having taught herself to speak the language; and Salvatrice "Sally" Liota, who spoke several languages, including Italian. Known for their fluency in multiple languages, the Sisters of Service assisted immigrants in every aspect of the arrival experience.[87]

Sister Kelly recalls that upon her arrival in the early 1950s, she found the immigration facility tremendously busy with the large volume of passenger traffic. On days when ships called on Halifax, the sisters were often distressed because they fell several books behind in typing the names of passengers and sending them out to various dioceses across the country that sought this information. Relief eventually came from Catholic Immigrant Services of Montreal in the form of a small tape recorder. The

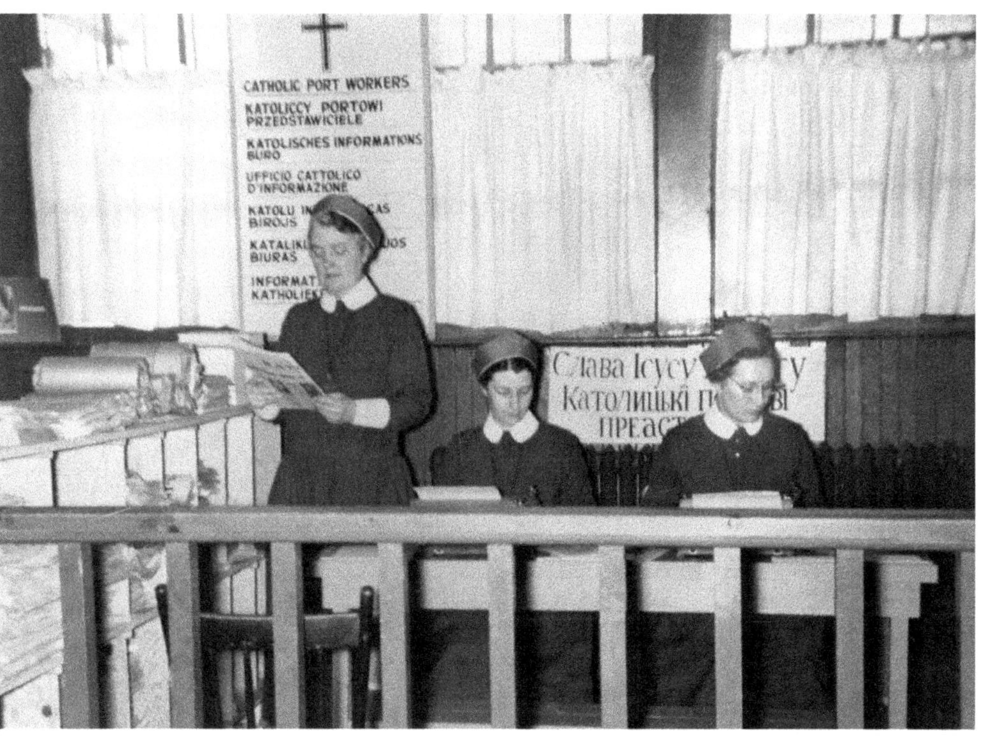

Sisters Veronica Gillis (left), Florence Kelly, (centre), and Josephine Dulaska (right) perform their duties at Pier 21, 1950s. *Source: Canadian Museum of Immigration Collection (DI1999.6.16)*

sisters verbally recorded the names of passengers from a ship's manifest instead of copying the names by hand, which took much longer.[88]

In 1955, Sister Liota, who had been assisting newly arrived immigrants at the port of Montreal, replaced Sister Kelly at Pier 21. She remembers spending long hours at the immigration shed, anywhere from eighteen to twenty-two hours at a time, to meet immigrants who disembarked from ships that arrived at all hours of the day and night. Along with Sister Dulaska, Liota arrived an hour ahead of time before a passenger ship docked at Pier 21 so that they could sell stamps, postcards, and stationary. The Catholic Women's League purchased the materials wholesale for the Sisters of Service to sell to immigrants who wished to write home while waiting for their train. Sister Liota also recalls making little cloth bags, with drawstrings, which would hold toiletries. These little bags were given as free samples to immigrants who might be in need of some of these basic necessities. Other "ditty bags" made of plastic or cellophane were put together for men and women, and included shoelaces, razor blades,

Sister Salvatrice Liota assists immigrants at the Canadian National Railway ticket office, Pier 21, 1955–1969. *Source: Canadian Museum of Immigration Collection (DI1999.6.14)*

ballpoint pencils, bars of soap, a washcloth, and lip balm. Bags included a rosary and a holy picture of Our Mother of Perpetual Help, with a list of Catholic clubs across Canada.

When the days were long, the Sisters of Service would seek out rest any way they could. Sister Liota recalls that her fellow sisters would take turns sleeping on benches in between ship arrivals in the early hours of the day. When the harbour commission gave the Sisters of Service a storeroom for their supplies, the sisters sometimes slept on the boxes in the storeroom. They often took naps to keep themselves going during the day. After completing her duties in the immigration facility, Sister Liota returned to the Sisters of Service's house in the city. Since she was a sacristan, Sister Liota was expected to help prepare for Mass every morning in the chapel, while the other sisters helped in the kitchen.[89]

Another voluntary service organization that made a significant contribution to the welfare of arriving immigrants at Pier 21 was the Jewish Immigrant Aid Society (JIAS). Established in 1922, JIAS stationed staff and volunteers at Pier 21 throughout its years of operation. Sadie Fineberg, an immigrant who spoke seven languages and later became a well-known philanthropist, volunteered at Pier 21 on behalf of JIAS for over three decades, beginning in the 1930s. Her husband, Morris, owned a food service business in the city, from which Fineberg often brought boxes of food to distribute for free to immigrants at Pier 21. Her dedication to recently arrived immigrants soon brought her accolades from the city of Halifax. In 1948, Mayor John Ahern presented Fineberg with a special silver badge and appointed her to represent the city as an official greeter and counsellor at Pier 21.[90]

Fineberg was there to welcome a future JIAS volunteer when she and her family arrived at Halifax aboard SS *Andania* on March 7, 1939. Marianne Ferguson (née Echt) immigrated to Canada from the Free City of Danzig (Gdańsk, Poland). Soon after Fineberg's appointment as the city's official greeter, Ferguson's mother, Meta, took over the role of welcoming immigrants at Pier 21 on behalf of JIAS. As a volunteer herself, Marianne helped immigrants claim their baggage and find their waiting trains that were to take them to their final destinations across Canada. She remembers that many immigrants arrived at Pier 21 with small children.

Volunteers from JIAS often took children to the Red Cross Seaport Nursery, where they received milk and cookies and took naps in the available cribs. Ferguson notes that JIAS also notified sponsors of the arrival times of newcomers for their final destination so that they could meet them at the local train station. For those immigrants who were not sponsored, the organization sent one of its workers to meet them once they disembarked from their train.[91]

Sadie Fineberg, a Jewish Immigrant Aid Society volunteer at Pier 21, and her husband, Morris, ca. 1945. *Source: Canadian Museum of Immigration Collection (DI2014.451.3)*

The Canadian Red Cross also played an important role in assisting newcomers at Pier 21.

One of the organization's first initiatives involved the introduction of a nursery for immigrant children. With the nursery open twenty-four hours per day, Red Cross staff supervised young newcomers, while their parents looked for food, secured train travel, used the facility's washrooms to freshen up, or caught up on some much needed rest. Meanwhile, the YWCA organized special clubs for war brides and their children—where they could find support and comradery from others like themselves. The YWCA also provided a baby clinic for recent mothers, many of whom were war brides or displaced persons. The organization helped newcomers find employment if they chose to resettle locally, and offered English-language training.[92] Volunteers with the Imperial Order Daughters of the Empire operated a canteen and provided displaced persons with a place to purchase food and small items on their way to their final destination across Canada.[93] Lesser-known volunteer organizations included the Charitable Irish Society, and the North British Society, who provided information and financial assistance, and would contact British or Irish authorities if an immigrant was detained in Halifax.[94]

Ordinary Haligonians were also employed in various capacities at Pier 21. Under the headline "Serves New Canadians," the *Halifax Mail-Star* published a photo of Ross D. Taylor, who worked as the Department of Citizenship and Immigration's caterer at the immigration facility.[95] Pier 21's catering department was responsible for operating a cafeteria in the detention quarters and a small grocery store, often referred to by staff as the "canteen," in the Annex building. On "boat days," when ships arrived, several hundred immigrants would descend on the store. According to Malcolm MacLeod, who served as a clerk cashier in the catering department for over a year beginning in 1954, the canteen's shelves were stocked with "the simplest of foodstuffs: bread, canned meat and fruit, soft drinks, cookies, crackers and spreads. Our sandwiches were usually cheese or ham or sometimes, when a fit of creativity struck the boss, ham and cheese. Making these sandwiches was a marvel of efficiency. The two managers, myself, and three or four casual workers brought in for boat day worked at it all together. Slices from two or three loaves of bread at a time were spread on a large surface. We buttered each slice, cost-effectively, by melting the butter first and applying it very sparingly with a brush."[96] The *Halifax*

Mail-Star reported that, before taking a train to their final destination, immigrants purchased large quantities of food. The canteen also carried a "two-dollar-special," which consisted of a cardboard box containing all the essentials for the long train journey across Canada.[97]

Voluntary service workers acted as intermediaries between officials and immigrants by guiding, steering, comforting, and translating for newcomers. Their actions demonstrate that the immigration process through Pier 21 was not a linear or monolithic practice. However, Canadian immigration and customs officials adhered to a defined process of arrival, examination, detention, and admission or deportation. Yet the varied experiences of newcomers indicate that the practice of processing immigrants was also adaptable to the particular circumstances of the individual.

POSTWAR EXPERIENCES OF ENTERING CANADA THROUGH PIER 21

The transatlantic voyage was an important part of an immigrant's non-linear experience of coming to Canada. As a child, English immigrant Maureen Pettigrew (née McDermott) arrived at Halifax aboard RMS *Aquitania* in June 1948. She recalls that her "most vivid memory, however, is the night we weighed anchor in Halifax Harbour. We children were allowed to stay up, and scrambled up to the funnels and around everywhere previously forbidden. The lights on Halifax Hill is still one of my most cherished memories. A child coming from Britain and a lifetime of darkness to see the hill of lights was truly like a miracle."[98]

For other immigrants, simply arriving to find volunteers waiting with food and treats was a welcome sight. Hungarian Jewish refugee Bill Gluck survived the Auschwitz-Birkenau and Dachau concentration camps. In June 1948, at the young age of seventeen, he boarded SS *Marine Falcon* in Bremerhaven, occupied Germany, for its voyage to Halifax. When Gluck disembarked at Halifax, the young Holocaust survivor remembers that several people were waiting for the ship's passengers with oranges and chocolates.[99]

For other newcomers, entering Canada through Halifax was more problematic. In June 1948, Mary de Jong and her family left Andijk,

Netherlands, for Canada. Her father had sailed previously to Canada after signing a labour contract to work on a farm in Elora, Ontario. Upon arrival at Pier 21, Mary's father discovered that the job had been given to someone else. He remained in Halifax until he could find other employment. In July, de Jong and her family disembarked from SS *Tabinta* at Pier 21. She recalls that her family's confinement in Pier 21's quarters dampened the initial excitement of leaving the ship and disembarking. During their two-day stay, they were not permitted to leave the facility except for one short walk. De Jong notes that the bars and cages in the immigration facility were similar to a jail. As a result of their detention, de Jong's father held a long grudge against the Canadian government for his family's temporary loss of freedom.[100]

Sixteen-year-old Dutch immigrant Dori van Schagen remembers her father learning that his sponsor had backed out of his farm labour contract while the family was crossing the Atlantic Ocean. Upon landing at Halifax, the family of nine spent six weeks in Pier 21's accommodations until another sponsor could be found. It was a difficult time for the family with only a few dollars in their pockets and no knowledge of the English language. Similar to many Dutch families who travelled with large wooden crates known as *kists*, which often contained clothing, personal items, furniture, sinks, and bicycles, the van Schagen family had their clothes and other belongings stored in their *kist* within Pier 21's baggage hall. During her stay in Halifax, van Schagen recalls that kitchen staff gave her and her father a glass of water and a bottle of ketchup as they went to Pier 21's kitchen for lunch. Neither newcomer knew what to do with the items and thought that maybe they had to make their own tomato juice, so they stirred the ketchup into the water.[101]

While some newcomers stayed at Pier 21 while they waited to secure employment, others were quarantined due to illness. In February 1951, six-year-old Dutch immigrant Gerry Van Kessel, his parents, and four siblings arrived at Pier 21 aboard SS *Volendam*. Unfortunately for the family, medical officers under the auspices of the Department of National Health and Welfare screened the Van Kessels, found that two of Van Kessel's younger brothers had the mumps, and put them into quarantine. The family remained at the immigration facility for approximately three weeks. While there, Van Kessel remembers celebrating his seventh birthday. Eventually, the family received clearance to leave and commenced their travels to Ontario.[102]

Immigrants could also be detained for a lack of paperwork, the possibility of being a security risk, or simply for a lack of "sufficient means to maintain" themselves until employment was secured. In June 1951, West German immigrants Harry and Heidi Kornelsen and their nine-month-old son disembarked at Pier 21 and headed for their civil examination. The family recalls that funds for their train tickets were supposed to be wired to Halifax for when they arrived, but the money had not arrived by the time of their disembarkation. Although the funds arrived the following morning, the Kornelsens remained at Pier 21 until July 2 due to a long weekend that included the Dominion Day holiday. With $10 American in their possession, the Kornelsens boarded a CNR train to Montreal.[103]

A *kist* belonging to the Timmerman family from the Netherlands is lifted off SS *Volendam* at Pier 21, 1950. *Source: Canadian Museum of Immigration Collection (DI2013.1529.12)*

Often, Pier 21 officers processed newcomers quickly through their civil examination, only to encounter difficulties during their customs inspection in the gangway between the immigration shed and the Annex building. Although some Canada customs officers had a working knowledge of the French language and were able to use a few expressions in other languages, they were at a loss when dealing with individuals of Slavic origin.[104] Customs officials relied on the Sisters of Service and other volunteers to communicate with immigrants.

Milan Gregor, following the communist takeover of Czechoslovakia in February 1948, escaped from his homeland to occupied Germany, where he later became a bookkeeper for the IRO. He arrived in Halifax aboard SS *Nelly* in May 1951. Gregor recalls that every immigrant was permitted to bring two pieces of luggage with limited weight. As a single adult, Gregor planned to bring only one piece of luggage with him. In Germany, a fellow countryman with a wife and child asked him whether he could bring an additional suitcase with him to Canada. Gregor subsequently agreed. After disembarkation and his civil examination, Gregor proceeded to customs for inspection, where he faced a customs officer behind a table. Gregor was asked to empty his pockets and place the contents on the table. Afterward, he opened his personal luggage and was shocked to find a woman's negligee, a bra, and a child's pee-pot. Fortunately for Gregor, the customs officer understood the situation and only smiled.[105] Although Gregor's customs experience was rather benign, newcomers' personal effects were often at risk of being taken away by Canadian customs officials.

German immigrant Wolfgang Christl departed Bremen for Halifax aboard MS *Anna Salén* in 1952. He remembers staff leading him down the gangway to be screened by Canadian customs officials. He was instructed to have his suitcase ready for inspection. After waiting his turn in line, the officer inspected Christl's personal items. He remembers observing "the officer checking my baggage, and there he grabbed a sausage… and not realising what was going on, I observed he threw that sausage in the garbage! No sooner did that one land, he grabbed a second one, and attempted to throw [it] too. And I was so upset, I pushed the officer. And I said, 'You can't do that.' And just to make a long story short… I was escorted into a room, and the door was locked."[106]

Religious organizations and voluntary service agencies also assisted immigrants in the Annex building, where newcomers could find several tables covered predominantly with religious literature and publications about Canada. Gregor recalls that the Imperial Order Daughters of the Empire occupied the largest table. He notes that regardless of their linguistic ability in either English or French, newcomers received a King James Bible before being led to other tables and the canteen.[107] Below, on the ground floor of the Annex building, immigrants, visitors, and returning Canadians located their larger pieces of luggage before boarding trains heading westward. There too, voluntary service agencies assisted newcomers in purchasing tickets and finding the proper train. Port chaplains and volunteers made sure that immigrants were comfortable aboard their trains prior to leaving Halifax.

However, immigrants had mixed views of train travel westward from Halifax. In June 1952, West German immigrant Peter Hessel arrived at Halifax aboard MS *Anna Salén*. He had a positive recollection of the journey westward: "We went through Nova Scotia, and it was still daylight for several hours. The countryside is beautiful and romantic-looking, with rugged rocks, clear lakes, huge forests, and brightly clean settlements. As soon as the sun set, it became dark very suddenly. We pulled out the seats and went to sleep. This morning we passed a long lake surrounded by wooded mountains."[108] Dutch immigrant William Kreeft landed at Halifax aboard SS *Groote Beer* in September 1952. He had a different recollection of his train journey to Alberta: "[T]he trains were dirty and very short on all of the amenities for daily life. When I entered Grade 1, the class was asked to draw a picture of a train. I did so and coloured the whole train black. The teacher spanked me for not using other colours, and for not taking a realistic view of trains. My mother later explained to her what my experiences of trains had been."[109]

RENOVATIONS TO THE IMMIGRATION SHED

Pier 21's immigration facilities were rebuilt after the 1944 fire and reoccupied in December 1946. During the period of reconstruction, Pier 21's detention quarters were hastily constructed army huts to the north of the Annex kitchen. The new quarters were erected in time for a significant movement of soldiers' dependents, European displaced persons, and political refugees.[110]

At the time, Canadian immigration officials debated the suitability of the waterfront shed for immigrant accommodation and detention. Pier 21's reconstruction provided federal immigration officials with an opportunity to substantially rearrange the site's interior. Changes to the arrangement of the assembly area did not alter the basic path of passenger traffic disembarking from a ship.[111] The gangway, assembly area, medical and civil examination spaces, and the use of the gangway connecting shed 21 to the Annex building remained in approximately the same relationship to each other.

However, bureaucratic views of immigrant desirability and the sociopolitical norms of the period influenced the changes made to the immigration quarters. The separate "British" and "Foreign" medical and detention quarters were removed from the reconstruction plans, and so were the separate detention spaces for men and women. Canadian immigration authorities chose to build five detention areas of similar size, with one space set aside for women. Although the other four spaces lacked a gender designation, they were all destined for men. In addition, three smaller detention rooms, with the dimensions of a bedroom, were added, as was a strong room specifically for women. Following these renovations, Pier 21 could hold a maximum of approximately 160 people in its accommodations and sixteen in its detention spaces.

Renovations after the 1944 fire included the construction of another airing gallery, and the relocation of the recreation room to be closer to all detention spaces. The recreation room also featured access to the newly built airing gallery. The completed renovations reduced the available space for offices in the accommodation and detention area of the immigration shed. The immigration department dealt with this shift by making some notable changes to the assembly area. After the Second World War, immigration officials took approximately a hundred feet—sixty feet for offices and secondary examination spaces, and forty feet for the washroom—out of the length of the assembly area.

The space became an open office space, with small offices and room for a stenographer along the waterside wall, and examination and storage rooms on the south wall toward the assembly area. The latter was reduced on its south end by the construction of a large set of washroom facilities—extending almost forty feet north into the assembly area space.[112] When the shed opened in 1928, the assembly area consumed half the interior length of the shed—more than 250 feet. After the Second World War, the assembly area was approximately a hundred feet shorter. Although passengers moved through the space in a similar fashion, the assembly area was no longer the airy gallery it had previously been during the interwar period. The facility was rebuilt with all of its former immigration services restored.

With the expansion in office space due to the renovations completed in 1946, the Department of Citizenship and Immigration's district offices moved to the quarters at Pier 21 in 1953.[113] The move was followed by a substantial renovation to the Annex building. The National Harbours Board, which was responsible for the Halifax Ocean Terminals, built a two-storey addition on the south end of the Annex building. This renovation increased the available floor space in the Annex building from 33,000 square feet to 55,000 square feet.[114] This new floor space was larger than the area inside shed 21. The new accommodations benefited the voluntary aid organizations that stationed their representatives at the immigration facility. When Pier 21 opened in 1928, religious organizations and service groups occupied an open office space near the north end of the ground level of the Annex building.

Following the 1953 renovation, these agencies moved their work to the second storey, near the entrance into the Annex building from the gangway.[115] The area was constructed with a large central waiting room and services around the outside walls, including various social services and a money exchange office, telegraph offices, and a railway ticketing office. The local detachment of the Canadian Red Cross also relocated to the new space. Its Seaport Nursery had previously been located near the north end of the Annex building.[116] After the completion of renovations, the nursery moved to a space directly at the bottom of the gangway from the immigration quarters to the Annex building. The previously mentioned voluntary service organizations later claimed that the space they moved into was not quite what they initially requested.[117]

The relocation of the voluntary service agencies reflects a changing understanding of the importance of immigration reception in the early postwar period. Another shift that speaks to this trend was the removal of the personal baggage cages from the immigration facility in 1956, which was an attempt to make the assembly area more welcoming to new arrivals.[118] Although the religious organizations and service agencies gained office space, the principal beneficiaries of the site renovations that expanded the immigration facility's overall space were the Canadian customs officials. Their baggage examination room on the ground floor at the south end of the Annex building more than doubled in length, to some 260 feet.[119]

Meanwhile, the expansion proved to be a major improvement to the baggage-handling capacity of the immigration facility, and would have complemented a planned component of the 1953 renovations that was never built: a tunnel linking the baggage space on the ground floor of shed 21 with the area in the Annex building.[120] The proposed tunnel would have permitted baggage handlers to avoid crossing five sets of train tracks to bring items into the Annex building from shed 21. However, with a projected grade of 10 per cent down at shed 21 and 8.5 per cent at the Annex building, and with both ramps leading to sharp curves, the proposed tunnel would have merely changed the nature of the challenges faced by stevedores, rather than eliminating them. The expansion did not change how travellers located their items in the baggage hall. They still found their baggage organized alphabetically by surname. The renovations and addition of the immigration district office in 1953 were the last major structural changes to the immigration facility for the remainder of its years of operation.[121]

During its peak years from the late 1940s to the early 1950s, Pier 21's facilities consisted of over 100,000 square feet of space and required a staff of over thirty individuals in addition to the stationed immigration and customs officials. Pier 21 was not only an immigration shed but a site of employment for twenty-two guards, a caterer, an assistant caterer, two cooks, four kitchen helpers, two janitors, two matrons, and two cleaning ladies.[122]

With the completion of the expansion to the baggage area on the ground floor of the Annex building in 1955, customs officials found ample room for their examinations over the coming years. As the busiest ocean port of entry in Canada between the late 1940s and early 1950s, Pier 21 was also well positioned to respond to a sudden large movement of ocean liner traffic. In 1956, Pier 21 officials were quick to respond when a strike by dockworkers forced dozens of ocean liners headed for American ports along the eastern seaboard to reroute their travel itineraries to Halifax. In one day as many as five passenger ships, including RMS *Queen Elizabeth*, docked at Pier 21, permitting approximately 3,800 travellers to disembark. With the assistance of United States immigration authorities stationed at Halifax, Canadian immigration officials were able to process this large amount of passenger traffic successfully.[123]

Despite the occasional increase in ocean liner traffic, the large movement of immigrants to Canada through Pier 21 in the late 1940s began to decrease in the mid-1950s. In his recollections of Pier 21, Canadian customs officer Arthur J. Vaughan noted that fewer ships were landing at Halifax and passenger lists were becoming shorter. Instead of immigrants, Vaughan found that, increasingly, Canadian residents, visitors, and businesspeople were being processed though the immigration facility. This trend would continue for the next sixteen years of Pier 21's existence as an immigration facility.[124]

The early 1950s were marked by government-promoted schemes to bring large numbers of immigrants, including displaced persons and political refugees, to Canada. By the end of the decade, 1.5 million immigrants had arrived in Canada.[125] The Canadian government passed a new Immigration Act that streamlined the administration of immigration and gave considerable discretionary power to the minister of immigration to determine the suitability and admissibility of prospective immigrants. Initially, Canadian officials attempted to prevent "undesirable" individuals, including communist sympathizers, individuals with criminal records, drug users and traffickers, and persons with non-traditional lifestyles, from entering the country. Soon, events behind the Iron Curtain in communist Hungary presented Canadian officials at Pier 21 with an opportunity to admit, detain, and help resettle refugees according to prevailing Cold War norms surrounding who was deemed to be an admissible and desirable immigrant. During the early postwar period, Pier 21 was a major port of entry for displaced persons and political refugees seeking safe haven, economic opportunity, and a better life in Canada.

OPPOSITE: Juliana Miller, a Hungarian-speaking Red Cross volunteer, briefs a Hungarian refugee about Canadian geography and travel customs, 1956–1957.

Source: Canada. Department of Employment and Immigration, Library and Archives Canada, PA-181009

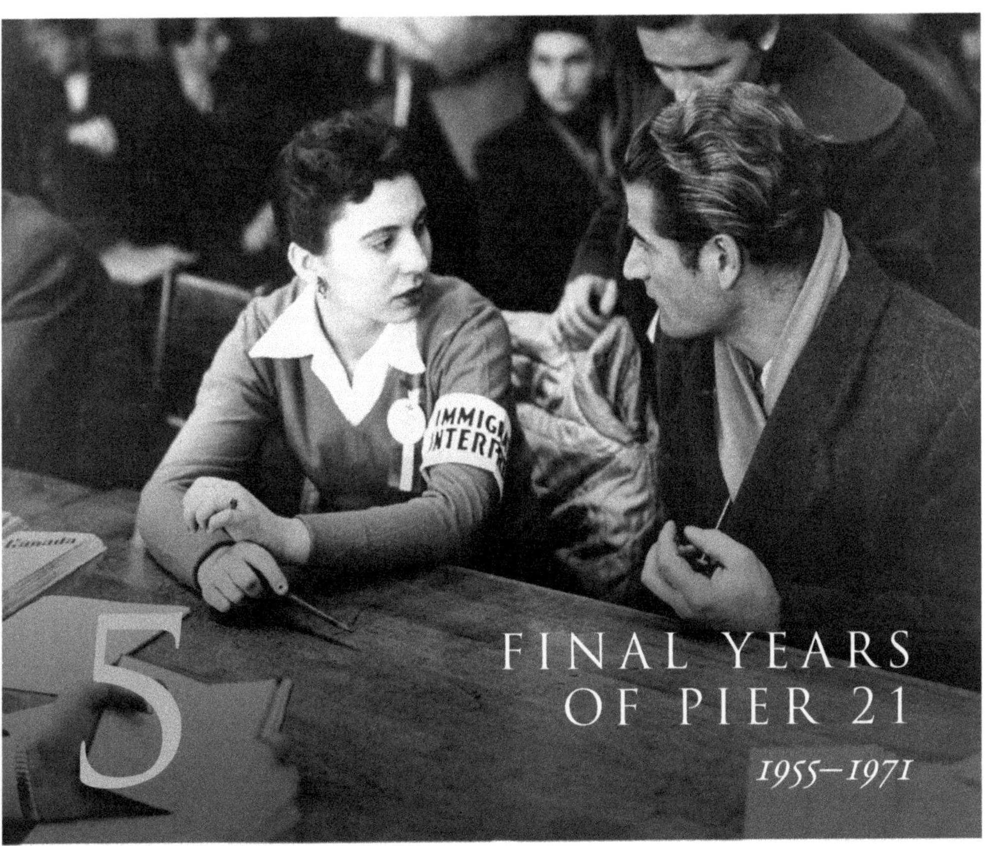

5 FINAL YEARS OF PIER 21

1955–1971

I loved the Italians; they were full of life... the babies were absolutely gorgeous... there were huge waves... where there would be a great many people coming in, and there would be smaller waves. When a Hungarian revolution happened, it was a different kind of immigrant there. More nervous, and more northern. The Italians are Mediterraneans and they... [had a]... kind of joie de vivre... [that]...the Hungarians didn't have—but the Hungarians had come out of a very bad situation and were very nervous.[1]

—Heather Wineberg (née Davis), an English immigrant who volunteered with Pier 21's Red Cross Seaport Nursery, 1956–1962.

In the 1950s, Pier 21 welcomed an average of 50,000 immigrants each year.[2] Between 1956 and 1971, the immigration facility saw the continued movement of British, Italian, American, West German, Greek, Portuguese, Dutch, French, and West Indian immigrants, among other groups, to Canada. Many of these individuals came in search of economic opportunity and to reunite with family members. These newcomers were joined by refugees who fled communist regimes in their homelands and sought safe haven in Canada. At Pier 21, the immigration process for new arrivals remained similar to previous years.

EXPERIENCES OF ARRIVAL TO (AND DEPARTURE FROM) PIER 21 IN THE 1950S AND 1960S

Before their departure from a European port of entry to their final destination in Canada, immigrants were still required to submit to a medical examination, as well as a vaccination. In some cases, immigrants were also screened prior to embarkation and on board their ocean liners before landing in Canada. In early August 1956, Wiebren Pijl, his wife, Jantje, and their three children arrived at the port of Rotterdam before continuing their journey to Halifax. The Pijl family were required to visit several control stations consisting of a health examination with a throat inspection, vaccination control, and distribution of landing documents. Upon having their travel documentation checked one final time, the family was allowed to proceed over the gangway onto their ship. In mid-August, the Pijls landed at Halifax. Almost immediately, immigration and customs officials came on board to inspect the passengers. Wiebren Pijl recalls coming to a long table surrounded by several Canadian immigration and customs officials. The travel documentation that Pijl had filled out the preceding day was examined by the officers and the family was later permitted to disembark from their ship.[3]

For some immigrants, the transatlantic voyage was a challenging period in their immigration from their old country to Canada. Emilio Poggi, his wife, Zolanda, and two children left their hometown of Genoa, Italy, for a new life in Canada. Poggi recalls that "the departure was one of the most horrid and disorganized experiences we have ever had to endure. It truly seemed as though they were embarking animals onto the ship and not passengers that had paid the full amount for their voyage." After a long and tumultuous voyage across the Atlantic Ocean, the Poggi family arrived at Pier 21 aboard MS *Saturnia* in December 1956. Upon receiving a warm welcome from Canadian authorities, Poggi viewed Halifax as a paradise after coming from such an agonizing experience in Naples.[4]

In an effort to help immigrants reach their final destinations more efficiently, volunteers at Pier 21 received individual ship manifests before the arrival of a ship and contacted their colleagues across the country, informing them that a particular immigrant was scheduled to arrive at their local railway station at a specific date and time. Michael McCarthy, who volunteered with the Sisters of Service at Pier 21 from 1960 to 1970, explains that the organization's volunteers each received a ship's manifest prior to its arrival. Consequently, voluntary aid organizations knew the nationality and, in some cases, the religious denomination of each passenger. When a newcomer arrived at Pier 21, they often found themselves in a considerable queue, and eventually a representative from the Sisters of Service or one of the other service organizations met them. McCarthy recalls that he would ask an immigrant for their name in order to find them in the ship's manifest. Subsequent questions usually involved identifying an arrival's religious background in order to determine which voluntary aid agency was best equipped to look after an immigrant's spiritual and personal needs.

McCarthy remembers that the Sisters of Service never turned anyone away, including individuals who were not of a Catholic background. The Sisters of Service attempted to provide assistance to anyone in need and answered as many of the newcomers' questions as they could. McCarthy observes that many of the immigrants arrived with a European mentality; believing that if they were headed to Toronto, for example, they would arrive the following day. Newcomers struggled to understand the length and the breadth of the country.[5] The practice of forwarding ship manifests to Pier 21 volunteers prior to a ship's arrival continued well into the 1960s and helped many newcomers navigate the immigration process through Pier 21 and reach their final destinations across Canada.[6]

In some cases, immigrants who experienced a smooth transatlantic voyage encountered difficulty upon reaching Pier 21. Twenty-nine-year-old Portuguese immigrant Amélia Vieira Da Silva and her four children arrived at Pier 21 aboard MS *Vulcania* in early April 1955. Canadian officials, who wrongly suspected that she had tuberculosis, quickly took Da Silva for X-rays. Pier 21's medical staff followed a system of certification outlined in the 1952 Immigration Act. In particular, they referred to section 5 ("prohibited classes") to determine whether an immigrant was inadmissible, including subsections for mentally or physically defective persons, and diseased individuals. If immigrants were certified according to one of these categories, immigration officials would then interview the newcomers to evaluate their admissibility according to the Immigration Act. In some cases, immigrants were deemed medically inadmissible and deported the day of their arrival. Da Silva's eldest daughter, nine-year-old Maria Manuela, was left to look after her younger siblings. After one day and one night in Pier 21's medical quarters, Da Silva was happily reunited with her children.[7]

Some immigrants were disoriented by the interior of the immigration shed and the large number of passengers being processed through the site. In late March 1959, four-year-old Frank Giorno, along with his mother, father, and six-year-old sister, left their home in Calabria, Italy, for a better life in Canada. After arriving at Pier 21, Giorno remembers that his family entered the immigration facility to find a crowd of passengers holding their personal baggage as they headed in every direction. His parents were concerned with recovering their items from the baggage hall in the Annex building. After walking down a ramp, the family entered what appeared to them to be a large unfinished basement to retrieve their possessions. Afterward, they went down a narrow tunnel and across the street toward the train that would take them to Toronto.[8]

Without the help of interpreters, newcomers had difficulty understanding Canadian officials. In May 1957, Martha Akmens (née Hochheimer) left West Germany aboard MS *Stockholm* to be reunited with her family in Canada. Sophia Maddalena recalls that her grandmother's voyage to Canada by ship lasted a week before she reached Pier 21 in Halifax. Upon arrival, the only words that Akmens could say in English were "yes" and "no." Luckily, there were interpreters to help her. Akmens had to wait for a long time for her name to be called in order to get her papers examined. After a Canadian immigration official stamped her papers with "Landed Immigrant," she was free to go. Akmens's brother Walter, who lived in Canada, was there to pick her up after she left the immigration facility.[9]

European immigrants often brought items from their homeland that did not survive the long journey to Canada and were also subject to seizure at the hands of Canadian customs officials. Immigrants often went to great lengths to conceal foodstuffs prohibited from entering Canada. If these items were discovered, they were immediately deemed to be contraband. Newcomers often wanted to bring to Canada food products that reminded them of their culture and homeland, and that they could share with their families and friends. They also worried that the foods available for purchase in their new country would be of lower quality than the items found back home.

Customs officers were tasked with searching an immigrant's personal baggage and checked luggage to seize contraband items considered to be a risk to the security of Canada, for example, weapons and communist propaganda; or detrimental to Canadian society, such as illicit and "immoral" literature. Customs inspection also attempted to prevent hoof-and-mouth disease, and protect agriculture from disease generally, often confiscating foreign plants, meats, and soils. Volunteer Heather Wineberg recalls that two customs officers came by one day to have coffee in the Seaport Nursery and informed her that they had run into a terrible incident in the baggage hall downstairs. One of the officers told Wineberg that they had isolated a terrible smell in the area to a blue-painted wooden box, similar to a trunk. Upon opening the box, they found a cooked baby pig. The recently arrived family, to which the box belonged, came from a village where they roasted the pig and placed it at the bottom of their box because they did not know whether they would receive food aboard their ship.[10]

Passengers at Pier 21 often smelled rotting foods in the assembly area or the baggage hall in the Annex building. On days when a large ocean liner docked at Pier 21, immigration officers would permit only 250 passengers at a time to enter the assembly area, due to its seating capacity. In one case, travellers refused to sit beside a Greek immigrant who sat with a rolled-up towel in his lap. Immigration officials soon discovered that the man possessed a decaying octopus, brought to Canada from Greece. Officials later seized the octopus, much to the relief of the passengers in the assembly area.[11]

Pier 21 officials also attempted to prevent a considerable amount of cured meat brought by ocean liner passengers from entering the country. Teresa Perri was nine years old when she arrived at Pier 21 with her mother and three brothers. In early May 1957, the family left Naples, Italy, aboard

MS *Vulcania*. Upon arriving in mid-May, Perri remembers that her mother became very concerned when a customs officer opened her suitcase. Prior to their departure, Perri's mother had hidden a capicollo (cured ham) inside the piece of luggage, but the official only discovered three bottles of liquor. Initially, the customs officer only permitted two bottles for entry into Canada, but after Perri's mother indicated that they were a family of five, the official allowed her to continue her journey with all three bottles of liquor and the cured ham, which left the immigration facility undeclared.

Other immigrants were less lucky. Perri claims that her mother witnessed Canadian customs officers puncture a mattress holding hidden containers of olive oil. According to Perri, the olive oil spilled out, onto the floor, causing the owners much anguish as their goods were confiscated. Further testing their luck with Canadian officials, Perri's mother had also hidden three salamis in her purse. Prior to customs inspection, she gave them to a young boy, who placed them in the pocket of his jacket. During the journey by train, the family enjoyed the salamis when they ran out of food.[12]

Meat was another item brought by immigrants to Pier 21 that was subject to further inspection. In early April 1959, eight-year-old Angela Crosdale (née Marchitto), along with her father and sister, landed at Pier 21 from Italy. Recognizing that the family was from Italy, where previous immigrants had tried to bring various meats, including salami, prosciutto, and sausages, to Canada, a customs officer asked through an interpreter whether the family had any meat in their possession. The official proceeded to search the family's belongings, discovering a small cloth bag of flour given to Crosdale's father by a neighbour who wanted it brought to a relative in Montreal as a gift. He indicated that the flour was cornmeal, unaware that a chunk of homemade pork sausage was hidden within the flour. The customs officer found the contraband meat and proceeded to thoroughly inspect the family's other possessions. In both pieces of luggage, Crosdale's grandmother had placed walnuts wherever there was remaining space. Crosdale vividly remembers how a cascade of walnuts fell from the trunk onto the polished floor. Crosdale and her sister attempted to recover the walnuts as quickly as possible before they came to rest at the feet of other passengers at Pier 21. Crosdale's father was too tired and disgusted by the incident to worry about the walnuts.[13]

Teresa Perri (right), her mother, Antonietta, and brothers Silvio (left), Achille (second from left), and Egidio (centre) aboard MS *Vulcania*, 1957. *Source: Canadian Museum of Immigration Collection (DI2016.399.5)*

Immigrants also concealed fruits and vegetables in their luggage. In November 1961, Maria Pagano, along with her daughter and son, arrived at Pier 21. Pagano left Italy to be reunited with her husband, Antonio, who had arrived in Canada in 1958. After an eleven-day transatlantic journey aboard MS *Saturnia*, the family went through the immigration and customs process. Upon descending into the Annex building's baggage hall to retrieve their checked items, Pagano located the family's luggage and called a customs officer to examine their possessions in order to have them marked as inspected. Pagano remembers seeing beans on the floor of the baggage hall and thinking that they resembled the bag of beans in one of the family's trunks. She recalls that people wondered how the beans ended up on the floor. After surviving the embarrassment of finding their beans on the floor of Pier 21's baggage hall, the Pagano family had their luggage examined by Canadian customs officers. Shortly thereafter, the family was directed to the train station. Pagano remembers passing by a long table in the warehouse full of confiscated items, including prosciuttos, sausages, cheeses, salamis, and bottles of liquor not permitted into Canada. While Pagano was unable to speak English, and Canadian officials did not understand Italian, they nevertheless made her feel welcome in Canada and helped her family locate their train.

Soon after, Maria Pagano learned from her children that there were differences in the taste of Italian and Canadian food. In preparation for the trip by train to Toronto, Pagano visited the store in the train station. She purchased bread and bologna in order to make some sandwiches for her children. Unaccustomed to Canadian food, her son and daughter found the bread and processed meat too sweet, and refused to eat them. After boarding the train, Pagano brought her children to the restaurant car and ordered each of them a plate of spaghetti. Once again, the children found the meal too sweet and refused to eat it. Pagano worried that if her children did not eat, they would get sick before arriving in Toronto. She then remembered packing some homemade biscuits prior to leaving Italy for Canada. The children happily ate the baked goods until they reached their final destination.[14]

In addition to confiscating contraband items, Canadian officials at Pier 21 were also concerned with preventing contagious diseases from entering the country. Quarantine was also used to prevent the spread of contagious diseases from passenger traffic, which included individuals and their pets. Canadian officials at Pier 21 could not afford to be lenient with recently arrived animals. In the 1962 National Film Board of Canada documentary *Strangers for the Day*, a recently arrived couple from France were asked about their dog being placed in quarantine upon arriving at Pier 21. Unaware of Canadian quarantine regulations, the couple claimed that their dog was underfed to the point of starvation aboard ship and was forced into quarantine for ninety days in Halifax. They went on to question why English dogs received no trouble entering the

Maria Pagano with her husband, Antonio, and daughter, Maria Grazia, and son, Luigi, before their immigration to Canada, 1958. *Source: Canadian Museum of Immigration Collection (DI2013.1420.7)*

country, while their dog had to "suffer the indignity of quarantine." Perhaps the French couple were unaware that Britain had yet to find a confirmed case of rabies, therefore British dogs did not have to go into quarantine. Nevertheless, their dog received ample attention and food while in quarantine, and the French couple continued their journey.[15]

In another case, Sister Liota had to interpret for an Italian immigrant who did not understand why her dog had to be quarantined. She remembers that the "dog had its paws around her neck, and she was crying, that the dog only understood Italian. I was, you know, putting the dog in quarantine, the dog understood Italian. And he only ate Italian food. So, it was heartbreaking. It was like tearing a child away from its mother."[16] Volunteers like Sister Liota were instrumental in ensuring that immigrants received the necessary advice, basic necessities, and spiritual guidance as they moved through the immigration facility.

As the flow of European immigrants to Canada continued through Halifax, voluntary aid agencies continued to provide newcomers with "ditty bags." As in previous years, the contents of the ditty bags remained much the same. Similar to the Sisters of Service, the United Church offered bags containing airmail stationery, stamps, notebook, pencil, soap, facial tissues, toothpaste, toothbrush, facecloth, candy, and a colouring book for children. Many ditty bags were made up on the spot to fit a newcomer's situation, such as a warm scarf and mittens during a winter arrival. Upward of two hundred ditty bags could be passed out in a single day.

As port chaplain for the United Church, Reverend J. P. C. Fraser had previous experience helping returning Canadian servicemen and their war brides adjust to postwar Canadian society. Along with his wife, Anna, he worked at Pier 21 throughout the 1960s. The couple handed out thousands of ditty bags containing useful necessities to many immigrants after they landed at Halifax. The bags were put together from countless donations to the United Church from across the country.[17]

Immigrants often came across volunteers handing out free samples of various products provided by Canadian companies. While Imperial Tobacco's products, including Ogden's tobacco and papers for men and Turret cigarettes for women, were well-received, Kellogg's cornflakes were largely misunderstood. Many immigrants were not aware that the cereal was a breakfast item and, given its dry contents, decided to discard the product. As children were usually given cornflakes, the food item was often found on the floor of the Annex building and the inside of train cars.[18]

For adults with young children, the child-minding services provided by the voluntary service agencies were welcome because they provided them with an opportunity to locate their checked baggage, secure train tickets, and purchase food for the journey across Canada. Wiebren Pijl recalls that inside the Red Cross Seaport Nursery, a volunteer spoke to them in their native language, while younger children played in playpens, older children coloured or drew, and exhausted mothers napped. The Pijls temporarily left their three children in the nursery in order to locate their baggage. On the way downstairs, other volunteers met them and gave them each a sample package of tea, Kellogg's cornflakes, and a small tin of Buisman's instant coffee. Upon entering the Annex building's baggage hall, they found that their six pieces of luggage were scattered across the hall. With their items in tow, the Dutch couple quickly reserved three double seats for their train trip to Victoria, British Columbia. In the waiting room, the couple noticed a self-service food store and decided to purchase bread, butter, sandwich fixings, and fruit, among other items, which they were able to store on the train prior to its departure.[19]

The Frasers, supported through a special fund provided by the United Church, helped immigrants who arrived with phony train tickets sold to them by unscrupulous travel agents overseas, or who had bought tickets for the wrong day or at an incorrect rate and could not pay the difference between the fares. The Frasers often helped to purchase tickets or supplement the difference in price. On most days, the couple was joined on the second floor of the immigration facility by Deacon Williams of the Anglican Church and Father J. R. Brown of the Catholic Church, where they would await incoming passenger ships and provide assistance to newcomers, sometimes until the early hours of the following day.[20]

For many immigrants, the journey by train to their final destination across Canada was an uncomfortable experience. In April 1957, Dutch immigrant W. A. T. Van den Byllaardt arrived at Pier 21 aboard SS *Rijndam*. Later that evening, he caught a train heading for Montreal. Van den Byllaardt remembers boarding the Colonist, a train pulled by

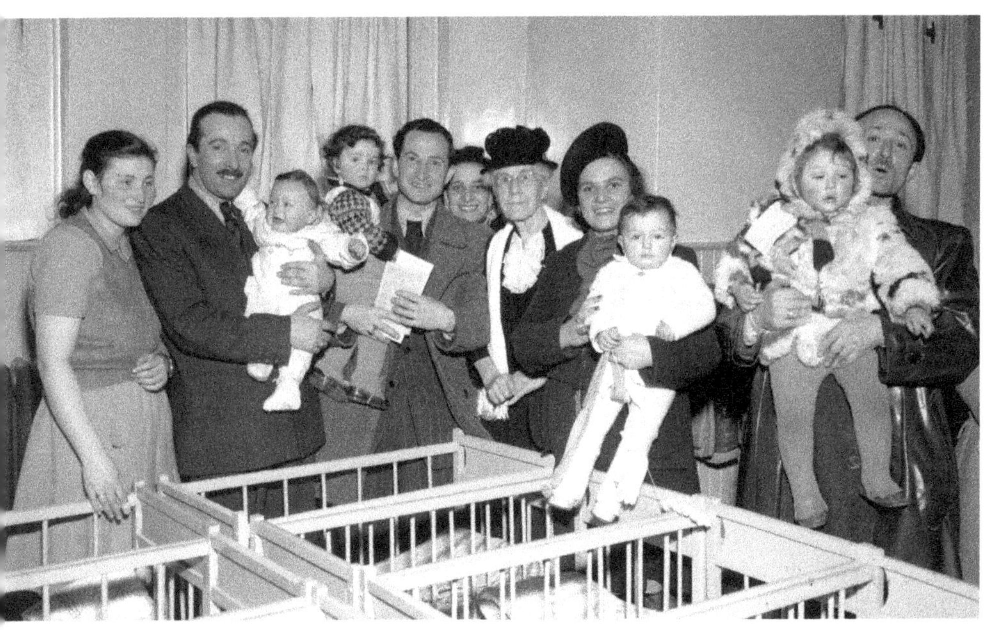

Immigrant families with a Red Cross worker in the Seaport Nursery at Pier 21, 1948.
Source: Canadian Museum of Immigration Collection (R2014.440.24)

a steam locomotive, with cars featuring hard benches, plugged toilets, and no heat. With numerous stops and long waits along the journey to Montreal, sleep was hard to attain and Van den Byllaardt found the entire experience uncomfortable. After reaching Montreal, he was picked up by his sister, who had arrived fourteen days earlier on SS *Maasdam* and rented a place in the city. In Montreal, the Dutch siblings boarded the Super Continental for Edmonton and found the meals to be expensive, but the service aboard the train was good and sleep was attainable.[21]

The Johansen family arrived at Pier 21 aboard MS *Stockholm* in late June 1957. They later boarded a train for Calgary. The Danish family recalls boarding an old train car that contained wooden benches. The Johansens later learned from other travellers that the train was referred to as the "cattle train" for its lack of comfort and space, and propensity to move large numbers of passengers. Upon reaching Montreal, the family happily transferred to a more modern train.[22]

While some immigrants like the Johansen family found the train experience from Halifax to be unsatisfactory, Wiebren Pijl claims that the seats were larger and more spacious than those found in his native Netherlands. The train cars had double windows, a toilet in both the front and the back, air conditioning for cold or heat, and taps offering ice-cold drinking

Immigrants await the departure of their train from Pier 21, 1965.
Source: Canadian Museum of Immigration Collection (R2013.1362.222)

water. Pijl describes the experience of leaving Pier 21 by train: "[T]hen at last we were actually rolling. 100 meters ahead, then back a bit, then ahead again... this went on for about 20 minutes which was totally foreign to our train travelling experiences in Holland. Gradually we gained more speed, under viaducts, along steep rock walls, along ravines, forests and lakes. Across the water we catch a glimpse of the city of Halifax, of which we had seen nothing except what we could from out at sea. All those houses against the mountainsides make a beautiful view. We steadily gain speed, passing lakeside cottages and masses of cars."[23] Often, a successful train departure also depended on the support of Pier 21's volunteers.

Sometimes immigrants arriving through Pier 21 had an unconscionably long delay. In November 1965, passengers aboard the Greek Liner SS *Queen Anna Maria* were made to wait more than fifteen hours aboard a train before their eventual departure from Pier 21. Within two hours of their 2:00 a.m. arrival, two hundred passengers, including forty-two children under the age of ten, disembarked from the ship. Delayed by bad weather, *Queen Anna Maria*'s Canada-bound passengers disembarked as quickly as possible before the ship headed to its final destination of New York City. Once the two hundred passengers were processed at Pier 21, they were forced to wait until 7:15 p.m. for a scheduled CNR train to Montreal because the noon train was fully booked and the size of the group was deemed to not warrant a special train departure.[24]

Despite such unfortunate circumstances, immigration and customs officers acknowledged the countless hours of service that volunteers provided in the immigration shed. Immigration official John Hood recognizes the long hours of service contributed by "these men and women [who] formed an amateur reception bureau; they watched over the needs of the passengers with such care that in all the tumult of moving vehicles and lengthy vistas of the open tracks of a great sea-port, in the passage of half a million people, not a child received an injury."[25] Alongside Canadian immigration and customs officials, voluntary aid organizations at Pier 21 were also vital to the reception and resettlement of successive refugee groups that fled communism in their homelands and sought safe haven in Canada.

HUNGARIAN REFUGEES

One of the largest groups of refugees to enter Canada through Pier 21 was the Hungarians who fled the Soviet invasion of their homeland. In October 1956, Hungarian students initiated a protest in central Budapest. The student delegation broadcast its demands, which included the removal of Soviet troops from Hungary and free elections.[26] Due to their demands, the students soon faced detention. When they were later imprisoned, the protesting crowd demanded their release and were subsequently fired upon by Hungary's state security police from within the building where the students were being held. The shooting led to one fatality, of a protesting student, whose body was subsequently wrapped in a Hungarian flag and raised over the crowd. As news spread of the protest, violence and disorder began to erupt throughout Budapest.[27] The student-led protest in Budapest quickly spread to the countryside and later became a national revolt against the communist regime. Ordinary citizens organized into militias and fought government forces. Impromptu workers' councils took control over cities and towns throughout the country.

Supporters of the revolt soon demanded that the ruling Hungarian Working People's Party liberalize the political system. In Moscow, the Soviet Politburo was initially reluctant to invade Hungary due to a belief that the demonstrations were part of a popular uprising in support of reforms to the communist system rather than a counter-revolution. Soviet leaders later changed their strategy and moved to crush the student-led uprising. On November 1, Soviet forces entered the country from the east and rapidly moved on Budapest. Two days later, they surrounded Budapest. On November 4, the national government fell. Sporadic fighting continued for approximately another week across Hungary before a Soviet-led hardline regime took hold.

The Soviet invasion spurred a refugee crisis. Approximately 200,000 Hungarians fled their homeland and sought safe haven in the West. Canadian officials believed the Hungarians would fit into their desired Cold War consensus as ardent democrats and anti-communists as refugees from communism. The special program for Hungarian refugees, which brought almost 38,000 professionals, workers, and students to Canada between November 1956 and December 1958, set an important precedent in the admission and resettlement of future refugee movements. Admissions criteria, including medical examination and security screening, were relaxed in order to quickly process and resettle highly sought-after professionals and skilled workers in Canada. By the time the special program ended, the Canadian government had resettled more Hungarian refugees per capita than any other country.[28]

In early February 1957, Judith Stoffman (née Bing) and her parents arrived in Halifax aboard SS *Arosa Sun*. She remembers how her parents had to decide whether to stay in Hungary or leave their home when it became apparent that the Soviets were going to crush the revolution. At first, Stoffman's father wanted to leave Hungary, but her mother wanted to stay. Then her mother hoped to leave, but her father wished to stay. She recalls that after lots of discussion about what to do, it was the reappearance of anti-Semitic slogans and graffiti in Budapest that led to her family's decision to leave Hungary. The Bing family fled to Austria, and Canada later accepted them as refugees.[29]

Some Hungarians chose to leave in the weeks following the reinstallation of a hardline communist government in Budapest. In early January

1957, Gabriella Niloff (née Lantos) and her parents, Erzsébet and Ferenc, arrived in Halifax aboard SS *Venezuela*. The journey of Niloff's family included a dangerous crossing of the border into Austria. Niloff remembers that the walk through the forest was cold and scary because she could see recurring flashlights, which made her believe that Hungarian border officials were nearby. Her fears dissipated when she realized that it was only other individuals attempting to leave. Upon reaching Vienna, the Lantos family applied to come to Canada as refugees because the queue to apply for immigration to the United States was too long.[30]

In early December 1956, the first group of Hungarian refugees to arrive in Canada by ship disembarked from SS *Arosa Sun* at the port of Québec. A week later, they were followed by the first group of refugees to dock at Halifax: 113 Hungarians disembarked from RMS *Ivernia* at Pier 21. The archbishop of Halifax, the Catholic port chaplain, and the Member of Parliament for Halifax welcomed them. Alongside Canadian political and religious officials, volunteers representing service organizations at Pier 21 also welcomed this initial group of Hungarian refugees to Canada.[31]

Gabriella Niloff (née Lantos) with her father, Ferenc (Frank), and mother, Erzsébet (Elizabeth) in Canada, ca. 1957. *Source: Canadian Museum of Immigration Collection (DI2016.11.6)*

The Hungarian refugee movement comprised professionals, skilled workers, and students, but it also included public officials. One was Imre Gregor, a thirty-year-old former member of Hungary's Országgyűlés (National Assembly), who fled with his wife, Julia, and nine-year-old daughter, Clara, and arrived in Canada through Pier 21. Carrying two pieces of luggage, with a Hungarian-language newspaper handed out by the Sisters of Service stuffed into Imre's coat pocket, the Gregors approached Sister Salvatrice Liota, who handed them some basic necessities.[32]

Although Sister Liota could not carry on a conversation in Hungarian, she learned a few phrases and key words so that she could help the Hungarian refugees whenever they needed anything. She recalls seeing the Hungarian refugees arrive at Pier 21: "[W]e had to control our emotions, as they disembarked. Because so many of the young men had on our cast-off army coats, you know the big khakis coats and pants. They just had the clothes they had on them and maybe a little suitcase... just watching them and seeing that—you could see the fear in their eyes, you could see—I'm a person who senses these things, you know? I had a hard time controlling my emotions and watching them come through. And the little children, they just broke my heart... yes, the women were [terrified as well]."[33]

The Canadian government attempted to provide adequate assistance to the Hungarian refugees, including paying for their trip by train to their final destination. Some refused to go where federal officials intended to resettle them because they had relatives in another location. Unfortunately for these refugees, their relatives had not come through with the required paperwork, and their final destination was not updated. Fearing a prolonged stay in detention or permanent resettlement to a place they did not wish to go, some of the refugees staged a sit-down strike at Pier 21. Canadian officials eventually brought an end to the protest and placed the refugees in detention until their individual cases were resolved.[34]

When Pier 21's accommodations were full, Rockhead Hospital was temporarily transformed into a detention centre. This had also been the case for earlier movements of displaced persons. Between 1956 and 1958, the hospital received Hungarian refugees with medical conditions, including tuberculosis. Florence Waldron, a staff nurse at Pier 21, recalls that the Hungarian refugees with tuberculosis were flown on specially chartered flights to Canada to avoid infecting other refugees. Some of these newcomers landed at Halifax and were brought to Rockhead for further examination. The refugees were kept at the hospital until available spaces could be found at a provincial sanatorium—a medical facility for long-term illness. Waldron remembers that the tubercular refugees were sent across the country.[35] Meanwhile, Pier 21's detention facilities only held healthy refugees.

Sisters Salvatrice Liota (left) and Josephine Dulaska (right) welcome former Hungarian Member of Parliament Imre Gregor, his wife, Julia, and daughter, Clara, at Pier 21, January 15, 1957. Photographer: Harry Cochrane/*Chronicle Herald*.
Source: Republished with permission from the Chronicle Herald

At Rockhead, officials maintained separate dormitories for men and women to deal with the overflow of recently arrived refugees. Canadian officials soon dealt with misunderstandings, including that of a young boy who continually attempted to gain entrance into the women's quarters. The short-haired boy confused immigration officials, who had identified him as male. Once a translator was found, the "young boy" explained that she was only able to escape from Hungary wearing her brother's clothing. The situation was soon resolved and she was able to enter the women's accommodations.[36]

Whether at Pier 21 or Rockhead, most immigrants spent from a few hours to a number of days under the authority of Canadian immigration officials. For one Hungarian refugee family, the stay in Pier 21's detention quarters lasted approximately five months. In January 1957, eleven-year-old Tibor Lukács fled Hungary with his parents and two older sisters. After living in an Austrian refugee camp for more than a year, the family

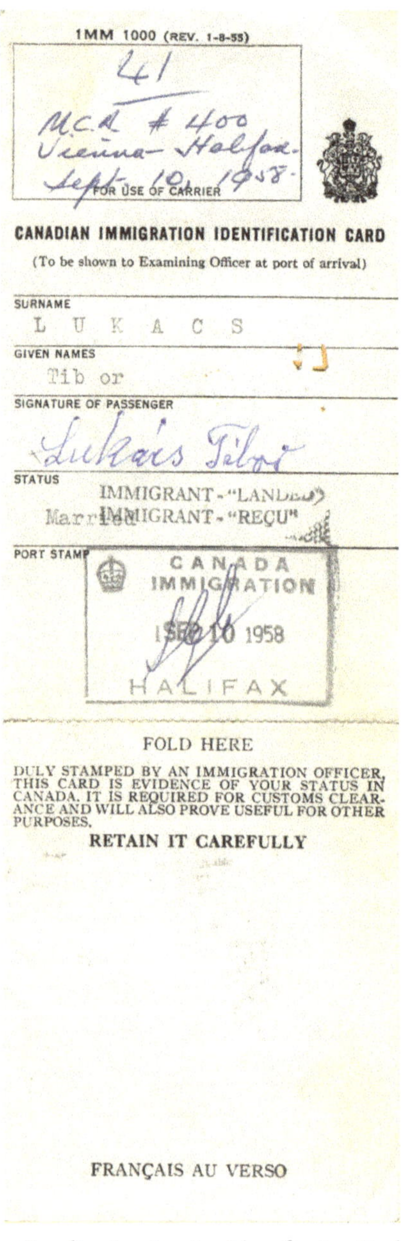

IMM 1000 (REV. 1-8-55)

41

M.C.A. # 400
Vienna–Halifax.
Sept. 10, 1958.

FOR USE OF CARRIER

CANADIAN IMMIGRATION IDENTIFICATION CARD

(To be shown to Examining Officer at port of arrival)

SURNAME
L U K A C S

GIVEN NAMES
Tib or

SIGNATURE OF PASSENGER
Lukács Tibor

STATUS
IMMIGRANT - "LANDED"
Married IMMIGRANT - "REÇU"

PORT STAMP
CANADA
IMMIGRATION
SEP 10 1958
HALIFAX

FOLD HERE

DULY STAMPED BY AN IMMIGRATION OFFICER, THIS CARD IS EVIDENCE OF YOUR STATUS IN CANADA. IT IS REQUIRED FOR CUSTOMS CLEARANCE AND WILL ALSO PROVE USEFUL FOR OTHER PURPOSES.

RETAIN IT CAREFULLY

FRANÇAIS AU VERSO

Canadian Immigration Identification Card issued to Hungarian refugee, Tibor Lukács, at Pier 21, 1958. *Source: Canadian Museum of Immigration Collection (DI2014.459.6)*

was approved for immigration to Canada in September 1958. They travelled by military aircraft, a DC-6, to Canada via Scotland, Iceland, and Newfoundland before arriving at Halifax Airport, from where they were transported by bus to Pier 21 for processing and detention. Lukács and his family entered the immigration facility, where an immigration official interviewed them in a small office. During the interview, Lukács's father had a flip folder with a list of political parties placed before him and was asked which of these organizations did he belong to in Hungary. Following the interview, Lukács and his family were further processed and then placed into Pier 21's detention quarters, where they were separated with the males in one room and the females in another.

While his family's immigration status was being determined, Lukács's parents were permitted to leave Pier 21. During the day, they searched for work, while Lukács and his two sisters went to school. Despite the ability to move freely during the day, the family had to respect a nightly curfew. They were also not permitted to bring anything from outside into the immigration facility. Lukács remembers that at the north end of Pier 21's detention facilities, the corridors led to small rooms with no doorknobs. In the middle of the door was a small square pane of reinforced glass with wires inside. Outside of the door, there were several latches, from the top to the bottom. Lukács was amazed that "on this side, on the dock side, there used to be a balcony and this balcony had bars, steel bars from top to bottom... we used to go out there to see the ships or whatever and, in fact, this was a prison."[37]

Lukács refers to the detention quarters' airing gallery, which provided immigrants with a way to step outside while remaining in the confines of the secured part of the immigration facility. Although Lukács asserts that Pier 21's detention quarters reminded him of a prison, he did not feel like a prisoner, since his family received every necessity. Pier 21 staff was kind to the family and provided them with three meals each day. According to Lukács, his parents were eventually billed for part of their stay since they decided to remain in Pier 21's detention quarters after they were officially admitted into the country. The family of five paid $25 a week to remain in Pier 21's detention quarters until they found suitable accommodations in Halifax. The detention quarters comprised small rooms with two or three sets of metal bunks with double beds, each consisting of a single mattress with a simple sheet, blanket, and pillow.[38]

While some Hungarian refugees were detained until their paperwork, immigration status, or medical and security screening could be verified, the immigration process through Pier 21 often also confounded Hungarian refugees who did not understand English or French. In December 1956, László Galambos, with his parents and brother, crossed the Hungarian border into Austria, where they found shelter in a refugee camp. The Galambos family later arrived at Pier 21 aboard MV *Britannic* in mid-February 1957. As a young boy, Galambos remembers feeling a mixture of confusion, terror, and curiosity. He was told that upon arriving, his family would be taken to a "hall." Galambos was immediately confused. In Hungarian, "*hal*" means "fish," so the young newcomer thought that his family would be put into a giant fish. Further increasing his anxiety, Galambos observes that "the smells upon arrival at Halifax did not do much to convince me otherwise. Halifax smelled of fish. Coming from Hungary, quite far from the ocean, these smells were noticeably strong.

So, Pier 21 for me evokes this old memory of fish smells, visions of giant fish and cold because I remember the weather then as being very cold."[39]

Including Galambos, many of the Hungarian refugees who came to Canada were young people. Nearly half of them were under the age of twenty-four. Approximately 30 per cent of the refugees were over forty-five years of age. Male refugees outnumbered their female counterparts almost three to two. Approximately two-thirds of the refugees were Roman Catholics, with the remainder comprising Protestants, Jews, and an unknown number of Roma.[40] Joseph Kage of JIAS recalls that 4,500 Jews were resettled in Canada, while historian Peter Hidas believes that upward of 7,000 Jews came to Canada within this refugee movement.[41] Canadian business and government officials found the socioreligious makeup of the refugees important, but occupational affiliation mattered even more. Canadian businesses hoped the refugees would meet their need for unskilled labour, while others hoped this wave of refugees would produce a large pool of domestic servants. In reality, a majority of the refugees were semi-skilled and skilled workers, professionals, and students. Canadian officials viewed them as a special class of refugees due to their ardent anticommunism, democratic values, education, and work experience.[42]

A majority of Hungarian refugees arrived in Canada in 1957. That year, immigration rose overall from nearly 165,000 to over 282,000 newcomers, which equalled 1.7 per cent of Canada's population.[43] Canadian immigration and customs officials remained vigilant as political refugees, some of whom were also stateless persons, arrived in Canada. At Pier 21, Canadian officials were on guard against communist sympathizers, spies, and individuals whose identities could not be immediately ascertained upon arrival. Individuals whose identities required further scrutiny were placed in Pier 21's detention facilities until their immigration status could be ascertained.

SPIES, LIES, AND COMMUNIST TIES? POSTWAR DETAINEES AT PIER 21

In the early 1960s, officials detained approximately one person per day in Pier 21's detention quarters.[44] Tibor Lukács remembers a young German

man named Carl, a spy who had tried to enter the country. Canadian immigration officials placed him in Pier 21's detention facilities until he could be deported to his home country. Lukács recalls eating meals with the deportee in the communal dining room.[45]

The food provided to detainees was organized by Pier 21's catering department, which operated a canteen in the Annex building that was open to the public and used by travellers, immigration officials, and individuals who worked along the waterfront. The department was also responsible for the cafeteria in the detention quarters and provided three meals per day to detainees. At one end of the cafeteria was a well-equipped kitchen with cold and normal storage, and at the other end a foyer led to a work station and the offices of the director and assistant director of catering. The kitchen staff consisted of two cooks and two or three servers and washers with an additional staff of casual workers. The number of staff fluctuated depending on the number of individuals in detention.[46]

Before staff could serve meals to the detainees, the detainees had to be properly inspected. Immigration officers strip-searched male detainees and checked their clothing for instruments that could aid escape. The matron searched female detainees. Possessions removed included writing utensils, radios, books, articles, and items considered dangerous, such as razor blades. Staff removed these items from the person to prevent them from causing harm to themselves or others, or using the instruments to escape. The RCMP received any weapons, while only a medical officer could handle narcotics, drugs, or other medicines. A detainee's travel documentation was placed in an envelope and delivered to Canadian immigration officials, while money and personal valuables were also placed in an envelope and delivered to the resident accountant, who secured the items in a safe. Detainees were also subject to unannounced searches at the discretion of Pier 21's officer-in-charge.[47]

Immigrants were often detained because of a lack of proper documentation, or were waiting for additional funds, certificates, or affidavits to arrive. Other individuals, who were ordered to be deported, remained at Pier 21 while awaiting transport. In the late 1950s, a Russian stowaway named Petrovich defected from an Italian ship once the vessel entered Halifax Harbour. The defector landed in Pier 21's detention facilities where he stayed for almost a year while his case was being decided. Upon learning of Petrovich's activities, Soviet diplomats demanded that they interview him without the presence of Canadian officials. Conversely, Canadian immigration officials advised that they would be present for any exchange between the detainee and Soviet representatives.[48] Immigration official Frank Wright, who served at the port of Halifax from 1948 to 1980, recalls the Petrovich affair: "[W]e had our first Russian defector… and we weren't too familiar [with] how to handle it, you know, it's the first one that came… he got to be one of the staff, you know, he got to know everyone by name and he defected off of one of the ships."[49] No longer deemed a security risk and unable to be sent back to the Soviet Union due to the likelihood of imprisonment, Petrovich was eventually permitted to enter Canada, and he resettled in Nova Scotia.

Not all individuals who sought to defect to the West were successful. In late March 1962, the fishing trawler *Eisenach*, from Rostock, East Germany, docked at Halifax to take on provisions. The vessel had been sent to fish on the Grand Banks near Newfoundland. Upon reaching Halifax, two crew members sought to defect to West Germany through Canada. According to an officer from the West German freighter *Silvia*, which was docked at Halifax's Pier 39 opposite the fishing vessel, the two would-be defectors approached him for further information on how to defect to West Germany. Canadian immigration officials soon discovered the pair and informed them that they would need to seek asylum in Canada, otherwise they would be sent back to East Germany. If the pair claimed asylum in Canada, they would be subject to immigration processing and detention at Pier 21 until their paperwork was in order. Two days later, the two returned to their ship, which left for the Grand Banks.[50] Throughout the Cold War, officials at Pier 21 witnessed hundreds of individuals in search of sanctuary in Canada. After seeking asylum in a second country or claiming asylum by disembarking from their ships or airplanes in Atlantic Canada, these individuals were brought to Pier 21's detention quarters, where they stayed until their immigration status could be determined. In the late 1950s and early 1960s, individuals who fled the emergence of communism in the Caribbean joined these refugees from the Eastern Bloc.

Cuban refugees who defected from a Cubana airliner at Gander, Newfoundland, arrive at Halifax International Airport, November 3, 1964. Photographer: Ferris/*Chronicle Herald*. *Source: Republished with permission from the* Chronicle Herald

CUBAN REFUGEES

In January 1959, Fidel Castro's Movimiento 26 de Julio (the 26th of July Movement) overthrew the dictatorship of Fulgencio Batista in Cuba. Canada and Mexico were the only two countries in the Western Hemisphere not to break diplomatic relations with Cuba following the emergence of a Castro-led communist state.[51] Between 1961 and 1963, large numbers of Cuban refugees left their planes at Gander International Airport, in Newfoundland, during routine refuelling stopovers. The refugees hoped that they would secure quick access to the United States but were later sent to Pier 21 for immigration processing while they waited for papers from their American sponsors. Since the process of acquiring a visa could take upward of six months, the Cubans were temporarily housed in Pier 21's detention quarters. On one occasion, more than a hundred Cuban refugees were detained at Pier 21. They comprised the largest group of detainees at Pier 21 since the arrival of the Baltic refugees in the late 1940s.[52]

The Cuban refugees came from diverse backgrounds, and included doctors, musicians, aircraft pilots, and agriculturalists. Since most of the refugees did not speak English or French, and found themselves in unfamiliar surroundings, they established their own committees, with two representatives who spoke on behalf of the entire group. One spokesperson was a criminal lawyer and the other was a commercial lawyer. The Cuban newcomers negotiated the use of a special bed for a compatriot with back trouble, and the use of a kitchen to prepare Cuban meals. They were pleased to find that salt cod was cheaper and more readily available in Halifax than back home. Soon, the refugees began basic language training.

During the winter of 1964, the Cuban refugees, Canadian immigration officers, and voluntary aid agencies came together to create a traditional Cuban Christmas celebration for all the children in detention. Attendees constructed an altar out of egg crates, covered it with a white tablecloth from the kitchen, and decorated a Christmas tree for the occasion. The Cuban refugees held a Christmas party with a dinner and gifts for all in attendance, which consisted of approximately fourteen children and twenty-four wives. Santa Claus also made an appearance, played by one of the refugees so that the children could understand him in their Spanish mother tongue.[53]

In 1964, the defection of Cuban refugees at Gander became a source of parliamentary debate. In mid-September, the MP for Trinity–Conception rose in the House of Commons and asked the minister of citizenship and immigration to confirm whether fourteen Cubans recently left a Czechoslovak Airlines flight at Gander. The fourteen defectors were part of the larger movement of Cubans who left their aircraft to request asylum in Canada.[54] The minister indicated that each Cuban who defected at Gander would receive an immigration hearing in order to obtain information about their intentions. The responsibility to decide whether each case was granted landed immigrant status or permitted to remain in the country under a minister's permit rested with him. Pending a final decision in their cases, the Cuban refugees and other Cold War defectors were to be temporarily housed in Pier 21's detention quarters.[55]

Soon, immigrants who were found inadmissible for entry into Canada and ordered deported also had a legal means of appeal. Following the

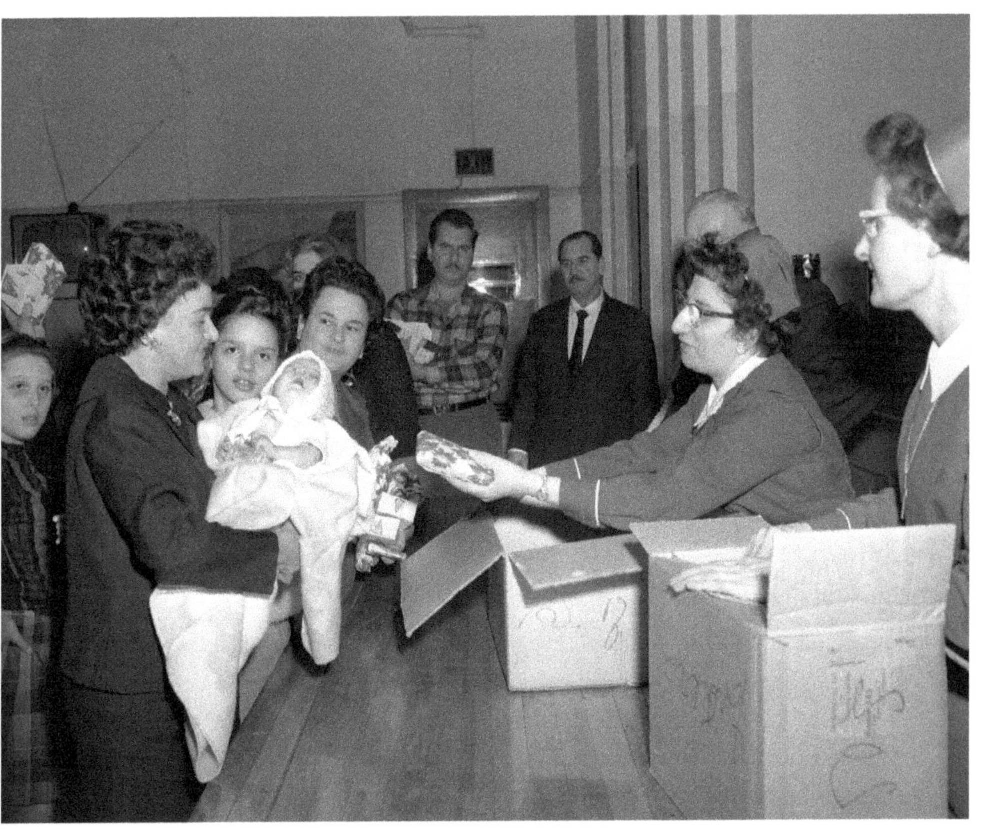

Sister Salvatrice Liota (second from right) hands out gifts to Cuban refugees during Christmas celebrations, December 25, 1964. Photographer: Ferris/*Chronicle Herald*. *Source: Republished with permission from the* Chronicle Herald

introduction of Order-in-Council P.C. 1967–1616, commonly referred to as "the points system," independent immigrants were assessed points in specific categories relating to their previous education, occupational skills, work experience, age, proficiency in English and French, and personal character. As the last vestiges of ethnoracial and geographic discrimination were removed from Canadian immigration policy, the federal government subsequently established the Immigration Appeal Board, in mid-November 1967. The board gave individuals who were ordered deported the right to appeal the decision.[56] The new regulations and the establishment of the appeals board soon played an important role in the admissions process for many refugees in search of safe haven in Canada. Less than a year later, another sudden Cold War crisis forced the Canadian government to respond to the plight of refugees fleeing communist Czechoslovakia.

PRAGUE SPRING REFUGEES

Early in January 1968, Alexander Dubček was elected as first secretary of the Communist Party of Czechoslovakia. Under his leadership, reformist members of the party seized an opportunity to effect change. Under a political program known as "socialism with a human face," civic freedoms were restored, press censorship was ended, and the economy was slowly liberalized. This period became known as the Prague Spring. After repeated warnings from Soviet leaders about their attempts to liberalize the communist regime from within, overnight on August 20–21, 1968, Warsaw Pact forces invaded the country to crush the Prague Spring reform movement.

In early September 1968, the Canadian government implemented a special program for Czechs and Slovaks who fled or were outside their homeland at the time of the Warsaw Pact invasion of Czechoslovakia. Using the special program for Hungarian refugees as a precedent, between September 1968 and January 1969, Canadian officials relaxed admissions criteria, including medical examinations and security screening, and chartered flights to bring close to 12,000 Prague Spring refugees to Canada.[57] This movement included close to two hundred families of Jewish origin, whom JIAS assisted upon arriving in Canada.[58]

A majority of the Prague Spring refugees arrived in Canada by air to major airports across Canada, but a small group of refugees found their way to Pier 21 by disembarking from their planes in Gander and requesting asylum. The refugees were brought to Pier 21 to be processed and housed until they could find suitable accommodations and employment in the city. The Catholic port chaplain, Father Brown, was heavily involved with detained Cold War refugees, defectors, and seamen. He provided them with clothes and toiletries, and tended to their spiritual needs.[59]

Brown recalls that the first couple from Czechoslovakia to approach him were full of smiles, holding out their papers in their hands. Brown's interpreter also soon began to smile. The Catholic port chaplain soon discovered that the papers were not travel documents but wedding invitations. The Czech couple had planned to be married in Prague the morning of the Soviet-led invasion, and their nuptials were still foremost on their minds. As Father Brown received special permission to marry the couple, the bride-to-be moved out of Pier 21 and into a boarding house in the city. Once her Greek landlady learned of the couple's upcoming wedding, she took it upon herself to borrow all the necessary items for a proper ceremony, including a white dress and a veil. All of the Prague Spring refugees living at Pier 21 or in Halifax attended the wedding festivities. One Halifax couple hosted a reception for the newlyweds, while another arranged for a honeymoon.[60]

Another couple, Libor and Jiřina (Irene) Roštík, defected to the West during a return flight from Havana to Prague. Libor, an engineer, and Jiřina, a technical illustrator and draftswoman, married in April 1968 and lived comfortably with steady employment and a lakeside cottage. The couple openly supported a return of democratic values to their homeland during the Prague Spring reform movement. The Warsaw Pact invasion of Czechoslovakia demonstrated to the couple that democratic ideals would not be permitted to flourish in their homeland, and they then decided to start a new life in the West. Libor had a brother-in-law who lived in Havana. The couple asked their relative to write a letter inviting them to Cuba for a visit. In early December 1968, the Roštíks, wearing only tropical clothing, deplaned from their Czechoslovak Airlines flight during a routine refuelling stopover at Gander, requested political asylum in Canada, and were sent to immigration processing.

They ended up in Pier 21's detention quarters. Once there, the Roštíks were separated: "[M]en to the left, women to the right and I will never forget Irene holding my hand and crying that she will not see me again. We were ushered to austere quarters with bunk beds, which served as a detention centre. Next morning we had to undergo health checks and obtain a medical clearance and we received a schedule for the immigration interviews." According to the Czech couple, the large number of diverse nationalities content to receive accommodations and food in the detention quarters spurred them to quickly learn English and find housing in Halifax. They did not want to prolong their stay in detention or depend on handouts. Upon being admitted into Canada, the couple enrolled in a six-month English-language course, which came with a weekly allowance of $35 if they successfully passed their tests. In

March 1969, only three months into their course, the Roštíks moved to Montreal after Libor secured a job as a project engineer with Dominion Engineering Works.[61]

POLISH SEAMEN

In late 1968, during the special program for Prague Spring refugees, nine Polish seamen left their ships in Halifax and requested asylum. Many of these individuals were not professional sailors but sought to defect from communist Poland. The Poles argued that they were defecting from an oppressive communist regime in their homeland. Defection from Poland was considered an illegitimate act by the communist authorities and punishable with imprisonment. Immigration officers at Pier 21 encouraged Father Brown to act on behalf of the refugees. Brown later assisted three Polish seamen from the group of nine who failed to qualify for legal aid. A subsequent legal hearing denied the defectors' request for asylum and ordered them to be deported from Canada.[62] The MP for Dartmouth–Halifax, Michael Forrestall, advocated for the seamen in the House of Commons but to no avail, as the Canadian government refused to provide the seamen asylum.[63]

Brown appealed the decision and announced that he would represent the three Polish seamen without legal aid; however, the decision was later overturned on appeal, and the seamen later resettled in Toronto. A second group of six Polish seamen had their request for asylum turned down. They then sought the assistance of church groups, the Canadian Polish community, and a Halifax lawyer. An emergency debate was held in Parliament to discuss their deportation. Altogether, the nine Poles were later granted immigrant status for humanitarian purposes.[64]

The Canadian government slowly recognized that refugee resettlement was becoming a necessity in immigration policy and further entrenched its commitment to finding a permanent solution to the international refugee crisis. In early June 1969, Canada signed the 1951 UN Convention Relating to the Status of Refugees and its 1967 Protocol Relating to the Status of Refugees. In essence, Canadian officials accepted asylum as an international right.[65] Four months later, the Canadian government streamlined immigration screening and customs inspection by designating Canada customs officers responsible for representing all federal departments in front-line operations at regular ports of entry.[66] Customs officials, along with the RCMP, continued to process Cold War defectors at Canadian ports of entry.

COLD WAR DEFECTIONS CONTINUE

Individuals in search of refuge continued to defect to the West by seeking asylum in Canada. In April 1970, a nineteen-year-old singer, Veronika Martenová Charles, and her band travelled by plane from Czechoslovakia to Cuba to tour the country. Their Czechoslovak Airlines flight included a refuelling stopover in Gander before reaching its final destination of Havana. While in Gander, the young performer was struck by how different Canada was from her homeland. Charles remembers that her band was given some food, including chopped celery, which she had never tasted before. These new experiences were enough for Charles to want to discover more about the world outside of the Eastern Bloc. While in Cuba, Charles decided to defect if her flight stopped for refuelling again at Gander. It did. She disembarked and, with the help of a dictionary, informed a Canadian immigration officer of her predicament, and that night she was placed in a local motel and transported the next morning to Pier 21 for processing.

Veronika Martenová Charles in Cuba before her defection in Gander, Newfoundland, 1970. *Source: Canadian Museum of Immigration Collection (DI2017.962.32)*

Detention proved to be a traumatic experience for Charles. She endured constant questioning at the hands of a Polish interpreter who had to determine if she was a communist spy or had links to communist intelligence services. In the detention quarters, Charles recalls feeling scared and lonely, and seeing many cockroaches—some of which crawled on her at night.[67] The immigration shed, as a converted waterfront warehouse with heat, shelter, and food, often attracted cockroaches. The insects were common in the immigration quarters as well as in the adjoining buildings, including the temporary buildings used after the Second World War.[68] Despite these circumstances, Charles spent approximately three months in detention, eventually being issued a temporary work permit in Canada. On Charles's Canada Manpower Division registration card, officials listed her occupation as "popular singer." She remains grateful to the volunteers, especially Sister Florence Kelly, Reverend J. P. C. Fraser, and his wife, Anna, who made life bearable for her in the cold environment of the immigration facility.[69]

Cold War defectors were often grateful for the assistance provided to them by church representatives and the voluntary service organizations. In 1968, Raphael Alcolado, a talented pianist, returned home to Cuba for a family visit, only to find deteriorating conditions and food rationing. Two years later, while studying in Poland, Alcolado again purchased an airline ticket to return home to Cuba. In December 1970, Alcolado disembarked from his Havana-bound flight during a routine refuelling stopover at Gander. He immediately approached a Canadian official to request asylum and demanded that he be held incommunicado until his flight left the airport. The following day, the Cuban refugee flew to Pier 21 in Halifax for immigration processing, including accommodations in the facility's detention quarters for several weeks. Alcolado remembers enjoying his first meal at Pier 21 and being shocked at the abundance of available food. The Cuban newcomer remembers the kindness of Catholic priest and port chaplain Father Brown, who gave him a bible and a small bag of necessities provided by the Sisters of Service for new immigrants. As a musician, what Alcolado required the most was access to a piano. Father Brown eventually found him a grand piano on which to practice in an auditorium at Mount Saint Vincent University, in Halifax.[70]

As Pier 21 staff and volunteers continued to provide assistance to immigrants and refugees, in mid-1970, federal immigration officials recommended closing the canteen and reducing access to the accommodation quarters. Immigration officials in Ottawa argued that newcomers with adequate financial means should secure their own accommodations, while arrivals dependent on assistance would be permitted to stay in Pier 21's accommodation quarters until they were able to permanently resettle in their final destination across Canada. In similar fashion, immigration officials also concluded that Pier 21's detention facilities, which were now underutilized, were no longer required. They agreed that the remaining detainees at Halifax would be sent to a local correctional centre or public jail.[71] These recommendations were based on a bureaucratic process initiated in the mid-1960s, which assessed the level of inefficiencies and surpluses found in Pier 21's operations in order to determine the immigration facility's future in light of declining ocean liner traffic.[72]

THE FUTURE OF PIER 21

Before federal officials began to assess Pier 21's future viability, the immigration facility underwent various modifications during its years of operation to reflect evolving attitudes toward the reception of immigrants and to simplify immigrant processing. In the mid-1950s, some immigration officials expressed their dismay with Pier 21's appearance. Immigration officer Bill Marks recalls that he was troubled by all the wire cages and the way in which immigrants were tagged with different coloured tags and moved about from one location to the next. Marks also remembers being uncomfortable with the bars on all the windows, which could often give staff and newcomers the impression that the immigration facility was a jail. The immigration officer-in-charge, Harry P. Wade, also doubted the usefulness of the cages. In 1956, Wade received permission from his superiors to ask the port manager to replace the cages with a counter and storage area, where immigrants' personal baggage could be stored during their medical and civil examinations. After approximately three decades of use, the locked wire cages located at the back of the assembly area were finally removed. Initially, the cages were used to hold newcomers' personal belongings as they proceeded through medical screening and a civil interview. However, for many immigrants, the cages signified interrogation or incarceration.[73]

Canadian officials were also forced to deal with repairs to Pier 21, when in late July 1960, a 41,000-ton United States aircraft carrier, USS *Essex*, completed a six-day stay in Halifax and began to leave port. A crowd gathered to watch and listen to the sounds of the US Navy's official march song, "Anchors Aweigh." Underestimating the length of its superstructure and without enough space to manoeuvre, the American naval vessel turned too quickly and a starboard catwalk hit the immigration building, creating a gaping hole in a doctor's office within Pier 21's medical facilities. At the time, the National Harbours Board, an administrative body responsible for business and service operations at major Canadian ports, found the United States Navy negligent in the incident and accountable for $5,000 in damages.[74]

Once repairs to Pier 21 concluded in the early 1960s, further improvements were made over the next several years, such as the addition of a sprinkler system in 1961. Renovations often stemmed from recommendations put forward by officials and volunteers who landed in Canada at Pier 21 or were stationed at the site. In the mid-1960s, William Stewart, an immigrant who had landed at Pier 21 four decades earlier and now served as director general with the Department of Citizenship and Immigration, ordered the removal of the bars located on the immigration facility's windows. Stewart disliked the barred windows and believed that they did not provide a warm welcome to arriving immigrants.[75]

In 1968, Pier 21 once again underwent renovations. The overhead pipes, which were previously covered in grime, were cleaned. The walls were painted green, and the ceiling above the entrance was covered in wire netting to prevent birds from reaching ocean travellers. Similarly, the wire cages that reached the ceiling were removed, while the rows of wooden seats in the assembly area were now upholstered in yellow, orange, and green plastic.[76] Subsequent renovations included an expansion of the medical clinic from two examination offices in 1928 to more than twenty rooms, supporting a laboratory, minor surgeries, and X-ray facilities by 1971.[77] These site renovations were made to improve the reception of immigrants and to support immigrant processing. Yet, these much-needed changes could not prevent the decline of ocean liner passenger traffic through the site.

THE CLOSURE OF PIER 21

By the late 1960s, immigration through Pier 21 was in steady decline. Immigrants were increasingly travelling by airplane to Canada rather than by ship. Due to the infrequent arrivals by a small number of ocean liner passengers, Canadian immigration officials were forced to split their time between Halifax's Ocean Terminals and the city's new international airport. Interest in a new civil airport for the city gained momentum after the Second World War, when in October 1945, city officials, with the help of the Department of Transport, searched for a site suitable for a new airport. On the recommendation of Trans-Canada Airlines, in fall 1954, a site near Kelly Lake was approved. Transport officials agreed to operate the new airport on the condition that city officials purchased the land and transferred it to the department for $1. With an agreement in place, construction began on two runways in November 1955. The Halifax International Airport opened in June 1960. The airport's air terminal building opened in September 1960. That same year, the airport received nearly 180,000 passengers. By the early 1970s, airport officials determined that the growth of air traffic and passenger travel at Halifax was far greater than other airports of a similar size. A developmental plan was implemented leading to the expansion of the original air terminal building.[78]

The emergence of affordable and accessible air travel signalled a shift from ocean liner passenger traffic to air travel, and the emergence of the Halifax International Airport as the main port of entry into the province hastened Pier 21's closure as an immigration facility.[79] By the end of the 1960s, three ocean liners per month docked at Halifax's immigration shed, with about a hundred immigrants disembarking from each vessel.[80] To further illustrate the decline in passenger traffic through Pier 21, in its last full year of operations in 1970, 2,281 travellers arrived at the site, compared to the height of passenger traffic in 1951, when 98,695 travellers were processed. In 1970, Halifax International Airport processed 50,700 passengers.[81]

Based on the bureaucratic process commenced in the mid-1960s that found inefficiencies and surpluses in Pier 21's operations, in late March 1971, William Stewart announced that Pier 21 would close its doors. Due to declining passenger traffic and to provide a more effective service to the public, Pier 21 ceased all immigration operations on April 1. The Halifax district immigration office, located at Pier 21, was moved to new quarters on Harvey Street in Halifax. Pier 21's accommodation quarters were subsequently closed in mid-April. Travellers who required an overnight stay were placed in other accommodations in the city.[82] Pier 21's detention facilities were closed for some time before operations were discontinued. Immigration detainees were held in the local jail or transferred to detention quarters at Quebec. During this period, passenger ships continued to arrive in Halifax, with a frequency of approximately one vessel per month. Passengers received their immigration examination on board ship.[83]

In order for Pier 21's facilities to be available for use by the federal government, the Department of Public Works renovated the site to permit the Dominion Bureau of Statistics to use the immigration facility for its 1971 Canadian census enumeration. During the summer of 1971, more than two hundred post-secondary students worked out of Pier 21, processing census returns from the Maritime provinces. After the end of the census program, the immigration facility returned to the auspices of the National Harbours Board.[84]

During its last fifteen years of operation, Pier 21 continued to serve as a major ocean port of entry into Canada. It welcomed immigrants from the United Kingdom and continental Europe, and increasingly processed arrivals from Mediterranean source countries. This chapter has illustrated some of the diverse views during this time from officials, volunteers, and immigrants of Pier 21 as an entry point into Canada, immigration shed, and mechanism of Canadian nation building and state regulation. Newcomers often spoke of their bewilderment, confusion, fear, relief, and excitement at finally reaching Halifax. Upon landing at Pier 21, they encountered officials from several branches of the federal government, including immigration, customs, health and welfare, agriculture, and the RCMP. At Pier 21, processing immigrants involved medical screening, civil interview, quarantine, detention, customs inspection, receiving social services, locating checked baggage, and boarding a train to their final destination in Canada. During the immigration process, newcomers also met individuals from various voluntary aid agencies, some of which represented Christian and Jewish organizations. These volunteers provided immigrants with basic necessities, food, newspapers, bibles, child minding, spiritual guidance and comfort, and translation services.

Similar to the early postwar period, when the immigration facility saw the arrival of thousands of individuals displaced in the aftermath of the Second World War and political refugees who fled the Eastern Bloc, in the mid-1950s, Pier 21's staff and volunteers received a significant movement of Hungarian refugees, who fled the Soviet invasion of their homeland. Many other Cold War refugees and defectors followed. They left their ships in Halifax Harbour or deplaned at Gander, Newfoundland, during routine fuelling stopovers between Cuba and Eastern Europe, and were brought to Pier 21's detention quarters until their immigration status could be determined. Immigrants without the proper financial means to maintain themselves or lack of proper documentation also lived at Pier 21, from a few days to several months. During the 1950s and 1960s, Pier 21's accommodations quarters, including its detention facilities, were in constant use.

The liberalization of Canadian immigration policy, with the introduction of the points system in 1967, and Canada's official recognition of asylum as an international right after signing the UN refugee convention and protocol in 1969, opened the country's doors to immigration from non-European source countries. This evolution in immigration policy could have also increased immigration through Pier 21, but the immigration shed along Halifax Harbour was already in gradual decline as immigrants, visitors, and returning Canadians increasingly opted for the convenience of air travel, which had become affordable and readily accessible. During this period, Canadian immigration officials commenced discussions about Pier 21's future in light of declining ocean liner traffic. As the immigration shed's operations were brought to a close, and resources and staff were relocated, the site began its slow transformation from an active ocean port of entry to a public site of commemoration of twentieth-century Canadian immigration.

OPPOSITE: View of Pier 21's front door, formerly a loading-bay door, and the ramp, 1990s.

Source: Canadian Museum of Immigration Collection (DI2013.1231.1)

CONCLUSION

Pier 21's closure in 1971 attracted the attention of the Nova Scotia Nautical Institute (NSNI). In 1973, the NSNI leased space in Pier 21's former detention quarters and, by early September that year, opened its doors to students. Six years later, the NSNI expanded to occupy the second floor (south end) of the Annex building, where Pier 21's ticket and social services area was once located. On the second floor, the institute ran courses on marine safety, firefighting, first aid, lifeboat, and life-raft training. While classes were held, ships continued to dock at Piers 20, 21, and 22 to load bags of grain and flour.

In 1984, Deputy Prime Minister Allan J. MacEachen announced that the NSNI would have a new building in Port Hawkesbury, Nova Scotia; in 1987, the institute moved its entry-level courses, previously located at Pier 21, to that new facility. The safety courses previously held in the Annex building were moved to Pier 21's second floor, which had been the immigration hall and detention quarters. In 1991, the remaining NSNI courses moved to Port Hawkesbury, along with the remaining instructors and student mariners. At the height of NSNI's tenancy, close to 350 students attended classes at Pier 21. With the institute's departure, the space became vacant, and artists later rented it for studio space.[1]

In the mid-1980s, J.P. LeBlanc, a director general with the Nova Scotia branch of the Department of Manpower and Immigration, began to promote Pier 21 as a site of history and memory. As a veteran of the Royal Canadian Air Force, LeBlanc had a personal connection to Pier 21. He had departed from Pier 21 aboard a troopship during the Second World War and later brought to Canada his wife, Trudy LeBlanc (née Tansey), a British war bride.

LeBlanc began to collect Pier 21 memorabilia and pushed for greater recognition of the former immigration shed as a public site to commemorate Canadian immigration. In 1987, the Historic Sites and Monuments Board of Canada (HSMBC) deferred its consideration of Pier 21 as a site of national historic significance pending the creation of a thematic study that would place the site in the larger context of overseas immigration to Canada. That same year, the HSMBC produced a report titled "Halifax Against the Background of Canadian Immigration, 1815–1970." It recommended that, while Pier 21 was not itself of national historic significance, postwar immigration through Halifax deserved to be commemorated by means of a plaque with at least a mention of the former immigration facility.

Despite this news, LeBlanc continued to raise awareness of Pier 21. In 1988, he organized an event to celebrate the sixtieth anniversary of the immigration facility's opening. Mayor Ron Wallace of Halifax attended, and Pier 21 received widespread media attention. With heightened interest in the history of the site, LeBlanc founded the Pier 21 Society and established a board of directors. Meanwhile, the HSMBC approved the plaque commemorating postwar immigration through Halifax and Pier 21, and installed it near the entrance to the building in 1994. The board later produced an expanded thematic paper that recommended the designation of Pier 21 itself as a National Historic Site of Canada. The reasons were its role as a major ocean port of entry and immigration facility during the interwar and postwar periods; its high degree of structural and site integrity as a specialized building constructed for the purposes of immigration;

and its embodiment of early-twentieth-century Canadian immigration policies, procedures, and attitudes. In 1996, these recommendations came to fruition when Pier 21 was thus officially designated.[2]

Ruth Goldbloom entered the scene in 1993 as LeBlanc's successor and president of the Pier 21 Society. During her tenure, the society prepared a feasibility study and a business plan as it lobbied government officials, at all levels, for support in reopening Pier 21 as an interpretive centre. In June 1995, during the last day of the G7 summit in Halifax, Prime Minister Jean Chrétien announced that the legacy gift to the host city would be a $4.5 million pledge toward the reopening of Pier 21 as such. In order to have the pledge fulfilled, the Pier 21 Society had to raise an equivalent amount.

Under Goldbloom's leadership, the society raised awareness of the history of Pier 21 among Canadians, and, in 1997, initiated a national fundraising campaign that ultimately led to financial commitments worth over $1 million. Subsequent donations from the private sector and ordinary Canadians helped the society reach its goal of $4.5 million. With fundraising well under way, in 1998 renovations to the former immigration facility began. On Canada Day 1999, Pier 21 reopened as an interpretive centre.[3] Hundreds of people gathered to witness the opening celebrations, which were broadcast live on television and included live music and storytelling. Chrétien spoke via satellite from Ottawa, and declared, "it's a great day for all Canadians to see this monument open." As part of the opening celebrations, HMCS *Preserver* sailed into Halifax Harbour with more than a hundred war brides, who re-enacted their arrival in Canada of a half-century earlier.

The interpretive centre flourished throughout the next decade, and the Pier 21 Society hosted a wide array of events. These included the March 2001 launch of "Our Canadian Millennium Quilt," which more than five hundred students from across the country created to "celebrate Canada's historic and geographic diversity at the start of a new millennium." In 2006, more than 250 war brides came to Pier 21 by train to commemorate the sixtieth anniversary of their arrival in Canada.[4]

The Pier 21 Society also hosted a number of conferences by groups like the Atlantic Jewish Council, hosted events like the International Day of the Lebanese Immigrant, and provided the backdrop for documentaries filmed by the Canadian Broadcasting Corporation and Radiotelevisione italiana. The facility also continued to act as a site of pilgrimage, for the war brides and Canadian service personnel who left from Pier 21 to serve on the European front during the Second World War. Immigrants and their families began to recognize more widely Pier 21 as the site of their first steps in Canada.[5] Across the country and abroad, descendants of immigrants who arrived through Pier 21 and other ports of entry were able to retrace their loved ones' journey to Canada through the museum's genealogical and family history resources.

In June 2009, Prime Minister Stephen Harper officially designated Pier 21 as a national museum. This announcement stemmed from a partnership agreement between the Canadian government, the Pier 21 Society, and the Halifax Port Authority. With federal funding, the new museum would fulfil an even greater role, as outlined by Governor General Michaëlle Jean: "[W]e are a country of immigrants. Our identities are bound up in the stories of ancestors from hundreds of lands. To share these stories, our Government will introduce legislation to establish Pier 21 in Halifax—the site where so many began their Canadian journey—as Canada's National Museum of Immigration."[6] In June 2010, the Canadian government introduced legislation to amend the *Museums Act* in order to add the Canadian Museum of Immigration to the list of national museums. The legislation passed through the House of Commons and the Senate with unanimous approval and received royal assent later that month.

The museum received the following mandate: "[T]he purpose of the Canadian Museum of Immigration at Pier 21 is to explore the theme of immigration to Canada in order to enhance public understanding of the experiences of immigrants as they arrived in Canada, of the vital role immigration has played in the building of Canada and of the contributions of immigrants to Canada's culture, economy and way of life."[7] In February 2011, the Canadian Museum of Immigration joined Canada's five other national museums to become the country's sixth national museum, only the second outside Ottawa.[8]

Today, the museum engages with visitors from all over the world through exhibits and public programs related to the museum's mandate. As a hub of expertise on Canadian immigration history, the museum maintains an

The central office bay at Pier 21, now the main entrance to the Canadian Museum of Immigration, 2015. *Source: Canadian Museum of Immigration, Communications*

active research program by conducting oral history interviews, publishing articles online, responding to public inquiries, and establishing partnerships with educational, cultural, and community organizations. The museum also contributes to the national collection with digitized oral histories, stories, archival documents and images, and objects. Immigration has had a profound impact on Canada. The Canadian Museum of Immigration builds awareness and facilitates conversations about this by preserving the memories of Canadian immigrant experiences and showcasing the role of immigration in building Canada.

Pier 21, as part of this museum and the last remaining example in Canada of an oceangoing immigration facility, where all others have been demolished, is a unique historic site and an important site of public memory.[9] During its years of operation, from 1928 to 1971, nearly a million immigrants entered Canada through the site. Few symbols represent the shared Canadian immigrant experience like Pier 21, as it has become a site of pilgrimage for many immigrants and their families. For them, it stands as a living embodiment of their loved ones' journey to Canada.

A visit to Pier 21 often elicits an emotional response in people. From recent museum comment cards:

> I came through these gates as a child. I have emotions that I cannot describe. Thank you for keeping the memories alive.
>
> Visiting Pier 21 has given me a newfound appreciation for what my ancestors went through to provide future generations with a peaceful and safe life.
>
> Pier 21 was the gateway to a new life for my family. The friendliness of the people was memorable—a good indication of what kind of country we would be calling "home."
>
> Could they have ever imagined that 59 years later their family would have grown to 136? There are lawyers, engineers, construction workers, teachers, students, tailors, retailers and many others. The things that bind all of us together are the values that mammanon and papanon instilled in all of us: family, respect, hard work, and caring for each other. It is with tears of joy that I say thank you and miss you.
>
> The museum is an educational and contemplative space in which we can look back on our shared history and forward to the future with hope that Canada will continue to be a beacon of light in a dark world for those seeking refuge and a better life for themselves and their children. In gratitude, faith and love.[10]

Pier 21 has played such an important role in the hearts and minds of Canadians. It began with the initial development of Halifax's South End Ocean Terminals as a multimillion-dollar project to improve railway infrastructure and shipping through the port of Halifax. The early development of Pier 21 in the 1910s was the result of private companies, public organizations, and government departments coming together to plan, construct, and eventually operate the site. When it opened in 1928, the immigration facility actually downsized from its previous iteration at

Pier 2 in Halifax's North End to about half the size. Nevertheless, the modern facility provided the necessary space for passenger examinations and inspections required for immigration, customs, health, agriculture, and public works to operate.

At Pier 21, the official process for immigrants included a medical screening, civil interview, and customs inspection. Volunteers representing churches and service organizations came to the aid of newcomers—some of whom could not understand English or French—with translation services, basic necessities, child minding, spiritual guidance, and comfort. Each organization was assigned a space within the immigration facility, which included a canteen and hospital. Over four decades, the immigration process through Pier 21 remained the same despite the facility undergoing several structural changes. Some of these modifications were caused by unforeseen circumstances, such as the 1944 fire. The fire shaped the rebuilding and use of the space; for example, the reorganization of the immigration quarters and the expansion of the adjacent Annex building.

Soon after opening, Pier 21 became a strategic link in the transatlantic network between Europe and Canada. As an official port of entry and border enforcement facility, Pier 21 served a function of the Canadian state in regulating immigration. The site reflected changing bureaucratic views of immigrant admissibility, including admission, detention, refusal, and deportation.

Evolving policy priorities and bureaucratic discretion affected the nature of immigration during Pier 21's years of operation. Approximately 44,000 immigrants entered Canada through Pier 21 in its first two years of operation. Soon the socioeconomic effects of the Great Depression forced the Canadian government to restrict immigration to agriculturalists and persons with American, Australian, British, Irish, Newfoundland, New Zealand, and South African citizenship. This policy change resulted in a drastic reduction in immigration through Pier 21.

With Canada's declaration of war on Germany in September 1939, the port of Halifax became a strategic port of call for Allied military operations, including the movement of war materiel and personnel to the European front.[11] It was also the principal embarkation point for Canadian service personnel during the Second World War. Notwithstanding its wartime role as a military site, Pier 21 continued to operate as an immigration facility that witnessed evacuated civilians, merchant mariners, refugees, and foreign military personnel processed through its doors.

After the Second World War, Pier 21 returned to full immigration operations. In the first decade after the war, over a million immigrants entered Canada, many of whom were processed at Pier 21. The height of immigration through Halifax in this early postwar period saw Pier 21 as the busiest port of entry into Canada for immigration. Large movements of European displaced persons and political refugees arrived, including more than 400,000 individuals who landed there between 1946 and 1955.[12] From the late 1940s until its closure in 1971, Pier 21 came to symbolize immigration to Canada. Successive movements of returning servicemen, war brides and their children, displaced persons fleeing the aftermath of war, and Cold War refugees were followed by immigrants in search of new and better opportunities.[13]

In March 1971, immigration operations ceased at Pier 21. Individuals held in the detention quarters were sent to the city jail or transferred to detention quarters in Québec City. After 1971, the building was renovated to provide facilities for the Nova Scotia Nautical Institute. When it fell into disuse, a local group of Haligonians established the Pier 21 Society and revitalized the former immigration facility into a public symbol of Canadian immigration, honouring its vital role in the development of Canada.[14]

ACKNOWLEDGMENTS

The Canadian Museum of Immigration has supported the research and writing of this book. Within the museum, Monica MacDonald has championed and led the project, including coordinating with outside reviewers and our partners at the Canadian Museum of History and the University of Ottawa Press. Nicole Dalrymple reviewed drafts and provided feedback, as well as specific research support.

We would also like to acknowledge the generosity of colleagues and partners outside the museum. We benefited from the early interest and enthusiasm of our colleagues at the Canadian Museum of History and the University of Ottawa Press, in particular John Willis, Mercury Series editor and coordinator of the anonymous peer review, and Lara Mainville, Director of the University of Ottawa Press. They provided advice and encouragement as we developed our plan to publish the work together. Immigration, Refugees and Citizenship Canada provided access to restricted files at Library and Archives Canada (LAC), which has been essential for research on the more recent operations of Pier 21. Archivists and staff at LAC and at the Nova Scotia Archives offered great assistance throughout the project. The LAC Halifax Public Services Branch deserves special thanks for their assistance in identifying and consulting material related to earlier immigration sites in Halifax, and to the later years of Pier 21's operations. Gary Shutlak, Lisa Chilton, Robert Vineberg, Laura Madokoro, Andrew Burtch, Marlene Epp, and Roberto Perin all offered insight and guidance on specific parts of the manuscript early in its development, much to the betterment of the work. The anonymous reviewers provided thoughtful and thorough responses that helped us reshape parts of the work. We were sad to hear in 2018 of the passing of Bill Naftel, who had contributed a generous and thought-provoking set of remarks related to the early history of Halifax's immigration sites.

Finally, we have personal connections to the web of stories surrounding Pier 21 and Canadian immigration more broadly. Jan immigrated to Canada as a young child with his family. They left communist Czechoslovakia by way of a "vacation" to Yugoslavia. Steve has family connections to Pier 21 through his grandmother (a war bride) and grandfather (a Canadian veteran), as well as to immigration more broadly through family links to German settlement in the Canadian West.

With those stories in mind, we acknowledge and thank our families and the many others who have chosen to share their personal experiences related to immigration with us and with the museum.

LIST OF ABBREVIATIONS

CEIC	Canada Employment and Immigration Commission
CGR	Canadian Government Railways
CMI	Canadian Museum of Immigration
CORB	Children's Overseas Reception Board
CNR	Canadian National Railway
CPR	Canadian Pacific Railway
CWB	Canadian Wives Bureau
DA	Department of Agriculture
DBS	Dominion Bureau of Statistics
DCI	Department of Citizenship and Immigration
DIC	Department of Immigration and Colonization
DMI	Department of Manpower and Immigration
DND	Department of National Defence
DNHW	Department of National Health and Welfare
DP	Displaced Person
DPW	Department of Public Works

DRC	Department of Railways and Canals
HPA	Halifax Port Authority
HSMBC	Historic Sites and Monuments Board of Canada
IB	Immigration Branch
ICR	Intercolonial Railway
IRO	International Refugee Organization
JIAS	Jewish Immigrant Aid Society
NHB	National Harbours Board
NSNI	Nova Scotia Nautical Institute
PCO	Privy Council Office
LAC	Library and Archives Canada
RCMP	Royal Canadian Mounted Police
YMCA	Young Men's Christian Association
YWCA	Young Women's Christian Association

NOTES

INTRODUCTION

1 Oral History with Mike Frederiksen, interviewed by Amy Coleman, Halifax, 17 August 2001, Canadian Museum of Immigration (hereafter cited as CMI) Collection (01.08.17MF), 00:00:06.

2 See, for instance, Mitic and LeBlanc, *Pier 21*; Linda Granfield, *Pier 21: Gateway of Hope* (Toronto: Tundra Books, 2000); Thompson and van de Wiel, *Pier 21*; Christine Welldon, *Quai 21 – Écoutez mon histoire* (Halifax: Nimbus Publishing, 2013); Renaud, *Pier 21*.

3 Among the many works on Grosse Île, Ron Rudin's short film *Remembering a Memory* is a great introduction, both to the site and to the complexities of public memory and commemoration surrounding it: http://rememberingamemory.cohds.ca/index.html. On William Head, see Peter Johnson, *Quarantined: Life and Death at William Head Station, 1872–1959* (Victoria: Heritage House Publishing, 2013). For information relating to other sites, see Greg Marquis, "Saint John as an Immigrant City, 1851–1951," Atlantic Metropolis Centre Working Paper Series, December 2009; Lisa Chilton, "Managing Migrants: Toronto, 1820–1880," *Canadian Historical Review* 92, no. 2 (2011), 231–62; Robert Vineberg, "Welcoming Immigrants at the Gateway to Canada's West: Immigration Halls in Winnipeg, 1872–1975," *Manitoba History*, no. 65 (Winter 2011), 12–22; and the authors' short papers and blogs on Canadian immigration facilities at Quebec City, Victoria, Saint John, and Halifax at http://www.pier21.ca.

1. IMMIGRATING TO CANADA THROUGH PIER 21, 1928–1971

1 Immigration Story of Bronisława Glod, CMI Collection (S2012.735.1), with revisions based on Steven Schwinghamer's personal correspondence and telephone conversation with Mrs. Glod and her daughter, Barbara Billingsley, 5–7 June 2019.

2 Library and Archives Canada (hereafter cited as LAC), Immigration Branch (hereafter cited as IB) fonds, RG 76, vol. 666, file C1594, pt. 2 "Immigration Building – Halifax, NS," memo from F.C. Blair, acting Deputy Minister, Department of Immigration and Colonization (hereafter cited as DIC) to Charles A. Stewart, Minister, DIC, 23 February 1926.

3 Oral History with Carmen Wood, interviewed by Amy Coleman, Halifax, 5 July 2000, CMI Collection (00.07.05CW), 00:04:53.

4 Oral History with Maria Scornaienchi, interviewed by Cassidy Bankson, Halifax, 6 June 2010, CMI Collection (10.06.06MS), 00:47:21.

5 Immigration Story of William Waterhouse, CMI Collection (S2012.534.1).

6 LAC, IB fonds, RG 76, vol. 666, file C1594, pt. 2 "Immigration Building at Halifax, Nova Scotia (map) (plans)," telegram from T.B. Willans, Travelling Immigration Inspector to J.S. Fraser, Atlantic District Commissioner, DIC, 2 March 1928.

7 LAC, IB fonds, RG 76, vol. 666, file C1594, pt. 2 "Immigration Building at Halifax, Nova Scotia (map) (plans)," W.L. Barnstead, Immigration Agent to J.S. Fraser, 21 March 1928.

8 LAC, IB fonds, RG 76, vol. 666, file C1594, pt. 2 "Immigration Building at Halifax, Nova Scotia (map) (plans)," J.S. Fraser to A.L. Jolliffe, Commissioner of Immigration, DIC, 14 December 1925; and A.L. Jolliffe to W.J. Egan, Deputy Minister, DIC, 4 May 1926.

9 Oral History with Charles Dwyer, interviewed by James H. Morrison, Halifax, 24 March 1998, CMI Collection (98.03.24CD), 00:37:27. Passengers were also occasionally disembarked onto the brow of the pier when the gangway and assembly area were occupied.

10 LAC, IB fonds, RG 76, vol. 666, file C1594, pt. 2 "Immigration Building at Halifax, Nova Scotia (map) (plans)," telegram from W.L. Barnstead to J.S. Fraser, 8 February 1929.

11 Oral History with Bill Marks, interviewed by James H. Morrison, Halifax, 24 April 1998, CMI Collection (98.04.24BM), 00:05:59.

12 LAC, IB fonds, RG 76, vol. 666, file C1594, pt. 1 "Immigration Building at Halifax, Nova Scotia (map) (plans)," H.J. Crudge, Building Engineer, Atlantic Region, CNR to J. S. Fraser, 20 May 1927; Oral History with Charles Dwyer, 00:01:04.

13 H.J. Crudge, Architectural Drawing, "CNR Halifax Ocean Terminals Shed No 21 Proposed Screen Partitions and Pipe Railings," 4 August 1927, Halifax Port Authority (hereafter cited as HPA) document #8655.

14 Immigration Story of the Schlechta Family, CMI Collection (S2012.2350.1).

15 Oral History with Charles Dwyer, 00:15:48; Oral History with Bill Marks, 00:07:35.

16 Crosman, *Recollections*, 34.

17 LAC, Department of Citizenship and Immigration (hereafter cited as DCI) fonds, RG 26, vol. 934, file "First Immigration Manual," binder 8, section 9.05, "Chapter 9: Primary and Secondary Examination at Ports of Entry," 1953. Regarding the manuals, Fenton Crosman participated in the drafting of the First Immigration Manual, and encapsulates the process in his memoir with a quote from Shakespeare's *Macbeth*: "Confusion now hath made his masterpiece." See Crosman, *Recollections,* 195.

18 LAC, IB fonds, RG 76, vol. 790, file 544-23-35, pt. 2 "Examination of Immigrants at Halifax, Nova Scotia (1957–1966)," memo from G.R. Benoit, Chief, Operations Division, IB, DCI to Director, Chief of Operations Division, IB, DCI, 12 July 1955.

19 Immigration Story of the Johansen Family, CMI Collection (S2016.484.1).

20 LAC, IB fonds, RG 76, vol. 790, file 544-23-35, pt. 2 "Examination of Immigrants at Halifax, Nova Scotia (1957–1966)," Rev. W.J. Gallagher, General Secretary, Canadian Council of Churches to D.A. Reid, Chief, Operations Division, IB, DCI, 22 January 1963.

21 LAC, IB fonds, RG 76, vol. 790, file 544-23-35, pt. 2 "Examination of Immigrants at Halifax, Nova Scotia (1957–1966)," telex from IB, Halifax to IB, Ottawa, 4 March 1963. In the mid-1960s, several transatlantic transportation companies voiced their displeasure at having to go through the added expense of disembarking a small number of passengers at Halifax or Quebec when the majority were destined for the United States. These itineraries often led to delays of several hours beyond the time allocated for a normal stopover, resulting in the loss of several thousand dollars and in some instances a deficit operation. In some cases, European transportation companies disembarked Canada-bound immigrants at American ports of entry, such as New York, in order to avoid incurring further costs and to keep their transatlantic operations on time, against the wishes of Canadian immigration officials. In its correspondence with the Canadian Council of Churches, the IB claimed that it was obliged to examine passengers whenever the transportation companies requested such service, and could only object to passenger disembarkation before inland transportation was available or within twenty-four hours of arrival at a Canadian port of entry, whichever occurred first. See LAC, IB fonds, RG 76, vol. 790, file 544-23-35, pt. 2 "Examination of Immigrants at Halifax, Nova Scotia (1957–1966)," J.R. Robillard, A/Chief of Operations, IB, DCI to Rev. W.J. Gallagher, 11 March 1963.

22 LAC, Department of National Health and Welfare (hereafter cited as DNHW) fonds, RG 29, vol. 766, file 412-2-213, pt. 1 "Quarantine Station Halifax, Nova Scotia–Reports of Vessels Arriving with Contagious Diseases on Board, 1920–1940," J.L. Cock, Immigration Medical Officer to C.P. Brown, Chief, Immigration Medical Service, DNHW, 10 December 1937.

23 LAC, DNHW fonds, RG 29, vol. 766, file 412-2-1, pt. A "Quarantine Station, Halifax, Nova Scotia – General, 1916–1948," Hon. James Ralston, Minister, Department of Health to Department of Railways and Canals (hereafter cited as DRC), 20 June 1930, file no. 2446; and memo from J.D. Pagé to Deputy Minister, Department of Pensions and National Health, 20 August 1930; LAC, DNHW fonds, RG 29, vol. 766, file 412-2-213, pt. 1 "Quarantine Station Halifax, Nova Scotia–Reports of Vessels Arriving with Contagious Diseases on Board, 1920–1940," J.L. Cock to C.P. Brown, 10 December 1937.

24 LAC, IB fonds, RG 76, vol. 798, file 546-2, pts. 1 to 3 "Medical Examination of Immigrants in Canada: Policy & Instructions," selected correspondence.

25 See, for example, Public Works Canada (hereafter cited as DPW), "Alterations to Port Medical Clinic," architectural drawing A1, May 1967, HPA #8470.

26 Immigration Story of Vera Weller, CMI Collection (S2012.2029.1).

27 In 1927, the Canadian government approved the hiring of an additional twenty-five medical officers to perform overseas medical screening that applied to all immigrants from the United Kingdom and continental Europe. On February 1, 1928, a system of overseas medical examination was implemented with the creation of an overseas immigration medical service. For further context, see Vineberg, "Healthy Enough," 288.

28 Immigration Story of the Bekkers Family, CMI Collection (S2012.1004.1).

29 Cameron, *Quarantine*, 31–58.

30 Pagé, "Medical Examination of Immigrants"; Vineberg, "Healthy Enough"; Bilson, "Dr Frederick Montizambert."
31 LAC, IB fonds, RG 76, vol. 666, file C1594, pt. 2 "Immigration Building at Halifax, Nova Scotia (map) (plans)," see reproduced article, "Best Immigration Facilities on the Continent Here," *Halifax Chronicle*, 10 November 1927. See also, DPW, "Dept of Immigration Pier 21 Halifax, NS, 2nd Floor Plan," March 1956, Drawing 51103-412, consulted from HPA digitized document #11000.
32 DPW, "Immigration, Pier 21, Halifax NS, Accommodations," 14 February 1969, Drawing 51103-101, consulted from HPA digitized document #10899.
33 Crosman, *Recollections*, 39.
34 United Kingdom National Archives, Board of Trade (UK), BT27/1476, Embarkation list, *Duchess of York*, 12 March 1937, www.findmypast.co.uk; Government of Nova Scotia, Nova Scotia Historical Vital Statistics, "Death Record for Stefania Piasta, 1937, Book 169, Page 224," http://www.novascotiagenealogy.com.
35 Oral History with Lloyd Hirtle, interviewed by James H. Morrison and Shelagh MacKenzie, Halifax, 17 April 1998, CMI Collection (98.04.17LH), 00:27:29.
36 Oral History with Lloyd Hirtle, interviewed by James H. Morrison and Shelagh MacKenzie, Halifax, 17 April 1998, CMI Collection (98.04.17LH), 00:27:29.
37 Oral History with Alison Trapnell, interviewed by James H. Morrison, Halifax, 16 April 1998, CMI Collection (98.04.16AT), 00:21:57, 00:23:12.
38 Crosman, *Recollections*, 108.
39 LAC, DNHW fonds, RG 29, vol. 766, file 412-2-213, pt. 1 "Quarantine Station Halifax, Nova Scotia–Reports of Vessels Arriving with Contagious Diseases on Board, 1920–1940," Immigration Quarantine Officer to J.D. Pagé, Chief, Division of Quarantine, Department of Health, 9 May 1929.
40 LAC, DNHW fonds, RG 29, vol. 766, file 412-2-213, pt. 1 "Quarantine Station Halifax, Nova Scotia–Reports of Vessels Arriving with Contagious Diseases on Board, 1920–1940," Immigration Quarantine Officer to J.D. Pagé, 9 May 1929. See "Smallpox on Steamer that Called Here," *Halifax Evening Mail*, 9 May 1929.
41 Cameron, *Quarantine*, 163.
42 Oral History with Jim Dauphinee, Marguerite Day and George LaRue, interviewed by James H. Morrison, Halifax, 16 April 1998, CMI Collection (98.04.16JDMDGL), 00:12:29.
43 Oral History with Charles Dwyer, 00:15:48.
44 Immigration Story of Fred von Ompteda, CMI Collection (S2012.2009.1).
45 Immigration Story of Connie A.H. Uyterlinde, CMI Collection (S2012.639.1).
46 Oral History with Bill Marks, 00:08:33.
47 Oral History with Charles Dwyer, 00:15:48.
48 Oral History with Ágnes Szabó, interviewed by Steven Schwinghamer, Halifax, 6 October 2007, CMI Collection (07.10.06AS), 00:53:02.
49 Oral History with James Braiden, interviewed by Steven Schwinghamer, Halifax, 6 June 2000, CMI Collection (00.06.06JB), 00:05:47.
50 Oral History with James Braiden, interviewed by Steven Schwinghamer, Halifax, 6 June 2000, CMI Collection (00.06.06JB), 00:05:47.
51 Oral History with Siegfried Speck, interviewed by Amy Coleman, Halifax, 21 June 2000, CMI Collection (00.06.21SS), 00:03:11. Direct police involvement with immigrants abroad was uncommon. In one case, the van Kooten family had a family friend who was a police officer keep an eye on their sixteen-year-old daughter, as they feared she might

run away to her friends rather than stay with the family to immigrate to Canada. See Oral History with Grace Bolding, interviewed by Steven Schwinghamer, Halifax, 28 September 2000, CMI Collection (00.09.28GB), 00:02:53.

52 Oral History with Corrado and Filomena Recchuti, interviewed by Cassidy Bankson, Halifax, 23 May 2009, CMI Collection (09.05.23CFR), 01:36:10.

53 Oral History with Nicholas Sbarra, interviewed by Cassidy Bankson, Halifax, 6 June 2009, CMI Collection (09.06.06NS), 02:09:15.

54 H.J. Crudge, "CNR Halifax Ocean Terminals Proposed Immigration Facilities, Sheds No. 21 & 22 General Layout," 31 October 1928, Drawing 16379-5, consulted from HPA digitized document #10882.

55 Oral History with Alison Trapnell, 00:08:44.

56 Oral History with Bill Marks, 00:19:11, 00:45:37. The 1906 Immigration Act established boards of inquiry at each port of entry into Canada to decide cases of immigrants seeking admission into the country. Section 31 of the Act states that an "immigration agent, medical officer, or any other officer or officers named by the Minister for such purpose, may act as a board of inquiry at any port of entry to consider and decide upon the case of any immigrant seeking admission into Canada. The decision of such a board touching the right of any such immigrant to land in Canada shall be subject to appeal to the Minister." See LAC, Statutes of Canada, *Act Respecting Immigration, 1906*, 115.

57 The extensive correspondence of travelling inspectors is on file at LAC; in relation to Halifax and Pier 21, the travelling inspector, T. B. Willans, offers key contributions to the assessment and development of the new Ocean Terminals site in LAC, IB fonds, RG 76, vol. 666, file C1594, pt. 1 "Immigration Building at Halifax, Nova Scotia (map) (plans)." Laval Fortier, later deputy minister of the DCI, is another notable correspondent as a senior inspector travelling the Maritime provinces before the Second World War.

58 Crosman, *Recollections*, 190.

59 LAC, IB fonds, RG 76, vol. 44, file 1328, pt.2 "Exchanging Money for Immigrants at the Port of Halifax (1914–1934)," Inspector-in-charge (Halifax) to Division Commissioner of Immigration, 16 September 1933.

60 Oral History with Charles Dwyer, 00:12:59.

61 Oral History with Mary Cecilia Catherine Wambolt Horwill, interviewed by Steven Schwinghamer, Halifax, 18 July 2000, CMI Collection (00.07.18MH), 00:12:26.

62 LAC, IB fonds, RG 76, vol. 666, file C1594, pt. 1 "Immigration Building at Halifax, Nova Scotia (map) (plans)," see reproduced article, "Splendid Facilities," *Halifax Chronicle*, 3 March 1928. For context, see Chilton, *Receiving Canada's Immigrants*, 25.

63 LAC, IB fonds, RG 76, vol. 666, file C1594, pt. 1 "Immigration Building at Halifax, Nova Scotia (map) (plans)," W.L. Barnstead to J.S. Fraser, 23 November 1926; H.J. Crudge, "CNR Halifax Ocean Terminals Proposed Immigration Facilities Shed No. 21 Gratings for Types 'A', 'B1' & 'B2' Windows," 25 November 1926, Drawing 51103-503, consulted from HPA digitized document #8647.

64 HPA #11000.

65 LAC, IB fonds, RG 76, vol. 668, file C19279 "Admission to Canada of the Corvette Walnut," H.P. Wade, Assistant Inspector-in-Charge, to H.U. McCrum, Atlantic District Superintendent, Department of Mines and Resources, 5 January 1949.

66 Oral History with Hans Leppik, interviewed by Cassidy Bankson, Halifax, 1 October 2008, CMI Collection (08.10.01HL), 00:26:25.

67 HPA #11000; Oral History with Alison Trapnell, 00:23:12.

68 Crosman, *Recollections,* 120, 128–30, 161.
69 See, for example, Oral History with Tibor Lukács, interviewed by Steven Schwinghamer, Halifax, 9 December 2006, CMI Collection (06.12.09TL), 00:49:37.
70 Oral History with Bill Marks, 00:59:55.
71 LAC, DCI fonds, RG 26, vol. 939, file "Immigration Manual: First Series," binder 22, sections 24.09 and 24.41, "Administration Chapter 24: Management of Immigration Halls and Detention Quarters," as amended 27 September 1954.
72 LAC, IB fonds, RG 76, vol. 513, file 800070, pt. 1 "E. Blake Robertson, Assistant Superintendent of Immigration, Ottawa Ontario. Deferred and rejected United States immigrants at Saint John, New Brunswick, and Halifax, Nova Scotia," T.B. Willans to W.L. Barnstead, 5 August 1920.
73 Oral History with Bill Marks, 00:36:07.
74 LAC, IB fonds, RG 76, vol. 745, file 507-5-35 "Catering – Policy and Instructions – Halifax, Nova Scotia," Acting Atlantic District Superintendent to Director of Operations, 7 November 1962. For example, in 1961 and 1962, the Annex dining area opened only thirty-seven times.
75 LAC, IB fonds, RG 76, vol. 745, file 507-5-35 "Catering – Policy and Instructions – Halifax, Nova Scotia," Administrator, Atlantic Region to Assistant Chief of Operations, 17 July 1964.
76 Oral History with Bill Marks, 00:27:10.
77 Raska, "Food Wars!"
78 Oral History with Jim Dauphinee, Marguerite Day and George LaRue, 01:15:20.
79 Immigration Story of Milan V. Gregor, CMI Collection (S2012.215.1).
80 Oral History with Jack Gladstone, interviewed by James H. Morrison, Toronto, 29 May 1998, CMI Collection (98.05.29JG), 00:01:00; Oral History with Sister Florence Kelly, interviewed by James H. Morrison, Toronto, 27 May 1998, CMI Collection (98.05.27FK), 00:15:39. See also Red Cross Nursery reports in LAC, IB fonds, RG 76, vol. 646, file 998369 "Rest rooms at Halifax, Nova Scotia (for immigrants) (Red Cross Nursery)."
81 H.J. Crudge, "Customs Examination & Waiting Room Building: General Plan, Elevations and Sections," 31 October 1928, Drawing 16436-3, as consulted from HPA digitized document #10912; NHB, "Ocean Terminals Facilities Leased By Canadian Immigration," 15 November 1954, Drawing 51103-110, as consulted from HPA digitized document #18196.
82 LAC, IB fonds, RG 76, vol. 666, file C1594, pt. 2 "Immigration Building at Halifax, Nova Scotia (map) (plans)," memo from T.B. Willans to J.S. Fraser, 17 January 1928. See attached "Memorandum Presented by the Social Workers at Halifax," n.d.
83 NHB, "Ocean Terminals Facilities Leased by Canadian Immigration," 15 November 1954, Drawing 51103-110, as consulted from HPA digitized document #18196.
84 Oral History with Sister Florence Kelly, 00:12:38.
85 For example, see Canada Employment and Immigration Commission (hereafter cited as CEIC), Public Affairs, Nova Scotia Region, "The Pier 21 Story: Halifax, 1924–1971," (Halifax: CEIC, 1978), 16.
86 Pier 21 Staff Story of Sister Adua Zampese, CMI Collection (S2012.1268.1).
87 Oral History with Sister Florence Kelly, 00:07:57.
88 LAC, IB fonds, RG 76, vol. 646, file 998369, pt. 1 "Rest rooms at Halifax, Nova Scotia (for immigrants) (Red Cross Nursery)," Gerry Congdon to J.S. Fraser, 21 January 1925; and T. McManus, Seaport Nursery Report, March 1928.

89 LAC, IB fonds, RG 76, vol. 666, file C1594, pt. 2 "Immigration Building at Halifax, Nova Scotia (map) (plans)," report quoted in J. Biggar, Chief Commissioner, Canadian Red Cross, to J.S. Fraser, 3 January 1928.
90 H.J. Crudge, "Customs Examination & Waiting Room Building: General Plan, Elevations and Sections," 31 October 1928.
91 A small sample series of reports representing the materials and food distributed, as well as other forms of aid provided by Red Cross staff, may be found in the above-mentioned citation: LAC, IB fonds, RG 76, vol. 646, file 998369, pt. 1 "Rest rooms at Halifax, Nova Scotia (for immigrants) (Red Cross Nursery)."
92 Immigration Story of Mary I. Bourgeois, CMI Collection (S2012.185.1).
93 NHB, "Ocean Terminals Facilities Leased By Canadian Immigration," 15 November 1954, Drawing 51103-110, as consulted from HPA digitized document #18196.
94 Oral History with Bill Marks, 00:24:08; Oral History with Heather Wineberg, interviewed by Steven Schwinghamer, Halifax, 10 August 2005, CMI Collection (05.08.10HW), 00:04:16.
95 Oral History with Heather Wineberg, 00:17:07.
96 LAC, IB fonds, RG 76, vol. 666, file C1594, pt. 2 "Immigration Building at Halifax, Nova Scotia (map) (plans)," memo from T.B. Willans to J.S. Fraser, 17 January 1928. See attached "Memorandum Presented by the Social Workers at Halifax," n.d.
97 McIntosh, *Collectors*, 139.
98 McIntosh, *Collectors*, 139.
99 Oral History with Charles Dwyer, 00:01:04, 00:47:10.
100 Immigration Story of Tynne Johanna Saarinen, CMI Collection (S2012.729.1).
101 Ken Elliott photograph, July 1965, CMI Collection (R2013.1362.4); Ken Elliott photograph, July 1965, CMI Collection (R2013.1362.5); Ken Elliott photograph, July 1965, CMI Collection (R2013.1362.350); Ken Elliott photograph, July 1965, CMI Collection (R2013.1362.351); Oral History with William Martin and Frank Power, interviewed by James H. Morrison, Halifax, 2 April 1998, CMI Collection (98.04.02WMFP), 00:02:33.
102 Immigration Story of Gerda Kiel, CMI Collection (S2012.1906.1).
103 Oral History with Bill Marks, 00:09:18.
104 Oral History with Jim Dauphinee, Marguerite Day and George LaRue, 00:26:53, 01:15:20.
105 Oral History with R. David Gray, interviewed by Steve Schwinghamer, Halifax, 25 July 2000, CMI Collection (00.07.25DG), 00:41:50.
106 Oral History with Patricia Leask, interviewed by Amy Coleman, Halifax, 5 July 2000, CMI Collection (00.07.05PL), 00:01:51.
107 H. J. Crudge, "Canadian National Railways Halifax Ocean Terminals Customs Examination & Waiting Room Building General Plan," 31 October 1928.
108 DPW, "Alterations and Additions, Customs Annex & Shed 21, Halifax, NS," 1 July 1953, Drawing 3, consulted in HPA digitized document #11025.
109 Oral History with Jim Dauphinee, Marguerite Day and George LaRue, 00:44:14.
110 Oral History with William Martin and Frank Power, 00:14:05.
111 Ken Elliott photograph, July 1965, CMI Collection (R2013.1362.27).
112 Oral History with Jim Dauphinee, Marguerite Day and George LaRue, 00:04:37.
113 Oral History with William Martin and Frank Power, 00:23:26.
114 Oral History with Jim Dauphinee, Marguerite Day and George LaRue, 00:56:06.
115 Oral History with Alison Trapnell, 01:00:45.

116 Oral History with Jim Dauphinee, Marguerite Day, and George LaRue, 00:50:13.
117 Oral History with Bill Marks, 00:38:05.
118 Oral History with William Martin and Frank Power, 01:28:39.
119 Oral History with Bill Marks, 00:37.17.
120 Immigration Story of Mary Leonetti Caravaggio, CMI Collection (S2012.961.1).
121 Immigration Story of the Pijl Family, CMI Collection (S2012.1992.1).
122 Immigration Story of Celia Beemster, CMI Collection (S2012.2055.1).
123 Immigration Story of W.A.T. Van den Byllaardt, CMI Collection (S2012.239.1).
124 Immigration Story of the Johansen Family, CMI Collection (S2016.484.1).
125 For different views of train travel from Pier 21, see Immigration Story of Peter Hessel, CMI Collection (S2012.124.1); Immigration Story of Willem Kreeft, CMI Collection (S2012.178.1); Immigration Story of the Pijl Family; Immigration Story of W.A.T. Van den Byllaardt; Immigration Story of the Johansen Family; "Immigrants Kept Waiting 15 Hours in Rail Coaches: Protests Sent to Ottawa," *Halifax Mail-Star*, 6 November 1965, 3.

2. PIER 2 AND THE EARLY YEARS OF PIER 21, 1890–1939

1 LAC, Statutes of Canada. *An Act Respecting Immigration, 1910*. Ottawa: SC 9–10 Edward VII, chapter 27, section 31.3.
2 Fingard, Guildford, and Sutherland, *Halifax*, 95.
3 Carrigan, "Immigrant Experience in Halifax," 30.
4 LAC, Department of Agriculture (hereafter cited as DA) fonds, RG 17, vol. 610, file 69092, "J.S. Blogdon & Son, Halifax: Estimate for new immigration shed at Halifax; with memo from Mr. Lowe," memo of John Lowe, 23 April 1889. From Confederation until 1892, immigration matters fell under the DA.
5 LAC, DA fonds, RG 17, vol. 626, file 70944, "Acknowledging letter of 14th instant re erection of new Immigration Shed at Halifax," Secretary, DPW, to H.B. Small, Secretary, DA, 7 October 1889; LAC, DA fonds, RG 17, vol. 665, file 75843, "Urging the immediate fitting up of the new Immigration Shed," E.M. Clay, Halifax immigration agent, to John Lowe, 15 November 1890.
6 LAC, DA fonds, RG 17, vol. 645, file 73377, "Office at Railway Station necessary in addition to Office at new Sheds," E.M. Clay to H.B. Small, Halifax, 6 June 1890; LAC, DA fonds, RG 17, vol. 701, file 80377, "Desirable to lower covered way between Intercolonial Railway freight shed and Halifax Immigration Building," unattributed memo (possibly H.B. Small or John Lowe), 19 September 1891.
7 LAC, IB fonds, RG 76, vol. 15, file 142, pt. 1 "Immigration Building, Halifax, Nova Scotia," E.M. Clay to A.M. Burgess, Deputy Minister of the Interior, 21 October 1892. Responsibility for immigration matters passed to the Department of the Interior in 1892.
8 LAC, IB fonds, RG 76, vol. 15, file 142, pt. 1 "Immigration Building, Halifax, Nova Scotia," J.M. Gordon to A.M. Burgess, 15 March 1893; and P. Doyle, Immigration Agent, to J.R. Hall, Secretary of the Department of the Interior, 6 April 1893.
9 LAC, IB fonds, RG 76, vol. 15, file 142, pt. 2 "Immigration Building, Halifax, Nova Scotia," E.M Clay to A.M. Burgess, 27 February and 12 March 1895.
10 LAC, IB fonds, RG 76, vol. 15, file 142, pt. 2 "Immigration Building, Halifax, Nova Scotia," E.M. Clay to A.M. Burgess, 4 and 21 March 1895.

11 LAC, IB fonds, RG 76, vol. 15, file 142, pt. 2 "Immigration Building, Halifax, Nova Scotia," E.M. Clay to L.M. Fortier, inspector of government agencies, 23 April 1895; and A.M. Burgess to T. Mayne Daly, Superintendent-General of Indian Affairs and Minister of the Interior, 25 April 1895.

12 LAC, IB fonds, RG 76, vol. 15, file 142, pt. 2 "Immigration Building, Halifax, Nova Scotia," E.M. Clay to J.R. Hall, Halifax, 1 October 1896; LAC, IB fonds, RG 76, vol. 15, file 142, pt. 3 "Immigration Building, Halifax, Nova Scotia," J.A. Kirk, Halifax immigration agent, to Clifford Sifton, Minister of the Interior, 18 September 1897; F.W. Annand, Halifax immigration agent, to Frank Pedley, Secretary, Department of the Interior, 20 November 1901; F.W. Annand to W.D. Scott, Superintendent of Immigration, 10 August 1903; and LAC, IB fonds, RG 76, vol. 15, file 142, pt. 4 "Immigration Building, Halifax, Nova Scotia," F.W. Annand to W.D. Scott, 30 December 1904.

13 LAC, IB fonds, RG 76, vol. 15, file 142, pt. 3 "Immigration Building, Halifax, Nova Scotia," Lyndwode Pereira, Assistant Secretary, Department of the Interior, to H. and A. Allan, 5 March 1897; "One of the Finest: The New Immigrant Shed at the Terminus," *Halifax Daily Echo*, 14 January 1895; LAC, IB fonds, RG 76, vol. 15, file 142, pt. 3 "Immigration Building, Halifax, Nova Scotia," G. Hannah, Montreal agent for Allan Lines, to A.M. Burgess, 23 February 1895; unattributed diagram of proposed addition to immigration wharf at Halifax, May 1898; T.E. Clay to L.M. Fortier, 13 April 1897; and memo by W.D. Scott, 3 June 1897.

14 LAC, IB fonds, RG 76, vol. 15, file 142, pt. 3 "Immigration Building, Halifax, Nova Scotia," J.A. Kirk to Clifford Sifton, 20 October 1897.

15 LAC, IB fonds, RG 76, vol. 15, file 142, pt. 4 "Immigration Building, Halifax, Nova Scotia," L.M. Fortier to J.A. Smart, Deputy Minister, Department of the Interior, 21 October 1902.

16 LAC, IB fonds, RG 76, vol. 15, file 142, pt. 4 "Immigration Building, Halifax, Nova Scotia," J.A. Smart to D. Ewart, Chief Architect, DPW, 9 January 1904; F.W. Annand to J.A. Smart, 12 April and 2 June 1904; and D. Ewart to J.A. Smart, 7 and 15 April 1904.

17 To track the progress of construction at Pier 2, see images and correspondence from December 1913, December 1914, and September 1915 in LAC, DRC fonds, RG 43, vol. 451, file 12795, "Canadian National Railway–Construction of Shed and Pier No. 2–Halifax, NS."

18 LAC, IB fonds, RG 76, vol. 15, file 142, pt. 6 "Immigration Building, Halifax, Nova Scotia," F.P. Gutelius to W.D. Scott, 12 April 1915. Gutelius's note is interesting in that he gives his opinion on prospective tenants and their capacity to pay. For instance, he commented on US officers claiming the expense of invitations to be in Halifax from the railways, and opined that the Salvation Army, although generally a charity, made "considerable money out of the people that they look after."

19 LAC, DRC fonds, RG 43, vol. 613, file 19403, "Canadian National Railway–Halifax, NS–Accommodation for Federal Government Departments at railway terminals," "General Plan of Offices and Baggage Equipment in Upper Storey of Shed No 2," Plan 882, 4 July 1913.

20 Gauvin and Gentzell Studio, Halifax, for Foley Bros. et al., *Ceremony of dedicating work by Sir Robert Borden*, 20 October 1915, Nova Scotia Archives 1986-490, Photograph F44.

21 LAC, DRC fonds, RG 43, vol. 613, file 19403, "Canadian National Railway–Halifax, NS–Accommodation for Federal Government Departments at railway terminals," F.P. Gutelius, General Manager, Intercolonial Railway, to John Kennedy, Consulting

Engineer (ordinarily Kennedy consulted for the Montreal Harbour Commission), 18 June 1913; and J. Kennedy to F.P Gutelius, 30 July 1913. Kennedy discusses the vulnerability to fire of the shed based on use of cheaper, combustible partitions and fittings; in 1933, the shed was consumed by fire. See also LAC, IB fonds, RG 76, vol. 15, file 142, pt. 6 "Immigration Building, Halifax, Nova Scotia," unattributed memo, 2 September 1914.

22 LAC, IB fonds, RG 76, vol. 15, file 142, pt. 8 "Immigration Building, Halifax, Nova Scotia," W.L. Barnstead to W.D. Scott, 18 December 1917; and memo of T.W. Puller, Assistant Chief Architect, DPW, 26 December 1919.

23 LAC, IB fonds, RG 76, vol. 666, file C1594, pt. 1 "Immigration Building – Halifax, NS," R.C. Wright to W.J. Egan, Deputy Minister, DIC, 24 October 1925.

24 LAC, IB fonds, RG 76, vol. 666, file C1594, pt. 1 "Immigration Building – Halifax, NS," A.F. Stewart, Chief Engineer, CNR, to W.J. Egan, Deputy Minister, DIC, 31 October 1925.

25 Cowie, *Report*, 25.

26 Cowie, *Report*, 8–10.

27 Cowie, *Report*, 46–49.

28 "Railway Terminals and Union Station for South End, Is Cochrane Plan," *The Morning Chronicle*, 31 October 1912, 1–2.

29 Headline and extensive coverage, *Halifax Herald*, 31 October 1912, 1–6.

30 "Hon. Mr. Cochrane's Announcement," *Halifax Herald*, 31 October 1912, 1.

31 M.O. Hammond, "Nova Scotia Rejoices in Growing Pains," *The Globe* (Toronto), April 26, 1913, 12. Perhaps as a nod to the possible incursion on public space at Point Pleasant and the consequent impact on quality of life in the city, the initial project was intended to have a pedestrian promenade on top of the terminal buildings, some 2,000 feet long and 40 feet wide.

32 "The Terminals Approved By The Council," *Halifax Herald*, 19 November 1912, 1.

33 "Great Terminals for Halifax Will Not Hurt Appearance of Halifax," *Halifax Herald*, 23 November 1912, 3.

34 Sir Sandford Fleming to F.P. Bligh, Mayor of Halifax, 15 November 1912, as recorded in Halifax, *Minutes of City Council for the Civic Year 1912–1913* (Halifax, NS: Office of the City Clerk, 1912–1913), 359; Canada, Parliament, *House of Commons Debates*, 26 May 1913 (Alexander Maclean, Liberal), http://parl.canadiana.ca/view/oop.debates_HOC1202_06/309?r=0&s=1. MacLean has a prolonged exchange with Cochrane on the topic of the construction of the Ocean Terminals, including the compromise of water and sewage systems.

35 "Why Not Put the Terminals in The North End?" *The Morning Chronicle*, 21 November 1912, 3.

36 Halifax, Minutes of City Council for the Civic Year 1916–1917 (Halifax, NS: Office of the City Clerk, 1916–1917), 86.

37 LAC, IB fonds, RG 76, vol. 666, file C1594, pt. 1 "Immigration Building – Halifax, NS," A.F. Stewart, Chief Engineer, CNR, to T.B. Willans, Travelling Inspector, DIC, 18 November 1925.

38 "Hon. Messrs. Borden and Cochrane Are the Best Friends Nova Scotia Ever Was Blest With," *Halifax Herald*, 31 October 1912, 3; "New Terminals Used," *The Globe* (Toronto), 27 November 1916, 1.

39 One source from 1913–1914 places the payments for lands related to the project at almost $800,000: Cowie, *Report*, 22–23; "Three Quarter Million Dollars were paid out for

properties in connection with terminals," clipping in Nova Scotia Archives, MG 1, vol. 1501, item 13. Charges of profiteering tainted the process of expropriating the needed land, with Halifax's *Morning Chronicle* noting in 1912 that "leading members of the Tory Party" knew some details of the waterfront plan in advance and so were able to cash in on insider knowledge by buying up land liable to government expropriation during the course of construction. The manipulation of real-estate prices did lead to numerous claims proceeding through the Exchequer Court and to the Supreme Court. This process stretched into the mid-1920s, long after the foundations of the Ocean Terminals and the associated rail cut were completed.

40 LAC, Department of Transport fonds, RG 12, vol. 4816, file 3570-11 "Railway – Terminals – New Terminal Facilities at Halifax, N.S.," C.O. McDonald to Frank Cochrane, Minister of Railways and Canals, 31 October 1913.

41 Forbes, *Maritime Rights Movement*, 8–12.

42 "What Prominent Liberals Think of the Minister's Splendid Announcement," *The Halifax Herald*, 31 October 1912, 2.

43 Halifax, *Minutes of City Council for the Civic Year 1916–1917* (Halifax, NS: Office of the City Clerk, 1916–1917), 85–87; quote from 86; emphasis added.

44 LAC, DRC fonds, RG 43, vol. 511, file 15927C, "Halifax Ocean Terminals – Claims of Contractors – Foley Bros., Welch, Stewart & Fauquier," Foley Bros., Welch, Stewart & Fauquier, to James McGregor, 5 April 1916; and A.C. Brown, Resident Engineer, Canadian Government Railways (hereafter cited as CGR), to W.A. Duff, Assistant Chief Engineer, CGR, 18 Oct 1916.

45 LAC, DRC fonds, RG 43, vol. 511, file 15927C, "Halifax Ocean Terminals – Claims of Contractors – Foley Bros., Welch, Stewart & Fauquier," memo re Contractors Claim, McGregor, 23 September 1919; Charles Murphy, lawyer for Foley Bros., Welch, Stewart & Fauquier, to E.E. Fairweather, Departmental Solicitor, DRC, 17 September 1920, 15; memo by McGregor and attached schedule, 23 September 1919; Foley Bros., Welch, Stewart & Fauquier, Dredging Report, Dredge "Cynthia," 5 July 1919; memo re Contractor Claims, McGregor, Halifax NS, 23 September 1919.

46 LAC, DRC fonds, RG 43, vol. 511, file 15927C, "Halifax Ocean Terminals – Claims of Contractors – Foley Bros., Welch, Stewart & Fauquier," Foley Bros, Welch, Stewart & Fauquier, to F.P. Gutelius, 1 June 1916; Charles Murphy to E.E. Fairweather, 17 September 1920, 15.

47 LAC, DRC fonds, RG 43, vol. 511, file 15927C, "Halifax Ocean Terminals – Claims of Contractors – Foley Bros., Welch, Stewart & Fauquier," Foley Bros., Welch, Stewart & Fauquier to Major General Sir William Otter, Officer Commanding Internment Operations, 1 June 1916; McGregor to Gutelius, 17 June 1916.

48 LAC, DRC fonds, RG 43, vol. 511, file 15927C, "Halifax Ocean Terminals – Claims of Contractors – Foley Bros., Welch, Stewart & Fauquier," CGR, Halifax Ocean Terminals – Docks (First Unit), Form of Tender, Contract and Specification, September 1913; LAC, DRC fonds, RG 43, vol. 511, file 15927C, "Halifax Ocean Terminals – Claims of Contractors – Foley Bros., Welch, Stewart & Fauquier," Foley Bros, Welch, Stewart & Fauquier, to Hames [*sic*] McGregor, 2 July 1919; LAC, Department of Justice fonds, RG13, vol. 260, item 1443, "Claim of Foley Bros., Welch, Stewart, & Fauquier re: extra cost of docks – Halifax Ocean Terminals," correspondence file.

49 LAC, DRC fonds, RG 43, vol. 511, file 15927C, "Halifax Ocean Terminals – Claims of Contractors – Foley Bros., Welch, Stewart & Fauquier," Order-in-Council P.C. 3013, 28

November 1913; J. Robertson, "Steel Design and Erection on Transit Sheds at Halifax Ocean Terminals," *Contract Record*, Toronto, 24 March 1920, 268. Robert Vineberg offered the reference to this useful article.

50 LAC, DRC fonds, RG 43, vol. 511, file 15927C, "Halifax Ocean Terminals – Claims of Contractors – Foley Bros., Welch, Stewart & Fauquier," F.P. Brady to J.W. Pugsley, Secretary, DRC, 28 July 1919; LAC, DRC fonds, RG 43, vol. 613, file 19403, "Canadian National Railway – Halifax NS – Accommodation for Federal Government Departments at Railway Terminals," C.A. Hayes to J.W. Pugsley, 13 March 1918; LAC, DRC fonds, RG 43, vol, 642, file 20451, "Construction of Docks, Marginal and other roads at Halifax Ocean Terminals," Boville to Little, 23 September 1919; Pugsley to Boville, 16 October 1919.

51 LAC, Department of Transport fonds, RG 12, vol. 4816, file 3570-11 "Railway – Terminals – New Terminal Facilities at Halifax, N.S.," S.J. Hungerford, Vice President, CNR Operating and Maintenance Department, to G.A. Bell, 29 July 1922; LAC, DRC fonds, RG 43, vol. 511, file 15927, "Canadian National Railway – Halifax Ocean Terminals – General File," D.E. Galloway, Chief Assistant to the President, CNR, to G.W. Yates, Assistant Deputy Minister, DRC, 1 May 1924.

52 LAC, IB fonds, RG 76, vol. 666, file C1594, pt. 1 "Immigration Building – Halifax, NS," G.A. Bell to R.C. Wright, Chief Architect, DPW, Ottawa, 3 November 1920; LAC, DRC fonds, RG 43, vol. 535, file 16914, "Intercolonial Railway at Halifax – Immigration Department re Accommodation," G.A. Bell to F.P. Brady, 2 November 1920; and F.P. Brady to G.A. Bell, Ottawa, ON, 2 November 1920.

53 LAC, IB fonds, RG 76, vol. 666, file C1594, pt. 1 "Immigration Building – Halifax, NS," DIC to Undersecretary of State, 28 March 1924.

54 Forbes, "Origins," 55–56.

55 Fingard, Guildford, and Sutherland, *Halifax*, 145. At this time, in 1926, the Royal Commission on Maritime Claims took evidence on the state of the Ocean Terminals, trade, and immigration reception. The representative of the Halifax Board of Trade emphasized that Halifax was generally well-suited to be a passenger destination but that the new sheds at the Ocean Terminals were built to handle freight, not passengers. He stated that nothing proposed—and indeed nothing he thought possible—would make the immigration quarters at Pier 21 the equal of the 1915 building at Pier 2.

56 Canada, Parliament, *House of Commons Debates*, 19 June 1924 (Arthur Meighen, Conservative), http://parl.canadiana.ca/view/oop.debates_HOC1403_04/390?R=0&S=1; 26 January 1926 (Felix Quinn, Conservative), http://parl.canadiana.ca/view/oop.debates_HOC1501_01/433?R=0&S=1; and 26 January 1926 (William Duff, Liberal), http://parl.canadiana.ca/view/oop.debates_HOC1501_01/461?R=0&S=1.

57 LAC, DRC fonds, RG 43, vol. 511, file 15927, "Canadian National Railway – Halifax Ocean Terminals – General File," L.V. Hummel, Assistant to the President, CNR, to G.W. Yates, Assistant Deputy Minister, DRC, 29 April 1925.

58 "Port Facilities to Be Improved," *Halifax Herald*, 18 November 1925.

59 LAC, IB fonds, RG 76, vol. 666, file C1594, pt. 1 "Immigration Building – Halifax, NS," Fraser to Jolliffe, 14 December 1925; and Willans to Fraser, Halifax, 20 November 1925.

60 LAC, Royal Commission fonds, RG 33, Royal Commission on Maritime Claims, vol. 1, Evidence of Mr. Cornell, Halifax, 29 July 1926, page 799.

61 Canada, *House of Commons Debates*, 19 June 1924 (Robert Finn, Liberal), http://parl.canadiana.ca/view/oop.debates_HOC1403_04/390?R=0&S=1.

62 LAC, IB fonds, RG 76, vol. 666, file C1594, pts. 1-3 "Immigration Building – Halifax, NS," A.F. Stewart, Chief Engineer, CNR, to W.J Egan, Deputy Minister, DIC, 31 October 1925; and H.M. Grant to J.S. Fraser, 7 April 1933.

63 LAC, IB fonds, RG 76, vol. 666, file C1594, pt. 1 "Immigration Building – Halifax, NS," J.S. Fraser to Jolliffe, 19 February 1926; LAC, DRC fonds, RG 43, vol. 613, file 19403, "Canadian National Railway–Halifax, NS–Accommodation for Federal Government Departments at railway terminals," Minutes of Meeting, Board of Directors of CNR, 22 October 1926; LAC, Department of Transport fonds, RG 12, vol. 4816, file 3570-11 "Railway – Terminals – New Terminal Facilities at Halifax, N.S.," G.A. Bell to J.B. Hunter, 13 November 1926.

64 LAC, IB fonds, RG 76, vol. 666, file C1594, pt. 1 "Immigration Building – Halifax, NS," Barnstead to Fraser, 21 February 1926.

65 LAC, IB fonds, RG 76, vol. 666, file C1594, pt. 2 "Immigration Building – Halifax, NS," H.J. Crudge to J.S. Fraser, 20 May 1927; and H.J. Crudge to J.S. Fraser, 19 July 1927.

66 LAC, DRC fonds, RG 43, vol. 613, file 19403, "Canadian National Railway–Halifax, NS–Accommodation for Federal Government Departments at railway terminals," J.W. Pugsley to Gerard Ruel, Vice President, CNR, 23 September 1927; and James A. Yates, General Treasurer, CNR, to G.A. Bell, 19 March 1928; "Splendid Facilities for Development of Halifax as a Passenger Port," *Halifax Chronicle*, 3 March 1928.

67 LAC, IB fonds, RG 76, vol. 666, file C1594, pt. 2 "Immigration Building at Halifax, Nova Scotia (map) (plans)," see reproduced article, *Halifax Chronicle*, 8 November 1927; and telegram from T.B. Willans to J.S. Fraser, 8 March 1928; Schwinghamer, "Early Facility History," 2. See also Schwinghamer, "Altogether Unsatisfactory," 63; Thompson and van de Wiel, *Pier 21*, 28.

68 "Examine First Liner at New South Docks," *Halifax Evening Mail*, 8 March 1928, 1.

69 LAC, Department of Transport fonds, RG 12, vol. 4816, file 3570-11 "New Terminal Facilities at Halifax, N.S.," A. Wright, Operations Department, CNR to E.R. Williams, Secretary to Deputy Minister, DRC, 20 February 1928.

70 LAC, Department of Transport fonds, RG 12, vol. 4816, file 3570-11 "New Terminal Facilities at Halifax, N.S.," Deputy Minister, Department of Marine and Fisheries, to G.A. Bell, Minister, Department of Marine and Fisheries, 3 May 1928 (with attached schedule, CNR valuation of properties); and Order-in-Council P.C. 1456, 16 August 1928. The copy of Order-in-Council P.C. 1456 is present as listed, and has no other title, but concerns the transfer of properties from the Department of Railways (for CNR) to the Department of Marine and Fisheries (for the Halifax Harbour Commissioners). The Department of Marine and Fisheries sought to administer the Deep Water Terminus and Pier 2, which were valued at about $2.7 million, as well as the Halifax Ocean Terminals, which were valued at $6.5 million.

71 LAC, IB fonds, RG 76, vol. 666, file C1594, pt. 2 "Immigration Building at Halifax, Nova Scotia," J.B. Hunter, Deputy Minister, DPW to F.C. Blair, Deputy Minister, DIC, 21 March 1929.

72 LAC, IB fonds, RG 76, vol. 666, file C1594, pt. 2 "Immigration Building at Halifax, Nova Scotia," J.C. Elliot, Minister, DPW to Robert Forke, Minister, DIC, 30 November 1929; LAC, IB fonds, RG 76, vol. 666, file C1594, pt. 3 "Immigration Building at Halifax, Nova Scotia (map) (plans)," Alan Martin, Secretary, Halifax Harbour Commissioners to DIC, 3 December 1932. The issue of the immigration department creating unresolved debts was a sore spot in government at the time. At the port of Quebec, unpaid debts related to

the immigration sheds on the Louise Embankment accrued interest over a period of twenty years, which added some $3 million in interest to an original debt of $2.6 million.

73 Mitic and LeBlanc, *Pier 21*, 30.

74 LAC, IB fonds, RG 76, vol. 666, file C1594, pt. 2 "Immigration Building at Halifax, Nova Scotia (map) (plans)," J.S. Fraser to W.L. Barnstead, 12 February 1929.

75 Oral History with Norwood Akerlund, interviewed by Steven Schwinghamer, Halifax, 8 July 2000, CMI Collection (00.07.08NA), 00:09:40.

76 LAC, IB fonds, RG 76, vol. 352, file 381766, pt. 1, "Detention Hospital, Victoria, British Columbia," Peter H. Bryce, Chief Medical Officer, DIC to W.D. Scott, Superintendent of Immigration, DIC, 27 October 1906; LAC, IB fonds, RG 76, vol. 12, file 76, pt. 1, "E.M. Clay, Immigration Agent, Halifax, Nova Scotia," E.M. Clay, Dominion Immigration Agent, Department of the Interior to A.M. Burgess, Deputy Minister, Department of the Interior, 28 September 1893; Oral History with Norwood Akerlund, 00:09:14, 00:11:39.

77 This reciprocity was important. Prior to 1908, many immigrants to Canada came from the United States, or arrived at American ocean ports from Europe, before moving freely across the Canada-United States border. In 1908, Canada introduced a border inspection service to better regulate the flow of immigration between both countries. For context, see Knowles, *Strangers at Our Gates*, 121–22; LAC, "Border Entries."

78 LAC, IB fonds, RG 76, vol. 646, file 998369 "Red Cross Nurseries (at entry ports) (publications)," T. McManus, Seaport Nursery Report, March 1928, "A Letter Concerning Pier 21's History by Helen Creighton from Fabien O'Brien," CMI Collection (S2012.1019.1).

79 Statistics Canada, *Historical Statistics of Canada*, "Immigration"; Canada, Dominion Bureau of Statistics (hereafter cited as DBS), *Canada Year Book 1930*, 170; Canada, DBS, *Canada Year Book 1937*, 200; Canada, DBS, *Canada Year Book 1939*, 164; LAC, DCI fonds, RG 26, vol. 24, file b "Statement of Total Arrivals," see charts "Number of Arrivals, via Ocean Ports, Classified by Port of Entry and Class, for the Calendar Year 1938" and "Number of Arrivals, via Ocean Ports, Classified by Port of Entry and Class, for the Calendar Year 1939."

80 Fields, "Closing Immigration," 671.

81 LAC, Privy Council Office (hereafter PCO) fonds, RG 2, vol. 1479, file "Orders in Council – Décrets du Conseil," Order-in-Council P.C. 1931-695, 21 March 1931.

82 Thompson and van de Wiel, *Pier 21*, 35.

83 LAC, Statutes of Canada, *An Act to Amend the Immigration Act, 1919*, 8; LAC, IB fonds, RG 76, vol. 395, file 563236, pt. 14 "Deportation of undesirables from Canada (lists)," A.L. Jolliffe to T. Gelley, 27 May 1930.

84 For context, see Roberts, *From Whence They Came*.

85 LAC, IB Fonds, LAC, IB fonds, RG 76, vol. 646, file 998369 "Rest rooms at Halifax, Nova Scotia (for immigrants) (Red Cross Nursery) 1928–1934," T. McManus, Seaport Nursery Report, December 1931.

3. PIER 21 AT WAR, 1939–1946

1 Crosman, *Recollections*, 140.

2 Naftel, *Halifax at War*, 17.

3 LAC, IB fonds, RG 76, vol. 666, file C1594, pt. 1, "Immigration Building – Halifax, NS," J.B. Hunter, Deputy Minister, DPW, to G.A. Bell, Deputy Minister DRC, 5 November 1920; Crosman, *Recollections*, 98.

4 Naftel, *Halifax at War*, 84–86.

5 CEIC, "The Pier 21 Story,"17; Deployment Story of Graham Scase, CMI Collection (S2012.842.1); "Fire-Gutted Pier Had Colorful History," *Halifax Mail*, 6 March 1944, 1, 3, 13.

6 Statistics Canada, Historical Statistics of Canada, "Immigration."

7 LAC, "Orders-in-Council – Décrets-du-Conseil." RG2-A-1-a, vol. 1479, P.C. 1931-695 21 March 1931, http://www.pier21.ca/research/immigration-history/order-in-council-pc-1931-695-1931.

8 LAC, DCI fonds, RG 26, vol. 16, "Jewish Immigration 1899–1939," table "Jewish Immigration to Canada, from April 1, 1925 to March 31, 1941."

9 LAC, IB fonds, RG 76, vol. 391, file 541782, pt. 5 "Immigration to Canada of Jews from Europe," Massey to King, 29 November 1938.

10 The foundational work on the Canadian context of this voyage is Abella and Troper's *None is Too Many*. Laura Madokoro has pointed to the direct impact this work has had on the department of immigration itself; see Madokoro, "Remembering."

11 LAC, IB fonds, RG 76, vol. 440, file 670224, "Department of External Affairs–Confidential telegrams to Prime Minister at Washington, D.C., United States, on immigration matters (German Jews on SS *St. Louis*)," King to Skelton, 8 June 1939; Blair to Skelton, 8 June 1939; and Blair to Skelton, 16 June 1939; Hillmer, *O.D. Skelton*, 282–98; Ogilvie and Miller, *Refuge Denied*, 174.

12 LAC, DCI fonds, RG26, Office of Departmental Legal Advisor, vol. 87, "Orders-in-Council – Immigration Branch, 1940–1945," Canada, P.C. 6403, 13 November 1940.

13 LAC, DCI fonds, RG26, Office of Departmental Legal Advisor, vol. 87, "Orders-in-Council – Immigration Branch, 1940–1945."

14 LAC, DCI fonds, RG 26, vol. 24, "Statement of Arrivals via Ocean Ports and from USA, 1937–38 to 1951–52."

15 LAC, IB fonds, RG 76, vol. 468, file 712710, pt. 2 "The Merchant Seaman Order, 1941," Brigadier R.J. Orde, Judge Advocate-General, to Minister of National Defence for Naval Services, 8 December 1941.

16 Naftel, *Halifax at War*, 24.

17 LAC, IB fonds, RG 76, vol. 468, file 712710, pt. 1, "The Merchant Seaman Order, 1941," A.L. Jolliffe, Commissioner of Immigration, to McCrum, 6 December 1941; G.G. Congdon, Atlantic District Superintendent, to H.M. Grant, Inspector-in-Charge Halifax, 10 December 1941; and McCrum, memo for file, 10 December 1941; and LAC, IB fonds, RG 76, vol. 448, file 676701, "War circulars (to immigration officers)," A.L. Jolliffe, War Circular No. 9, 2 December 1941.

18 LAC, IB fonds, RG 76, vol. 468, file 712710, pt. 2 "The Merchant Seaman Order, 1941," Brigadier R.J. Orde, Judge Advocate-General, to Minister of National Defence for Naval Services, 8 December 1941; LAC, IB fonds, RG 76, vol. 468, file 712710, pt. 1, "The Merchant Seaman Order, 1941," Joliffe to Crerar, 9 September 1940 and P.C. 4751, 12 September 1940.

19 LAC, IB fonds, RG 76, vol. 468, file 712710, pt. 1, "The Merchant Seaman Order, 1941," Congdon to Jolliffe, 9 April 1941; Crosman, *Recollections*, 115, 161–62.

20 Crosman, *Recollections*, 108, 128.

21 Oral History with Alison Trapnell, 00:02:42.
22 Crosman, *Recollections*, 100; LAC, IB fonds, RG 76, vol. 468, file 712710, pt. 1, "The Merchant Seaman Order, 1941," Jolliffe to Blair, 20 September 1940; Contract of September 1940 between the City of Halifax and the Crown (Minister of Mines and Resources).
23 Crosman, *Recollections*, 130; LAC, IB fonds, RG 76, vol. 468, file 712710, pt. 1, "The Merchant Seaman Order, 1941," A.G. Christie to Congdon, 2 August 1941; and Grant to Congdon, 7 December 1940.
24 Oral History with Alison Trapnell, 00:21:57; Crosman, *Recollections*, 149.
25 Halstead, "Dangers behind, pleasures ahead," 164.
26 Oral History Adrienne Downs, interviewed by Steven Schwinghamer, 2 July 2002, CMI Collection (02.07.02AD), 00:07:03.
27 Baumel, "Twice a Refugee," 175.
28 Bilson, *Guest Children*, 10–15.
29 Bilson, *Guest Children*, 5; Cull, *Selling War*, 92.
30 Bilson, *Guest Children*, 58–60; LAC, DCI fonds, RG 26, vol. 16, "Evacuees to Canada, 1940–1941"; Fethney, *Absurd and the Brave*, 151–56, 304; National Archives (UK), "Evacuation to Canada," online resource, http://www.nationalarchives.gov.uk/education/lessons/lesson35.htm.
31 Evacuation Story of Diana Cape, CMI Collection (S2012.2470.1); Evacuation Story of Patricia and Pamela Pyle, CMI Collection (S2012.1462.1); Evacuation Story of Stella Marion Bates, CMI Collection (S2012.1676.1).
32 Immigration Story of Mary Hume, CMI Collection (S2012.360.1); Immigration Story of Margaret Smolensky, CMI Collection (S2012.377.1); Immigration Story of Catherine Read, CMI Collection (S2012.431.1).
33 Immigration Story of R. Stanley Goat, CMI Collection (S2012.304.1); Oral History with Thelma Freedman, interviewed by James H Morrison, Halifax, 28 May 1998, CMI Collection (98.05.28TF), 00:20:01; Evacuation Story of Daphne Levy, CMI Collection (S2012.1662.1).
34 Evacuation Story of Daphne Levy; Immigration Story of Peter Clarke, CMI Collection (s2012.1129.1); Immigration Story of Donald Stephen Chandler, CMI Collection (s2012.219.1); LAC, DCI fonds, RG 26, vol. 143, file 3-40-21, extracts from the IB Annual Report, Fiscal Year 1946–47.
35 LAC, DEA fonds, RG 25, vol. 2803, file 837-40 "Entry into Canada of Polish officials, art treasures and radio equipment," Statement of Dr. Stanisław Świerz Zaleski, 20 November 1946; Victor Podoski to William Lyon Mackenzie King, 11 July 1940.
36 Nova Scotia Archives, 1992-304 489 A, H.B. Jefferson Journal, August 1943, https://novascotia.ca/archives/EastCoastPort/archives.asp?ID=341&Page=200900590.
37 Canadian Press, "Princess Juliana and Children Land in Halifax," *Halifax Mail*, 11 June 1940, 1, 5; Oral History with Alison Trapnell, 00:52:31.
38 Naftel, *Halifax at War*, 102–04.
39 LAC, DEA fonds, RG 25, vol. 2803, file 837-40 "Entry into Canada of Polish officials, art treasures and radio equipment," Zaleski statement.
40 Swager, *Strange Odyssey*, 29, 44; LAC, DEA fonds, RG 25, vol. 2803, file 837-40 "Entry into Canada of Polish officials, art treasures and radio equipment," Zaleski statement, 2.
41 Draper, *Operation Fish*, 215; LAC, DEA fonds, RG 25, vol. 2803, file 837-40 "Entry into Canada of Polish officials, art treasures and radio equipment," Zaleski statement; Swager,

Strange Odyssey, 55, 62; LAC, DND fonds, RG 24, Directorate of Movements, HQS-63-303-12, file "Batory W-12," July 1940.

42 LAC, CNR fonds, RG 30, vol. 10149, file 8000-30-10, "Timber Ramp to Upper Floor at Shed 22, Halifax Harbour," J.F. Pringle, CNR, to S.W. Fairweather, Chief of Research and Development, CNR, 18 March 1942.

43 Stacey, *Canadian Army, 1939–1945*, 6.

44 "Armada of Troopships is Welcomed" and "As Canadians Embarked," *Halifax Herald*, December 19, 1939, 1.

45 C.-A. Smith, "We'll Meet Again"; Oral History with Victor Gray, interviewed by Amy Coleman, Halifax, 10 July 2001, CMI Collection (01.07.10VG), 00:04:53; Stacey, *Canadian Army*, 1; Parks Canada, "Backgrounder: Pier 21, Halifax," updated 26 September 2013, http://bit.ly/2hMVd4j; Oral History with Kenneth MacLaren, interviewed by Steven Schwinghamer, Halifax, 27 June 2000, CMI Collection (00.06.27KM), 00:10:10.

46 Oral History with Harold Hayward, interviewed by Steven Schwinghamer, Halifax, 15 January 2011, CMI Collection (11.01.15HH), 00:35:35; Oral History with James Gregg, interviewed by Steven Schwinghamer, Halifax, 2 October 2009, CMI Collection (09.10.02JG), 00:09:50; Oral History with Aubrey Young, interviewed by Steven Schwinghamer, Halifax, 21 August 2003, CMI Collection (03.08.21AY), 00:09:04.

47 Oral History with Gaston Audy, interviewed by Steven Schwinghamer, Halifax, 10 November 2002, CMI Collection (02.11.10GA), 00:08:38.

48 Oral History with James Cormier, interviewed by Steven Schwinghamer, Halifax, 25 March 2010, CMI Collection (10.03.25JC), 00:00:01.

49 Oral History with Reginald Bruce Crowe, interviewed by Steven Schwinghamer, Halifax, 6 June 2008, CMI Collection (08.06.06RMC), 00:03:52.

50 Deployment Story of Donald H. MacKenzie, CMI Collection (S2012.1979.1); Deployment Story of William Barker, CMI Collection (S2012.149.1); Oral History with Reginald Bruce Crowe, 00:07:41; Oral History with Claude Cowan, interviewed by Amy Coleman, Halifax, 22 August 2001, CMI Collection (01.08.22CC), 00:04:53.

51 Deployment Story of Dorothy Chartrand, CMI Collection (S2012.432.1).

52 Oral History with James Cormier, 00:25:35.

53 Oral History with Douglas Power, interviewed by Steven Schwinghamer, Halifax, 8 August 2000, CMI Collection (00.08.08DP), 00:16:03.

54 Oral History with Della Johansen, interviewed by Steven Schwinghamer, Halifax, 12 June 2000, CMI Collection (00.06.12DJ), 00:04:25.

55 Oral History with Everett MacLeod, interviewed by Nick Langley, Halifax, 24 July 2004, CMI Collection (04.07.24EM), 00:00:30; Oral History with Horace MacAulay and Gordon Dysart, interviewed by Steven Schwinghamer, Truro, 18 May 2004, CMI Collection (04.05.18HMGD), 00:00:01.

56 Oral History with Douglas Power, 00:16:03.

57 Oral History with Sheila and Robert Linden, interviewed by Kevin Lohnes, aboard commemorative train from Ottawa to Halifax, 7 November 2006, CMI Collection (06.11.07SRL), 00:12:45.

58 Immigration Story of J. Fred Havinga, CMI Collection (S2012.1696.1).

59 Deployment Story of Leland M. Pratt, CMI Collection (S2012.1299.1).

60 Crosman, *Recollections*, 98.

61 Oral History with Joyce Woodford, interviewed by Amy Coleman, Halifax, 28 May 2003, CMI Collection (03.05.28JW), 00:08:59.

62 Oral History with Gerald Porter, interviewed by Kevin Lohnes, Halifax, 14 August 2007, CMI Collection (07.08.14GP), 00:05:18.
63 Hatch, *Aerodrome*, epigraph and 202; Canada, Veterans Affairs Canada, "Air Training Plan."
64 Hatch, *Aerodrome*, 37, 208; Immigration Story of Ivor William Thomas, CMI Collection (S2012.1602.1).
65 Auger, *Prisoners*, 3.
66 Immigration Story of G. John Schönfelder, CMI Collection (S2012.1290.1).
67 Crosman, *Recollections*, 134; Naftel, *Halifax at War*, 92–94; LAC, IB fonds, RG 76, vol. 648, file A85451 "Admission of 4000 former Polish soldiers for agricultural work in Canada"; Kelley and Trebilcock, *Making of the Mosaic*, 340.
68 Koch, *Deemed Suspect*, xv, 73.
69 Draper, "'Camp Boys'," 171–72; Auger, *Prisoners*, 31–33; Koch, *Deemed Suspect*, 255.
70 Auger, *Prisoners*, 58.
71 Deployment Story of Edward J. Weaver, CMI Collection (S2012.1324.1).
72 "Fire-Gutted Pier Had Colorful History," *Halifax Evening Mail*, 6 March 1944, 1, 3, 13; LAC, National Harbours Board (hereafter cited as NHB) fonds, RG 66, Minutes of the Board, Box 23 No 83-84/130, Minutes of Meeting Held at Ottawa, 1 May 1944; LAC, IB fonds, RG 76, vol. 666, file C1594 pt. 1 "Immigration Building – Halifax, NS," W.L. Barnstead to J.S. Fraser, 23 November 1926. In connection with fire prevention duties, a 1942 order-in-council approved paying "an expenditure not exceeding $10.00… for the purpose of replacing one pair of uniform trousers damaged by Guard Yeates in his efforts to quell a fire on December 22, 1941, in the recreation room of the Immigration Building at Halifax, Nova Scotia." LAC, DCI fonds, RG26, Office of Departmental Legal Advisor, vol. 87, "Orders-in-Council – Immigration Branch, 1940–1945," Order-in-Council P.C. 29/2757, 11 April 1942.
73 "Fire-Gutted Pier Had Colorful History," *Halifax Evening Mail*, 6 March 1944, 1, 3, 13; Mitic and LeBlanc, *Pier 21*, 73; Oral History with Alison Trapnell, 00:08:44.
74 LAC, NHB fonds, RG 66, Minutes of the Board, Box 23 No 83-84/130, Minutes of Meeting, Ottawa, ON, 1 May 1944; Mitic and LeBlanc, *Pier 21*, 73; CEIC, "Pier 21 Story," 18.
75 LAC, DND fonds, RG 24, file HQS-8536-1 "Return to Families of Canadian Officers and Service Personnel to Canada, 1940–1951," unpublished report, "History of S.A.A.G. Office and Directorate of Repatriation, 1942–1947," 19-24, on microfilm C-5220. S.A.A.G. was an acronym for Special Assistant to the Adjutant General.
76 Oral History with John Gerald Connolly, interviewed by Steven Schwinghamer, Halifax, 5 July 2000, CMI Collection (00.07.05JC), 00:01:46.
77 Deployment Story of Walter Adlam, CMI Collection (S2012.855.1); Oral History with Colin Hunt, interviewed by Steven Schwinghamer, Halifax, 14 September 2000, CMI Collection (00.09.14CH), 00:48:23.
78 Oral History with Nick Wiebe, interviewed by Steven Schwinghamer, Halifax, 5 July 2000, CMI Collection (00.07.05NW), 01:07:28.
79 Oral History with Keith Craig, interviewed by Amy Coleman, Halifax, 26 July 2001, CMI Collection (01.07.26KC), 00:24:47.
80 Oral History with Alfred Cassidy, interviewed by Amy Coleman, Halifax, 16 June 2000, CMI Collection (00.06.16APC), 00:23:37.
81 Oral History with Victor Gray, 00:13:44.
82 Oral History with Joyce Woodford, 00:20:05.

83 Oral History with Victor Gray, 00:14:30; D. Smith, "Bringing Home the Wounded," 64; Deployment Story of Howard Michael Street, CMI Collection (S2012.2078.1).
84 Oral History with Floyd De Nicola, interviewed by Amy Coleman, Halifax, 30 June 2000, CMI Collection (00.06.30FD), 00:16:33ff.
85 Deployment Story of William Barker.
86 LAC, DND fonds, RG 24, file HQS-8536-1 "Return to Families of Canadian Officers and Service Personnel to Canada, 1940–1951," unpublished report, "History of S.A.A.G. Office and Directorate of Repatriation, 1942–1947," 32.
87 Oral History with Iris Shortell, interviewed by Steven Schwinghamer, Halifax, 14 May 2004, CMI Collection (04.05.14IS), 00:28:37.
88 Oral History with Paul and Joan Dumaine, interviewed by Steven Schwinghamer, aboard commemorative train from Halifax to Ottawa, 9 November 2006, CMI Collection (06.11.09PJD), 00:03:36.
89 Oral History with Patricia Ann Risley and Brenda Burton, interviewed by Kevin Lohnes, Halifax, 12 October 2006, CMI Collection (06.10.12ARBB), 00:07:05; Oral History with Margaret Hurley, interviewed by Kevin Lohnes, Halifax, 11 June 2007, CMI Collection (07.06.11MH), 00:11:34; Oral History with Florence Frantsi, interviewed by Kevin Lohnes, Halifax, 21 July 2006, CMI Collection (06.07.21FF), 00:17:17; Oral History with Dorothy Scott, interviewed by Steven Schwinghamer, Halifax, 10 August 2007, CMI Collection (07.08.10DS), 00:33:03.
90 Oral History with Jean Slater and Patricia Casselman, interviewed by Kevin Lohnes, Halifax, 13 August 2007, CMI Collection (07.08.13.JSPC), 00:08:19; Oral History with Iris Shortell, 00:53:48; Oral History with Sylvia Power, interviewed by Steven Schwinghamer, Halifax, 7 August 2000, CMI Collection (00.08.07SP), 00:22:12.
91 Oral History with Doreen Daley, interviewed by Steven Schwinghamer, Halifax, 16 August 2004, CMI Collection (04.08.16DD), 00:23:48.
92 Oral History with Mary Hamilton, interviewed by Kevin Lohnes, Halifax, 23 November 2006, CMI Collection (06.11.23MH), 00:21:15.
93 Oral History with Veronica Mitenko, interviewed by Steven Schwinghamer, Halifax, 16 July 2000, CMI Collection (00.07.16VM), 00:30:50.
94 Oral History with Jean Slater and Patricia Casselman, 00:10:26; Oral History with Petronella VanderDonk-Muise, interviewed by Amy Coleman, Halifax, 15 June 2001, CMI Collection (01.06.15PDM), 00:31:41; Oral History with Veronica Mitenko, 00:21:41.
95 Oral History with Hugh and Marjorie Asher, interviewed by Steven Schwinghamer, Halifax, 1 August 2000, CMI Collection (00.08.01HMA), 00:12:10; Oral History with Dorothy Scott, 00:37:30.
96 LAC, DND fonds, RG 24, 1903 Army Headquarters Central Registry, file HQS-8536-1-3, "Dependents Cdn Army Personnel Returning from Overseas – Nominal Rolls," Defensor to Canmilitry, 18, 19 and 31 July 1946; O'Hara, *From Romance to Reality*, 290; LAC, DND fonds, RG 24, file HQS-8536-1 "Return to Families of Canadian Officers and Service Personnel to Canada, 1940–1951," unpublished report, "History of S.A.A.G. Office and Directorate of Repatriation, 1942–1947," 34.
97 LAC, DND fonds, RG 24, 1903 Army Headquarters Central Registry, file HQS-8536-1-1, "Transfer to Canada of Dependents of Members of the Armed Forces serving Overseas, Canadian Red Cross Society," George Ellis, Director of Repatriation, to B.W. Browne, Assistant National Commissioner, Canadian Red Cross, 29 January 1947; LAC, DND fonds, RG 24, file HQS-8536-1 "Return to Families of Canadian Officers and Service

Personnel to Canada, 1940–1951," unpublished report, "History of S.A.A.G. Office and Directorate of Repatriation, 1942–1947," 26–27.

98 LAC, DND fonds, RG 24, file HQS-8536-1 "Return to Families of Canadian Officers and Service Personnel to Canada, 1940–1951," unpublished report, "History of S.A.A.G. Office and Directorate of Repatriation, 1942–1947," 28; LAC, DND fonds, RG 24, 1903 Army Headquarters Central Registry, file HQS-8536-1-1, "Transfer to Canada of Dependents of Members of the Armed Forces serving Overseas, Canadian Red Cross Society," Ellis to Browne, 29 January 1947; *Canadian War Bride Cookbook*, Division of Women's Voluntary Services, CMI Collection (R2015.376.1); *Money Hints for the Serviceman's Wife*, Bank of Montreal, CMI Collection (DI2015.154.17); Oral History with Veronica Mitenko, 00:31:54.

99 Oral History with Joyce Andersen, interviewed by Steven Schwinghamer, Halifax, 24 July 2000, CMI Collection (00.07.24JA), 00:21:08.

100 Oral History with Veronica Mitenko, 00:31:54.

101 LAC, DND fonds, RG 24, file HQS-8536-1 "Return to Families of Canadian Officers and Service Personnel to Canada, 1940–1951," unpublished report, "History of S.A.A.G. Office and Directorate of Repatriation, 1942–1947," 32.

102 LAC, Statutes of Canada, *An Act Respecting Citizenship, Nationality, Naturalization and Status of Aliens, 1946*, Ottawa: SC 10 George VI, chapter 15, sections 5 (a) and (b); 9(c); Matrix, "Mediated Citizenship," 68–75.

103 W.E. Sutherland, Note of Appreciation, HMT *Queen Mary*, 4 July 1946, CMI Collection (DI2014.433.31).

104 DBS, *Canada Year Book, 1945* (Ottawa: Edmond Cloutier, 1945), 168; DBS, *Canada Year Book, 1946* (Ottawa: Edmond Cloutier, 1946), 185; LAC, DND fonds, RG 24, file HQS-8536-1 "Return to Families of Canadian Officers and Service Personnel to Canada, 1940–1951," unpublished report, "History of S.A.A.G. Office and Directorate of Repatriation, 1942–1947," 30; Jarratt, "War Brides of New Brunswick" 12.

4. HEIGHT OF POSTWAR IMMIGRATION, 1946–1955

1 Immigration Story of Ilse Koerner, CMI Collection (S2012.169.1).

2 Statistics Canada, *Historical Statistics of Canada*, "Immigration." More specifically, 1,544,642 immigrants entered Canada during the 1950s. In 1942, 7,576 immigrants entered Canada. By 1948, this figure had increased to 125,414.

3 Canada, Department of Manpower and Immigration (hereafter cited as DMI), *Immigration Statistics 1966*, 26. From 1946 to 1955, 1,222,319 immigrants entered Canada.

4 LAC, DCI fonds, RG 26, vol. 24, file "Total Arrivals from U.S.A. and Overseas (By Port & Class), 1938–1952," statistical table "Number of Arrivals, via Ocean Ports, Classified by Port of Entry, Class, for the Calendar Year 1946," see subsequent tables for years 1947 to 1951; LAC, RG 26, vols. 21–22, files "Monthly Statistical Report – Immigration," see statistical tables for 1952–1954. These sources indicate that between 1946 and 1951, 297,566 individuals were given landed status at Halifax. From 1952 to 1954, a further 126,823 persons received landed status at Halifax. In total, 424,389 immigrants entered Canada through Pier 21 between 1946 and 1954.

5 Mitic and LeBlanc, *Pier 21*, 49, 61, 93. See also Thompson and van de Wiel, *Pier 21*, 111; Renaud, *Pier 21*, 30.

6 Hawkins, *Canada and Immigration*, 90.
7 Shephard, *Long Road Home*, 335–36.
8 LAC, IB fonds, RG 76, vol. 648, file A85451, pt. 2, "Admission of 4000 former Polish soldiers for agricultural work in Canada, 1946," Department of Labour Press Release, "Selection of Polish Veterans in Italy for Farm Work in Canada," 5 December 1946. The release is based on commentary from H.R. Hare, the head of the selection team sent from Canada to Italy to support the movement.
9 LAC, IB fonds, RG 76, vol. 648, file A85451, pt. 2, "Admission of 4000 former Polish soldiers for agricultural work in Canada, 1946," H.R. Hare, "Report of the Activities of Canadian Polish Movement Unit," 26 November 1946.
10 Margolian, *Unauthorized Entry*, 50–66. Facing a possible invasion by Hitler, in June 1940, British officials asked Canadian officials to accept approximately 3,000 German Prisoners of War and 4,000 civilian internees. See Canadian War Museum, "Democracy at War: Canadian Newspapers and the Second World War," http://www.warmuseum.ca/cwm/exhibitions/newspapers/canadawar/prisoners_e.shtml.
11 Gebhard, "Polish Veterans," 13.
12 LAC, DA fonds, RG 17, vol. 3191, file 126-2 "Entry of Polish Army Veterans into Canada," telegram from Norman Alexander Robertson, Acting High Commissioner for Canada in Great Britain to Secretary of State for External Affairs, 9 September 1946.
13 LAC, DCI fonds, RG 26, vol. 143, file 3-40-21, "Statistics: Ten Years of Post-War Immigration," report, George E. Fincham, "A Statistical Survey of Immigration to Canada," April 1952, 34.
14 Margolian, *Unauthorized Entry*, 62–63.
15 "Polish War Veterans Who Will Make Canada New Home Arrive at Halifax," *Globe and Mail*, 14 November 1946, 10.
16 LAC, IB fonds, RG 76, vol. 648, file A85451, pt. 1 "Admission of 4000 former Polish soldiers for agricultural work in Canada, 1946." Correspondence of October and November 1946 establishes amounts and mechanisms between Departments of Labour, National Defence, and External Affairs.
17 LAC, IB fonds, RG 76, vol. 648, file A85451, pt. 2 "Admission of 4000 former Polish soldiers for agricultural work in Canada, 1946." File contains correspondence and a detailed draft of the diplomatic note to be given to Viscount Addison, the United Kingdom's Secretary of State for Dominion Affairs, from Canadian representatives at Canada House in London, England.
18 Margolian, *Unauthorized Entry*, 54–56.
19 Gebhard, "Polish Veterans," 14. For further context, see Interview with Stanisław Kendzior, © Multicultural History Society of Ontario, Polish Collection, 5 November 1977 POL-3577-KEN.
20 LAC, IB fonds, RG 76, vol. 648, file A85451, pt. 1 "Admission of 4000 former Polish soldiers for agricultural work in Canada, 1946," McCrum, personal memo, 7 November 1946.
21 LAC, IB fonds, RG 76, vol. 648, file A85451, pt. 2 "Admission of 4000 former Polish soldiers for agricultural work in Canada, 1946," A.L. Jolliffe, memo for file, Ottawa, 27 November 1946; and Secretary of State for External Affairs to High Commissioner for Canada in the United Kingdom, Ottawa, 19 November 1946.
22 LAC, IB fonds, RG 76, vol. 648, file A85451, pt. 2 "Admission of 4000 former Polish soldiers for agricultural work in Canada, 1946," Munroe to Smith, Winnipeg, 5 December 1946.

23 LAC, IB fonds, RG 76, vol. 648, file A85451, pt. 2 "Admission of 4000 former Polish soldiers for agricultural work in Canada, 1946," newspaper clipping, "More than 1,000 Poles with TB Kept Off Farms," *Globe and Mail*, 14 December 1946.

24 LAC, IB fonds, RG 76, vol. 648, file A85451, pt. 2 "Admission of 4000 former Polish soldiers for agricultural work in Canada, 1946," C.F. Bentley to J.A. Glen, Ottawa, 15 December 1946.

25 LAC, IB fonds, RG 76, vol. 648, file A85451, pt. 2 "Admission of 4000 former Polish soldiers for agricultural work in Canada, 1946," Brigadier C.S. Thompson, Director General of Medical Services, confidential circular to District Medical Officers in Military Districts 1-4, 6, 10, 11, and 13, 12 November 1946; and Major General E.G. Weeks, Adjutant General, circular to Officers Commanding MD 1-4, 6, 10, 11, and 13, 15 November 1946.

26 LAC, IB fonds, RG 76, vol. 648, file A85451, pt. 2 "Admission of 4000 former Polish soldiers for agricultural work in Canada, 1946," Saskatchewan Provincial Labor-Progressive Party, "Resolution re Polish Fascist Immigrants," 2–3 November 1946; and North-West Council Labor-Progressive Party to W.L. McKenzie King, 17 November 1946.

27 Fincham, "A Statistical Survey of Immigration to Canada," 34.

28 Knowles, *Forging Our Legacy*, 67; Margolian, *Unauthorized Entry*, 62–63; Kelley and Trebilcock, *Making of the Mosaic*, 340. See also Dirks, *Canada's Refugee Policy*, 141–44, 152.

29 LAC, Department of Labour fonds, RG 27, vol. 628, file 23-7-17-5-1 "Polish Veterans – Health and Welfare – Issuance of Landing Permits to Individual Poles," Walter E. Harris, Minister of Citizenship and Immigration to Hon. Milton F. Gregg, Minister of Labour, Department of Labour, 12 March 1954.

30 LAC, DCI fonds, RG 26, vol. 143, file 3-40-21, "Statistics: Ten Years of Post-War Immigration," report, George E. Fincham, "A Statistical Survey of Immigration to Canada," April 1952, 34. In total, 4,112 Polish veterans received landed immigrant status and permanent residency in Canada.

31 Avery, *Reluctant Host*, 200.

32 Hawkins, *Canada and Immigration*, 90; Dirks, *Canada's Refugee Policy*, 151–64; Knowles, *Strangers at Our Gates*, 165.

33 Shephard, *Long Road Home*, 341. Canadian officials in Allied-occupied Germany soon demonstrated a preference for Baltic refugees, who were viewed as hardworking, healthy, and clean applicants.

34 Epp, *Refugees in Canada*, 10. The DP movement brought a total of 186,154 persons to Canada between 1947 and 1953.

35 LAC, IB fonds, RG 76, vol. 790, file 544-23-35, pt. 1 "Examination of Immigrants at Halifax, Nova Scotia (1941–1956)," pamphlet, Cunard White Star Line, "Important: Landing Arrangements," RMS *Aquitania*, Halifax, 23 August 1948. In 1970, the cities of Port Arthur and Fort William were amalgamated with the townships of Neebing and McIntyre to form the city of Thunder Bay, Ontario.

36 LAC, IB fonds, RG 76, vol. 790, file 544-23-35, pt. 1 "Examination of Immigrants at Halifax, Nova Scotia (1941–1956)," Irene Baird, Administration and Personnel Branch, Department of Mines and Resources to Miss. M. McEnaney, Talks Department, Canadian Broadcasting Corporation, 12 November 1948.

37 Canada, Parliament, House of Commons, *House of Commons Debates: Official Report, Third Session*, 2644–46; Whitaker, *Canadian Immigration Policy*, 14.

38 Knowles, *Forging Our Legacy*, 68.

39 Canada, *House of Commons Debates: Official Report, Third Session – Twentieth Parliament, Vol. 3*, 2644–46; Whitaker, *Canadian Immigration Policy* 14.
40 Knowles, *Forging Our Legacy*, 68.
41 Mitic and LeBlanc, *Pier 21*, 61.
42 Pier 21 Staff Story of Arthur J. Vaughan, CMI Collection (S2012.808.1).
43 Mitic and LeBlanc, *Pier 21*, 62.
44 Danys, *DP*, 95.
45 Mitic and LeBlanc, *Pier 21*, 62–63. The department had an ongoing internal discussion about its obligations regarding the health and welfare of immigrants who became indigent.
46 Taylor, *Polish Orphans of Tengeru*, 9–10, 223; Jack Regan, "'Kidnapped' Polish War Orphans Reach Halifax,'" *Halifax Mail-Star*, 8 September 1949, 1, 6.
47 Dirks, *Canada's Refugee Policy*, 167; Lappin, *Redeemed Children*, 10–11.
48 Abella and Troper, *None is Too Many*, 270–74; Lappin, *Redeemed Children*, 12–14; Vancouver Holocaust Education Centre, "Open Hearts, Closed Doors," see pages 3–6. The Jewish Immigrant Aid Society later changed its name to Jewish Immigrant Aid Services of Canada. In total, 1,123 Jewish war orphans were brought to Canada. More specifically, 783 orphans survived the concentration camps, while 229 orphans were in hiding during the Second World War.
49 Mitic and LeBlanc, *Pier 21*, 68–69.
50 Immigration Story of Celina Lieberman, CMI Collection (S2012.176.1).
51 Vancouver Holocaust Education Centre, "Open Hearts, Closed Doors," 4. More specifically, 790 orphans were resettled in Toronto and Montreal. Meanwhile, Manitoba received 131, British Columbia 38, Alberta 28, and Saskatchewan 12.
52 Immigration Story of Paul Kagan, CMI Collection (S2012.1395.1).
53 "Jewish War Orphans are Entertained at Synagogue, *Halifax Mail-Star*, 25 January 1949, 3.
54 Weinfeld, "Jews," 862–63. More specifically, 11,064 were displaced persons.
55 Znaimer, "Our Remnant of a Family," 236–37. See also Znaimer, "D.P. with a Future."
56 Immigration Story of Ann Kazimirski, CMI Collection (S2016.126.1).
57 Oral History with Jackie Eisen, interviewed by Amy Coleman, Halifax, 16 July 2003, CMI Collection (03.07.16JE), 00:21:19. According to her oral history, Eisen later filed a formal request under the *Access to Information Act* with the Canadian Security Intelligence Service to gain access to her family's security records. She later learned that their detention at Pier 21 was not due to her brother's strep throat, but rather her uncle's past membership in the Communist Party.
58 Shephard, *Long Road Home*, 336.
59 LAC, DCI fonds, RG 26, vol. 143, file 3-40-21, "Statistics: Ten Years of Post-War Immigration," report, George E. Fincham, "A Statistical Survey of Immigration to Canada," April 1952, 38.
60 Mitic and LeBlanc, *Pier 21*, 63–65.
61 Immigration Story of Ernests Kraulis, CMI Collection (S2012.160.1).
62 Dirks, *Canada's Refugee Policy*, 166.
63 For further context on SS *Walnut*, see Mannik, *Photography, Memory, and Refugee Identity*.
64 LAC, IB fonds, RG 76, vol. 668, file C19279 "Admission to Canada of the Corvette WALNUT with 261 refugee passengers (from Sweden) (Estonians) (Latvians) (Lithuanians)

(Finns) (Austrians) (Poles) (lists)," microfilm reel C-10602, Dr. Alfred A. Valdmanis, "Report on 347 Refugees from Sweden arriving on S.S. 'Walnut' on the morning of December 13th, 1948, at the port of Halifax, N.S."

65 "347 Refugees, Fleeing Reds, Believed On Way To Halifax," *Halifax Mail*, 11 December 1948, 1, 3.

66 Oral History with Florence Waldron, interviewed by Shelagh MacKenzie and James H. Morrison, Halifax, 21 April 1998, CMI Collection (98.04.21FW), 00:38:58. In her oral history interview, Waldron mentions the arrival of SS *Sarabande* in either November or December. However, the *Sarabande* landed on 19 August 1949. SS *Walnut* was the only Viking Boat to arrive late in the year. The vessel landed at Halifax on 13 December 1948. Therefore, it is likely she was referring to the *Walnut*.

67 LAC, IB fonds, RG 76, vol. 668, file C19279 "Admission to Canada of the Corvette WALNUT with 261 refugee passengers (from Sweden) (Estonians) (Latvians) (Lithuanians) (Finns) (Austrians) (Poles) (lists)," microfilm reel C-10602, memo for file, W.A. McFaul, Department of Mines and Resources, 11 December 1948.

68 Oral History with Alison Trapnell, 00:46:04.

69 LAC, IB fonds, RG 76, vol. 668, file C19279 "Admission to Canada of the Corvette WALNUT with 261 refugee passengers (from Sweden) (Estonians) (Latvians) (Lithuanians) (Finns) (Austrians) (Poles) (lists)," microfilm reel C-10602, Valdmanis, "Report on 347 Refugees from Sweden arriving on S.S. 'Walnut' on the morning of December 13th, 1948, at the port of Halifax, N.S."

70 Aun, *Political Refugees*, 24–25. Aun lists 355 passengers, while the archival record indicates 347 refugees.

71 LAC, IB fonds, RG 76, vol. 668, file C19279 "Admission to Canada of the Corvette WALNUT with 261 refugee passengers (from Sweden) (Estonians) (Latvians) (Lithuanians) (Finns) (Austrians) (Poles) (lists)," microfilm reel C-10602, memo "Appeal of Grigori Kattai" from Director, IB to Minister of Mines and Resources, 18 February 1949. See also, memo "Appeal of Johannes Liivamees" from Director, IB to Minister of Mines and Resources, 18 February 1949.

72 LAC, IB fonds, RG 76, vol. 668, file C19279 "Admission to Canada of the Corvette WALNUT with 261 refugee passengers (from Sweden) (Estonians) (Latvians) (Lithuanians) (Finns) (Austrians) (Poles) (lists)," microfilm reel C-10602, McCrum to C.E.S. Smith, Commissioner of Immigration, Department of Mines and Resources, 15 January 1949.

73 LAC, IB fonds, RG 76, vol. 668, file C19279 "Admission to Canada of the Corvette WALNUT with 261 refugee passengers (from Sweden) (Estonians) (Latvians) (Lithuanians) (Finns) (Austrians) (Poles) (lists)," microfilm reel C-10602, C.E.S. Smith to McCrum, 13 December 1948.

74 "Refugees Hold Farewell Party," *Halifax Mail-Star*, 31 January 1949, 3.

75 Oral History with Ausma Levalds Rowberry, interviewed by Steven Schwinghamer, Halifax, 31 July 2002, CMI Collection (02.07.31ALR), 01:14:01.

76 "Canada's 50,000th DP Starts New Life in New Home," *Globe and Mail*, 26 February 1949, 17.

77 Oral History with Ausma Levalds Rowberry, 01:14:01.

78 Mitic and LeBlanc, *Pier 21*, 65–66, 69–70.

79 Immigration Story of Ilmar Rakfeldt, CMI Collection (S2012.358.1).

80 Canadian Immigration Historical Society, "Canada's Refugee Programme," 7; Wyman, *DPs*, 190. This postwar movement was comprised of Poles (23 per cent), Ukrainians (16

per cent), Germans and Austrians (11 per cent), Jews (10 per cent), Latvians (6 per cent), Lithuanians (6 per cent), Hungarians (5 per cent), Czechs and Slovaks (3 per cent), Dutch (3 per cent), and Russians (3 per cent). These groups represented 86 per cent of all Europeans permitted to enter Canada in this period. See Knowles, *Forging Our Legacy*, 68–69.

81 Kelley and Trebilcock, *Making of the Mosaic*, 328; LAC, "Immigration History."

82 Knowles, *Forging Our Legacy*, 72.

83 "100,000th European D.P. Welcomed at Halifax," *Halifax Mail-Star*, 5 May 1951, 1, 6.

84 Knowles, *Forging Our Legacy*, 69, 72–73.

85 Thompson and van de Wiel, *Pier 21*, 97. See also Tinkham, "Lasting Impressions"; Pier 21 Staff Story of Arthur J. Vaughan.

86 Mitic and LeBlanc, *Pier 21*, 73–74. The last chartered refugee transport arrived in Halifax aboard MS *Anna Salén*.

87 Thompson and van de Wiel, *Pier 21*, 100; Institute of the Sisters of Service of Canada, "Pier 21 in Halifax." Generally, when a new sister arrived at the immigration facility, another one departed. Sister Dulaska served from 1934 to 1942 and from 1947 to 1962, followed by Sister Kelly, who served from 1950 to 1955 and returned in time to assist with the closure of the facility, and Sister Liota, who served from 1955 to 1969.

88 Oral History with Sister Florence Kelly, 00:07:57.

89 Oral History with Sister Salvatrice Liota, interviewed by James H. Morrison, Toronto, 27 May 1998, CMI Collection (98.05.27SL), 00:05:55; 00:16:21.

90 Mitic and LeBlanc, *Pier 21*, 76–78.

91 Immigration Story of Marianne Ferguson, CMI Collection (S2012.122.1); Tinkham, "Lasting Impressions," 13; Mitic and LeBlanc, *Pier 21*, 78–80. Ferguson went on to become one of the longest-serving volunteers at Pier 21. She added to her work at the immigration facility when she returned to Pier 21 as a volunteer for the museum after 1999.

92 Thompson and van de Wiel, *Pier 21*, 102; Mitic and LeBlanc, *Pier 21*, 82.

93 Thompson and van de Wiel, *Pier 21*, 102.

94 Tinkham, "Lasting Impressions," 14.

95 "Serves New Canadians," *Halifax Mail-Star*, 8 March 1951, 18; CEIC, "Pier 21 Story," 11.

96 Pier 21 Staff Story of Malcolm MacLeod, CMI Collection (S2012.1773.1).

97 "Serves New Canadians," 18; CEIC, "Pier 21 Story," 11.

98 Immigration Story of Maureen Pettigrew, CMI Collection (S2012.128.1).

99 Renaud, *Pier 21*, 32. Once processed through civil and medical examination, Gluck travelled by train to Montreal, where with the help of the Canadian Jewish Congress, he was able to secure employment and save enough money to bring his surviving family members to Canada.

100 Hutten, *Uprooted*, 64. De Jong further asserts that "both bars and cages were controversial even with management. The cages were eventually removed in 1956, to be replaced by a friendlier counter. Not until the mid-1960s were the bars on the windows removed."

101 Immigration Story of Dorothy Van Helvert, CMI Collection (S2012.262.1); Hutten, *Uprooted*, 65.

102 Renaud, *Pier 21*, 34. Gerry Van Kessel later became director general of the refugees branch in the Department of Citizenship and Immigration, and coordinator of the Intergovernmental Consultations on Asylum, Refugees and Migration Policy, in Geneva, Switzerland.

103 Immigration Story of Harry and Heidi Kornelsen, CMI Collection (S2012.479.1).
104 Pier 21 Staff Story of Arthur J. Vaughan.
105 Immigration Story of Milan V. Gregor, CMI Collection (S2012.215.1).
106 Oral History with Wolfgang Christl, interviewed by Emily Burton, Vancouver, 20 February 2014, CMI Collection (14.02.20WC), 00:07:43.
107 Immigration Story of Milan V. Gregor.
108 Immigration Story of Peter Hessel.
109 Immigration Story of Willem Kreeft.
110 CEIC, "Pier 21 Story," 8; Mitic and LeBlanc, *Pier 21*, 73.
111 Comparisons drawn between interior plans for Shed 21 prepared by the CNR (1928), Halifax Harbour Commissioners (1934) and the NHB (1945), HPA #8489, 10882, 15646 and 15647.
112 HPA #10882 and 15646.
113 Crosman, *Recollections*, 190.
114 HPA #10979 and 10882.
115 HPA#10882; NHB, "Ocean Terminals Facilities Leased By Canadian Immigration," 15 November 1954, Drawing 51103-110, as consulted from HPA digitized document #18196.
116 LAC, IB fonds, RG 76, vol. 666, file C1594, pt. 2, "Immigration Building at Halifax, Nova Scotia (publication) (plans)," report quoted in letter from J. Biggar to J.S. Fraser, 3 January 1928.
117 NHB, "Ocean Terminals Facilities Leased By Canadian Immigration," 15 November 1954, Drawing 51103-110, as consulted from HPA digitized document #18196.
118 Mitic and LeBlanc, *Pier 21*, 151–52.
119 HPA #10882; DPW, "Customs Annex – Pier 21 – Halifax, Nova Scotia," 10 April 1956, as consulted from HPA #10998. While Pier 21 was undergoing renovations, customs inspections were carried out on the pier and passengers were routed directly to that area after they had completed their immigration examinations. Canadian customs officials did not permit passengers to disembark from their ships until all baggage was unloaded. As a result, disembarkation and immigration examination were often deferred until customs officers were ready to proceed. See LAC, IB fonds, RG 76, vol. 790, file 544-23-35, pt. 1 "Examination of Immigrants at Halifax, Nova Scotia (1941–1956)," memo from J.W. Pickersgill, Minister, DCI to John H. Dickey, M.P., 12 July 1955.
120 CNR, "Proposed Tunnel Between Shed 21 and Immigration Building at Halifax," 10 September 1953, as consulted from HPA digitized document #10886.
121 HPA #10899; Oral History with Jim Dauphinee, Marguerite Day and George LaRue, 00:04:37.
122 See HPA #10886.
123 CEIC, "Pier 21 Story," 12.
124 Pier 21 Staff Story of Arthur J. Vaughan.
125 Statistics Canada, *Historical Statistics of Canada*, "Immigration." More specifically, 1,544,642 immigrants entered Canada during the 1950s.

5. FINAL YEARS OF AN IMMIGRATION SHED, 1955–1971

1 Oral History with Heather Wineberg, 00:08:14.
2 CEIC, "Pier 21 Story," 13.

3 Immigration Story of the Pijl Family.
4 Immigration Story of Emilio Poggi, CMI Collection (S2012.247.1).
5 Oral History with Michael McCarthy, interviewed by Kevin Lohnes, Halifax, 7 August 2007, CMI Collection (07.08.07MM), 00:35:12.
6 CEIC, "Pier 21 Story," 15.
7 Immigration Story of Amélia Vieira Da Silva, CMI Collection (S2017.231.1); Oral History with Dr. Lloyd Hirtle, 00:16:36. For further context, see LAC, Statutes of Canada, *An Act Respecting Immigration and Immigrants, 1952* (Ottawa: SC 1 Elizabeth II, chapter 42), 239.
8 Immigration Story of Frank Giorno, CMI Collection (S2012.248.1).
9 Immigration Story of Martha Hochheimer, CMI Collection (S2015.276.1).
10 Oral History with Heather Wineberg, 00:08:14.
11 CEIC, "Pier 21 Story," 12.
12 Immigration Story of Teresa Perri, CMI Collection (S2012.1493.1).
13 Immigration Story of Angela Crosdale, CMI Collection (S2012.737.1).
14 Immigration Story of Maria Rosaria Pagano, CMI Collection (S2012.246.1).
15 *Strangers for the Day*, directed by Georges Dufaux and Jacques Godbout (National Film Board of Canada, 1962), documentary short film, http://www.nfb.ca/film/strangers_for_the_day.
16 Oral History with Sister Salvatrice Liota, 00:45:17.
17 CEIC, "Pier 21 Story," 15; Mitic and LeBlanc, *Pier 21*, 85–87.
18 CEIC, "Pier 21 Story," 12–13.
19 Immigration Story of the Pijl Family.
20 CEIC, "Pier 21 Story," 15; Mitic and LeBlanc, *Pier 21*, 85–87.
21 Immigration Story of W.A.T. Van den Byllaardt.
22 Immigration Story of the Johansen Family.
23 Immigration Story of the Pijl Family.
24 "Immigrants Kept Waiting," *Halifax Mail-Star*, 6 November 1965, 3. Pier 21 volunteers complained that the passengers should have been allowed to stay on board to wait.
25 CEIC, "Pier 21 Story," 9; Mitic and LeBlanc, *Pier 21*, 91–92.
26 Alexandra Zabjek, "How 'the 56ers' Changed Canada," *Ottawa Citizen*, 15 October 2006, B4.
27 Keyserlingk, introduction to *Breaking Ground*, vii; see also Kage, "Settlement," 100.
28 Dirks, *Canada's Refugee Policy*, 202; Hawkins, *Canada and Immigration*, 114. More specifically, 37,566 Hungarian refugees were resettled in Canada between November 1956 and December 1958.
29 Oral History with Judith Stoffman, interviewed by Emily Burton, Vancouver, 24 February 2014, CMI Collection (14.02.24JS), 00:06:11.
30 Oral History with Gaby Niloff, interviewed by Amy Coleman, Halifax, 7 February 2004, CMI Collection (04.02.07GN), 00:01:30.
31 "City Rises Early to Welcome Refugees," *Halifax Mail-Star*, 17 December 1956, 3.
32 "Hungarian MP Rebuilding Life in Canada," *Halifax Mail-Star*, 30 May 1957, 39. At Pier 21, Hungarian refugees were assisted by the following voluntary service organizations: Canadian Red Cross, Salvation Army, Baptist Federation of Canada, Sisters of Service, Imperial Order Daughters of the Empire, JIAS, YMCA, and YWCA.
33 Oral History with Sister Salvatrice Liota, 00:22:03.
34 Oral History with Sister Salvatrice Liota, 00:23:40.
35 Oral History with Florence Waldron, 00:15:43.

36 CEIC, "Pier 21 Story," 13; Mitic and LeBlanc, *Pier 21*, 107.
37 Oral History with Tibor Lukács, 00:47:52, 00:51:50.
38 Oral History with Tibor Lukács, 00:51:50.
39 Immigration Story of László Galambos, CMI Collection (S2012.154.1).
40 Dreisziger et al., *Struggle and Hope*, 207–08; Dreisziger, "Refugee Experience," 68. In "The Refugee Experience in Canada and the Evolution of the Hungarian-Canadian Community," Dreisziger notes that half of the refugees were under the age of twenty-four.
41 Keyserlingk, introduction to *Breaking Ground*, vii; Kage, "Settlement," 100; Hidas, "Canada," 75.
42 Dreisziger et al., *Struggle and Hope*, 207–08; Dreisziger, "Refugee Experience," 68.
43 Citizenship and Immigration Canada, *Canada Facts and Figures 2014*, https://bit.ly/36kwoGx. See page 3 of document.
44 LAC, IB fonds, RG 76, vol. 753, file 514-40 "Detained Immigrants – General File," memo, "Seamen Deserters – Methods of Apprehension" from Chief, Policy and Liaison Division, DCI to Acting Director of Immigration, DCI, 6 March 1963; and memo, "Use of Immigration Facilities – Halifax, N.S." from R.M. Casselman, Acting Atlantic District Superintendent, DCI to Director, Operations Division, DCI, 6 March 1963.
45 Oral History with Tibor Lukács, 00:50:31.
46 Pier 21 Staff Story of Malcolm MacLeod.
47 LAC, IB fonds, RG 76, vol. 719, file 510-8 "Administration of Immigration Halls & Detention Quarters," memo from Director, Pacific Region, DCI to Director, Canadian Service, DCI, 15 February 1965.
48 CEIC, "Pier 21 Story," 12; Mitic and LeBlanc, *Pier 21*, 114.
49 Oral History with Frank Wright, interviewed by Therese Lamie, Halifax, 1980, CMI Collection (80.--.--FW), 00:16:48.
50 "E. German pair unable to defect," *Halifax Chronicle Herald*, 28 March 1962, 1.
51 Embassy of Canada to Cuba, "Canada - Cuba Relations."
52 Oral History with Sister Salvatrice Liota, 00:08:59, 00:13:13; CEIC, "Pier 21 Story," 14.
53 CEIC, "Pier 21 Story," 14.
54 Canada, Parliament, *House of Commons Debates*, 17 September 1964 (James Roy Tucker, Liberal), https://www.lipad.ca/full/permalink/2317642/.
55 Canada, Parliament, *House of Commons Debates*, 17 September 1964 (René Tremblay, Liberal), https://www.lipad.ca/full/permalink/2317643/.
56 LAC, PCO fonds, RG 2, vol. 2380, file "Orders in Council – Décrets du Conseil," "Immigration Act, Immigration Regulations, Part 1, Amended," P.C. 1967-1616, 16 August 1967. For context, see Kelley and Trebilcock, *Making of the Mosaic*, 360–63; Hawkins, *Canada and Immigration*, 424.
57 For further context, see Raska, *Czech Refugees*, 139–73; Madokoro, "Good Material," 161–71.
58 Jewish Immigrant Aid Services of Canada, "JIAS Canada"—see page 6.
59 Mitic and LeBlanc, *Pier 21*, 82–83. Although the Catholic Church was well represented at Pier 21 by the Sisters of Service, a priest was also sent to Halifax's Ocean Terminals to serve as a port chaplain. The first Catholic priest to serve at Pier 21 was Father Pius, who began his service during the Great Depression. He was followed in this role by Father Ed Flaherty (1942–1945), Father Anthony DesLauriers (1945–1956), and Father Leo J. Burns (1956–1968). In 1968, Father J.R. Brown began his work as the Catholic

port chaplain, and stayed until his retirement in 1986. According to the *Mail-Star*, Father Joseph Hompes served as a Catholic port chaplain during the initial arrival of Hungarian refugees to Pier 21 in December 1956. His term of service is unclear.

60 CEIC, "Pier 21 Story," 15–16.

61 Immigration Story of Libor and Jiřina Roštík, CMI Collection (S2012.2110.1).

62 CEIC, "Pier 21 Story," 16; Mitic and LeBlanc, "Pier 21," 83.

63 Canada, Parliament, *House of Commons Debates*, 16 December 1968 (J. Michael Forrestall, Progressive Conservative), https://www.lipad.ca/full/permalink/2567073/; Canada, Parliament, *House of Commons Debates*, 16 December 1968 (J. Michael Forrestall, Progressive Conservative), https://www.lipad.ca/full/permalink/2567075/; Canada, Parliament, *House of Commons Debates*, 16 December 1968 (Allan Joseph MacEachen, Liberal), https://www.lipad.ca/full/permalink/2567076/.

64 CEIC, "Pier 21 Story," 16; Mitic and LeBlanc, "Pier 21," 83.

65 Kelley and Trebilcock, *Making of the Mosaic*, 365–66.

66 McIntosh, *Collectors*, 344–45.

67 CMI, "Escape to the Land Beyond the Wall," http://www.pier21.ca/canadian-stories/escape-to-the-land-beyond-the-wall.

68 Oral History with Alison Trapnell, 00:08:44; Oral History with Frank Wright, 01:36:25.

69 Identification card issued to Veronika Martenová Charles in Toronto, 1970, CMI Collection (DI2017.962.11); CMI, "Escape to the Land Beyond the Wall."

70 Immigration Story of Raphael Alcolado, CMI Collection (S2014. 188.1).

71 LAC, IB fonds, RG 76, vol. 1032, file 5003-1-35 "Immigration – Administration Ports & Posts – Halifax, N.S.," memo "Immigration Operations – Pier 21, Halifax" from J.C. Best, Assistant Deputy Minister, Operations, DMI to W.C. Stewart, Director General, Atlantic Region, DMI, 14 July 1970.

72 LAC, IB fonds, RG 76, vol. 1032, file 5003-1-35 "Immigration – Administration Ports & Posts – Halifax, N.S.," memo "Confidential Study Immigration Operations Pier 21" from W.C. Stewart to J.C. Morrison, Director General, Operations, DMI, 14 May 1968. See attached, R. Casselman, Director, Immigration Operations, "Report on Pier 21 Operations – Halifax District Office."

73 Mitic and LeBlanc, *Pier 21*, 113.

74 "Loud Farewell," *Halifax Mail-Star*, 28 July 1960, 1; "Essex Parting to Cost $5,000," *Halifax Mail-Star*, 29 July 1960, 7; Mitic and LeBlanc, *Pier 21*, 119.

75 Mitic and LeBlanc, *Pier 21*, 122. The sprinkler system was installed at a cost $24,800.

76 "Bill Shaw's gate to the Promised Land," *Maclean's*, January 1970, 30.

77 Mitic and LeBlanc, *Pier 21*, 113, 122; "Bill Shaw," *Maclean's*, January 1970, 30; HPA #10899.

78 Halifax International Airport Authority, "History," 3–4. By 1980, approximately 1.7 million passengers utilized the services of the Halifax International Airport.

79 Tinkham, "Lasting Impressions," 3.

80 "Bill Shaw," *Maclean's*, January 1970, 30.

81 Canada, DMI, *Immigration Statistics 1970*, 20; LAC, DCI fonds, RG 26, vol. 24, file "Total Arrivals from U.S.A. and Overseas (By Port & Class), 1938–1952," statistical table "Number of Arrivals, via Ocean Ports, Classified by Port of Entry, Class, for the Calendar Year 1951." Of the 98,695 ocean liner passengers who arrived at Pier 21 in 1951, 93,758 were landed immigrants, 3,592 were returning Canadians, 1,320 were tourists, and 25 were rejected from entering Canada. In comparison, of the 2,281 travellers who arrived

at Pier 21 in 1970, 1,187 were immigrants from overseas, 172 were immigrants from the United States, 595 were returning Canadian residents, 323 were non-immigrant travellers, while 4 individuals were denied entry into the country.

82 Clarence Roberts, "Immigration office moving," *Halifax Mail-Star*, 29 March 1971, 1.

83 LAC, IB fonds, RG 76, vol. 1168, file 5400-3-1/35, "Examination–General Series–Ocean Ports–Examination, Halifax, 1966–1971," memo from J.C. Best to Deputy Minister, DMI, 22 April 1971.

84 Roberts, "Immigration office moving," *Halifax Mail-Star*, 29 March 1971, 8.

CONCLUSION

1 Oral History with Margaret Aucoin and Tom Kearsey, interviewed by Steven Schwinghamer, Halifax, 22 June 2010, CMI Collection (10.06.22MATK), 00:41:21; 01:43:13; Tom Kearsey, former principal of NSNI, correspondence with Steven Schwinghamer, 10 April 2016. Kearsey provided authors with an unpublished report, "The Nova Scotia Nautical Institute at Pier 21," 1–6. The NSNI was the outcome of an integration of programs for education at vocational and technical colleges, including the Nova Scotia Institute of Technology.

2 Mitic and LeBlanc, *Pier 21*, 125–26; Parks Canada, "Pier 21," 1, 5, 9.

3 Tinkham, "Lasting Impressions," 3.

4 Mitic and LeBlanc, *Pier 21*, 127–29; CBC News, "Halifax celebrates." That same day, eighteen war brides and their husbands renewed their wedding vows in a special service.

5 Thompson and van de Wiel, *Pier 21*, 131.

6 Canada, Parliament, House of Commons Debates, 10 March 2010 (The Governor General), https://www.lipad.ca/full/permalink/4443169/.

7 CMI, "About." This reflects the mandate set in the *Museums Act*.

8 CBC News, "Halifax's Pier 21."

9 Parks Canada, "Champlain Maritime Station"; Pierre-André Normandin, "La Gare maritime Champlain sera démolie malgré son statut patrimonial," *Le Soleil* (Quebec City), 29 mars 2011, http://www.lapresse.ca/le-soleil/actualites/societe/201103/28/01-4384104-la-gare-maritime-champlain-sera-demolie-malgre-son-statut-patrimonial.php; Delsan-AIM, "Gare Maritime Champlain Deconstruction," http://www.delsan-aim.com/en/projects/gare-maritime-champlain/.

10 Comment card from Stefania, ca. 2018–2019, "What Pier 21 Means to Me," *The Pier 21 Story*, CMI. Stefania arrived at Pier 21 with her mother and two brothers on 21 March 1965; Comment card from anonymous, ca. 2018–2019, "What Pier 21 Means to Me"; Comment card from anonymous, ca. 2018–2019, "What Pier 21 Means to Me"; Comment card from Antonio Agostinelli, ca. 2018–2019, "What Pier 21 Means to Me." Agostinelli's grandparents, mother, Adelina, and some of her nine siblings arrived at Pier 21 from San Bartolomeo, Galdo, Italy, in March 1959; Comment card from Karen Scott, Toronto, 24 March 2019, "What Pier 21 Means to Me."

11 LAC, IB fonds, RG 76, vol. 666, file C1594, pt. 1 "Immigration Building – Halifax, NS," J.B. Hunter to G.A. Bell, 5 November 1920; Crosman, *Recollections*, 98.

12 LAC, DCI fonds, RG 26, vol. 24, file "Total Arrivals from U.S.A. and Overseas (By Port & Class), 1938–1952," statistical table "Number of Arrivals, via Ocean Ports, Classified by Port of Entry, Class, for the Calendar Year 1946." See subsequent tables for years 1947

to 1951; LAC, RG 26, vols. 21–22, files "Monthly Statistical Report – Immigration," see statistical tables for 1952–1954.

13 Mitic and LeBlanc, *Pier 21*, 49, 61, 93; Thompson and van de Wiel, *Pier 21*, 111; Renaud, *Pier 21*, 30.

14 Parks Canada, "Pier 21," 11.

BIBLIOGRAPHY

ARCHIVAL SOURCES

Canadian Museum of Immigration
Archival Collection
Digital Collection
Oral History Collection
Story Collection

Government of Nova Scotia
Nova Scotia Historical Vital Statistics

Halifax Municipal Archives
Minutes of City Council

Halifax Port Authority
Archival Collection

Library and Archives Canada
Canadian National Railway fonds (RG 30)
Department of Agriculture fonds (RG 17)

Department of Citizenship and Immigration fonds (RG 26)
Department of External Affairs fonds (RG 25)
Department of National Defence fonds (RG 24)
Department of National Health and Welfare fonds (RG 29)
Department of Railways and Canals fonds (RG 43)
Department of Transport fonds (RG 12)
Immigration Branch fonds (RG 76)
National Harbours Board fonds (RG 66)
Privy Council Office (RG 2)
Royal Commissions fonds (RG 33)
Statutes of Canada

Nova Scotia Archives
Critique of Plans for Ocean Terminals (MG 1, vol. 1501)
Foley Bros. et al. Construction of Ocean Terminals, 1986-490 (photograph series)
H.B. Jefferson fonds (MG 1, vols. 484–515, 1224–1228)

United Kingdom National Archives
Archival Collection

NEWSPAPERS AND MAGAZINES

Contract Record (Toronto)
Globe and Mail
Halifax Chronicle
Halifax Chronicle Herald
Halifax Daily Echo
Halifax Evening Mail
Halifax Herald
Halifax Mail
Halifax Mail-Star
Halifax Morning Chronicle
Le Soleil (Quebec City)
Maclean's
Ottawa Citizen
The Globe (Toronto)

GOVERNMENT PUBLICATIONS

Canada. Department of Manpower and Immigration. *Immigration Statistics 1966*. Ottawa: Queen's Printer and Controller of Stationery, 1967.

———. *Immigration Statistics 1970*. Ottawa: Information Canada, 1971.

———. Department of Railways and Canals and Canadian Government Railways. Frederick Cowie. *Report to the Honourable Frank Cochrane on Halifax Harbour and the Development of a Project of Modern Ocean Terminals*. Ottawa: Department of Railways and Canals, 1913.

———. Dominion Bureau of Statistics. *The Canada Year Book 1930*. Ottawa: Printer to the King's Most Excellent Majesty, 1930.

———. *The Canada Year Book 1937*. Ottawa: King's Printer, 1937.

———. *The Canada Year Book 1939*. Ottawa: King's Printer, 1939.

———. *The Canada Year Book 1945*. Ottawa: King's Printer, 1945.

———. *The Canada Year Book 1946*. Ottawa: King's Printer, 1946.

———. Employment and Immigration Commission. Public Affairs. Nova Scotia Region. "The Pier 21 Story: Halifax, 1924–1971." Halifax: Canada Employment and Immigration Commission, 1978.

———. Parliament. House of Commons. *House of Commons Debates*. Linked Parliamentary Data Project. http://www.lipad.ca.

———. Parliament. House of Commons. *House of Commons Debates: Official Report, Third Session – Twentieth Parliament, Volume 3*. Ottawa: King's Printer and Controller of Stationery, 1947.

———. Veterans Affairs Canada. "The British Commonwealth Air Training Plan." http://www.veterans.gc.ca/eng/remembrance/history/second-world-war/british-commonwealth-air-training-plan.

Canadian Museum of Immigration. "About the Canadian Museum of Immigration at Pier 21." http://www.pier21.ca/about.

———. "Escape to the Land Beyond the Wall." http://www.pier21.ca/canadian-stories/escape-to-the-land-beyond-the-wall.

Canadian War Museum. "Democracy at War: Canadian Newspapers and the Second World War." http://www.warmuseum.ca/cwm/exhibitions/newspapers/canadawar/prisoners_e.shtml.

Citizenship and Immigration Canada. *Canada Facts and Figures: Immigrant Overview Permanent Residents, 2014*. https://bit.ly/36kwoGx.

Embassy of Canada to Cuba. "Canada - Cuba Relations." http://www.canadainternational.gc.ca/cuba/bilateral_relations_bilaterales/canada_cuba.aspx?lang=eng.

Hatch, F. J., and Canada. Department of National Defence. Directorate of History. *Aerodrome of Democracy: Canada and the British Commonwealth Air Training Plan 1939–1945*. Ottawa: Directorate of History, Department of National Defence, 1983.

Library and Archives Canada. "Border Entries." https://www.bac-lac.gc.ca/eng/discover/immigration/immigration-records/Pages/border-entries.aspx.

———. "Immigration History: Ethnic and Cultural Groups: German." http://www.bac-lac.gc.ca/eng/discover/immigration/history-ethnic-cultural/pages/german.aspx.

———. Statutes of Canada. *An Act Respecting Citizenship, Nationality, Naturalization and Status of Aliens, 1946*. Ottawa: SC 10 George VI, chapter 15.

———. Statutes of Canada. *An Act Respecting Immigration, 1910*. Ottawa: SC 9-10 Edward VII, chapter 27.

———. Statutes of Canada. *An Act Respecting Immigration and Immigrants, 1906*. Ottawa: SC 6 Edward VII, chapter 19.

———. Statutes of Canada. *An Act Respecting Immigration and Immigrants, 1952*. Ottawa: SC 1 Elizabeth II, chapter 42.

———. Statutes of Canada. *An Act to Amend the Immigration Act, 1919*. Ottawa: SC 9-10 George V, chapter 25.

Parks Canada. "Backgrounder: Pier 21, Halifax." Updated 26 September 2013. http://bit.ly/2hMvd4j.

———. "Champlain Maritime Station: Recognized Federal Heritage Building, Québec, Quebec," http://www.pc.gc.ca/apps/dfhd/page_fhbro_eng.aspx?id=8499.

———. "Pier 21 National Historic Site of Canada: Commemorative Integrity Statement." Parks Canada, 2004.

Stacey, C. P. *The Canadian Army, 1939–1945: An Official Historical Summary*. Ottawa: Edmond Cloutier, King's Printer, 1948.

Statistics Canada. *Historical Statistics of Canada.* "Immigration: Immigrant Arrivals in Canada, 1852 to 1977 (Table A350)." http://www.statcan.gc.ca/pub/11-516-x/sectiona/A350-eng.csv.

PUBLISHED SOURCES

Abella, Irving, and Harold Troper. *None is Too Many: Canada and the Jews of Europe.* Toronto: University of Toronto Press, 2012.

Auger, Martin F. *Prisoners of the Home Front: German POWs and "Enemy Aliens" in Southern Quebec, 1940–46.* Vancouver: University of British Columbia Press, 2005.

Aun, Karl. *The Political Refugees: A History of the Estonians in Canada.* Toronto: McClelland & Stewart, 1985.

Avery, Donald H. *Reluctant Host: Canada's Response to Immigrant Workers, 1896–1994.* Toronto: McClelland & Stewart, 1995.

Baumel, Judith Tydor. "Twice a Refugee: The Jewish Refugee Children in Great Britain during Evacuation, 1939–1943." *Jewish Social Studies*, vol. 45 no. 2 (Spring 1983): 175–84.

Bilson, Geoffrey. "Dr Frederick Montizambert (1843–1929): Canada's first Director General of Public Health." *Medical History*, vol. 29, no. 4 (1985), 386–400.

———. *The Guest Children: The Story of British Child Evacuees Sent to Canada During World War II.* Saskatoon, SK: Fifth House, 1988.

Cameron, Ian. *Quarantine: What is Old is New: Halifax and the Lawlor's Island Quarantine Station, 1866–1938.* Halifax: New World Publishing, 2007.

Canadian Immigration Historical Society. "Canada's Refugee Programme – 1945–1970." *Canadian Immigration Historical Society Bulletin* 45 (January 2005): 7–14.

Carrigan, D. Owen. "The Immigrant Experience in Halifax, 1881–1931." *Canadian Ethnic Studies*, vol. 20, no. 3 (January 1988): 28–41.

CBC News. "Halifax celebrates gateway to Canada, Pier 21." https://www.cbc.ca/news/canada/halifax-celebrates-gateway-to-canada-pier-21-1.175078.

———. "Halifax's Pier 21 designated national museum." http://www.cbc.ca/news/canada/nova-scotia/halifax-s-pier-21-designated-national-museum-1.1032627.

Chilton, Lisa. *Receiving Canada's Immigrants: The Work of the State before 1930.* Ottawa: Canadian Historical Association, 2016.

Crosman, Fenton. *Recollections of an Immigration Officer: The Memoirs of Fenton Crosman, 1930–1968.* Ottawa: Canadian Immigration Historical Society, 1989.

Cull, Nicholas. *Selling War: The British Campaign Against American Neutrality in World War II.* New York: Oxford University Press, 1995.

Danys, Milda. *DP: Lithuanian Immigration to Canada after the Second World War.* Toronto: Multicultural History Society of Ontario, 1986.

Delsan-AIM. "Gare Maritime Champlain Deconstruction." http://www.delsan-aim.com/en/projects/gare-maritime-champlain/.

Dirks, Gerald E. *Canada's Refugee Policy: Indifference or Opportunism?* Montreal: McGill-Queen's University Press, 1977.

Draper, Alfred. *Operation Fish: Race to Save Europe's Wealth, 1939–45.* Don Mills, ON: General Publishing, 1979.

Draper, Paula J. "The 'Camp Boys': Interned Refugees from Nazism." In *Enemies Within: Italian and Other Internees in Canada and Abroad*, edited by Angelo Principe, Roberto Perin, and Franca Iacovetta, 171–93. Toronto: University of Toronto Press, 2000.

Dreisziger, Nandor F. "The Refugee Experience in Canada and the Evolution of the Hungarian-Canadian Community." In *Breaking Ground: The 1956 Hungarian Refugee Movement to Canada*, edited by Robert H. Keyserlingk, 65–86. Toronto: York Lanes Press, 1993.

Dreisziger, Nandor F., M. L. Kovacs, Paul Body, and Bennett Kovrig. *Struggle and Hope: The Hungarian-Canadian Experience*. Toronto: McClelland and Stewart, 1982.

Epp, Marlene. *Refugees in Canada: A Brief History*. Ottawa: Canadian Historical Association, 2017.

Fethney, Michael. *The Absurd and the Brave: CORB – The True Account of the British Government's World War II Evacuation of Children Overseas*. Sussex, UK: The Book Guild, 2000.

Fields, Harold. "Closing Immigration Throughout the World." *American Journal of International Law*, vol. 26, no. 4 (October 1932): 671–99.

Fingard, Judith, Janet Guildford, and David Sutherland. *Halifax: The First 250 Years*. Halifax: Formac Publishing, 1999.

Forbes, Ernest. *The Maritime Rights Movement, 1919–1927: A Study in Canadian Regionalism*. Montreal: McGill-Queen's University Press, 1979.

———. "The Origins of the Maritime Rights Movement." *Acadiensis*, vol. 5, no. 1 (October 1975): 54–66.

Gebhard, Krzystof M. "Polish Veterans as Farm Labourers in Canada, 1946–49." *Oral History Forum* 9 (1989): 13–16.

Halstead, Claire. "'Dangers behind, pleasures ahead': British-Canadian identity and the evacuation of British children to Canada during the Second World War." *British Journal of Canadian Studies*, vol. 27, no. 2 (2014): 163–79.

Halifax International Airport Authority. "History of Halifax [Stanfield] International Airport." https://halifaxstanfield.ca/wp-content/uploads/2015/12/History-in-English1.pdf.

Hawkins, Freda. *Canada and Immigration: Public Policy and Public Concern*. Kingston, ON: McGill-Queen's University Press, 1988.

Hidas, Peter I. "Canada and the Hungarian Jewish Refugees, 1956–57." *East European Jewish Affairs*, vol. 37, no. 1 (April 2007): 75–89.

Hillmer, Norman. *O.D. Skelton: A Portrait of Canadian Ambition*. Toronto: University of Toronto Press, 2015.

Hutten, Anne van Arragon. *Uprooted: the Story of Dutch Immigrant Children in Canada, 1947–1959*. Kentville, NS: North Mountain Press, 2001.

Institute of the Sisters of Service of Canada. "Pier 21 in Halifax." http://sistersofservice.ca/pier-21.html.

Jarratt, Melynda. "The War Brides of New Brunswick." MA thesis, University of New Brunswick, 1995.

Jewish Immigrant Aid Services of Canada. "JIAS Canada: Our History." http://jias.org/history.pdf.

Kage, Joseph. "The Settlement of Hungarian Refugees in Canada." In *Breaking Ground: The 1956 Hungarian Refugee Movement to Canada*, edited by Robert H. Keyserlingk, 99–108. Toronto: York Lanes Press, 1993.

Kelley, Ninette, and Michael Trebilcock. *The Making of the Mosaic: A History of Canadian Immigration Policy*. Toronto: University of Toronto Press, 2010.

Keyserlingk, Robert H. "Introduction." In *Breaking Ground: The 1956 Hungarian Refugee Movement to Canada*, edited by Robert H. Keyserlingk, vii-x. Toronto: York Lanes Press, 1993.

Knowles, Valerie. *Forging Our Legacy: Canadian Immigration and Citizenship, 1900–1977.* Ottawa: Public Works and Government Services, 2000.

———. *Strangers at Our Gates: Canadian Immigration and Immigration Policy, 1540–2015.* Toronto: Dundurn Press, 2016.

Koch, Eric. *Deemed Suspect: A Wartime Blunder.* Toronto: Methuen Publishing, 1980.

Lappin, Ben. *The Redeemed Children: The Story of the Rescue of War Orphans by the Jewish Community of Canada.* Toronto: University of Toronto Press, 1963.

Madokoro, Laura. "Good Material: Canada and the Prague Spring Refugees." *Refuge: Canada's Journal on Refugees*, vol. 26, no. 1 (2010): 161–71.

———. "Remembering the Voyage of the St. Louis." http://activehistory.ca/2017/02/remembering-the-voyage-of-the-st-louis/.

Mannik, Lynda. *Photography, Memory, and Refugee Identity: The Voyage of the SS Walnut, 1948.* Vancouver: University of British Columbia Press, 2013.

Margolian, Howard. *Unauthorized Entry: The Truth about Nazi War Criminals in Canada, 1946–1956.* Toronto: University of Toronto Press, 2000.

McIntosh, Dave. *The Collectors: A History of Canadian Customs and Excise.* Toronto: NC Press Limited, 1984.

Mitic, Trudy Duivenvoorden, and J. P. LeBlanc. *Pier 21: The Gateway that Changed Canada.* Halifax: Nimbus Publishing, 2011.

Naftel, William. *Halifax at War: Searchlights, Squadrons and Submarines, 1939–1945.* Halifax: Formac Publishing, 2008.

Ogilvie, Sarah, and Scott Miller. *Refuge Denied: The St. Louis Passengers and the Holocaust.* Madison: University of Wisconsin Press, 2006.

O'Hara, Peggy. *From Romance to Reality: Stories of Canadian WWII War Brides.* Cobalt, ON: Highway Book Shop, 1985.

Pagé, J.D. "Medical Examination of Immigrants to Canada." *British Medical Journal*, vol. 1, no. 3675 (1931): 1040–41.

Raska, Jan. *Czech Refugees in Cold War Canada: 1945–1989.* Winnipeg: University of Manitoba Press, 2018.

———. "Food Wars! Immigration and Food Confiscation at Pier 21." Canadian Museum of Immigration Blog. https://www.pier21.ca/blog/jan-raska/food-wars-immigration-and-food-confiscation-at-pier-21.

Renaud, Anne. *Pier 21: Stories from Near and Far.* Vancouver: Whitecap Books, 2015.

Roberts, Barbara. *Whence They Came: Deportation from Canada, 1900–1935.* Ottawa: University of Ottawa Press, 1988.

Schwinghamer, Steven. "'Altogether Unsatisfactory': Revisiting the Opening of the Immigration Facility at Halifax's Pier 21." *Journal of the Royal Nova Scotia Historical Society* 15 (2012): 61–74.

———. "Early Facility History." Unpublished report. Canadian Museum of Immigration, 2009. Word document.

Shephard, Ben. *The Long Road Home: The Aftermath of the Second World War.* London: Bodley Head, 2010.

Smith, Carrie-Ann. "We'll Meet Again: The Gracie Fields Story." Canadian Museum of Immigration Blog. http://www.pier21.ca/blog/carrie-ann-smith/we-ll-meet-again-the-gracie-fields-story.

Smith, Douglas. "Bringing Home the Wounded: Canadian Hospital Cars in the Two World Wars." In *Canadian Rail Passenger Yearbook, 1996–1997.* Ottawa: Trackside Canada, 1997.

Swager, Gordon. *The Strange Odyssey of Poland's National Treasures, 1939–1961*. Toronto: Dundurn Press, 2004.

Taylor, Lynne. *Polish Orphans of Tengeru: The Dramatic Story of their Long Journey to Canada, 1941–49*. Toronto: Dundurn Press, 2010.

Thompson, Alexa, and Debi van de Wiel. *Pier 21: An Illustrated History of Canada's Gateway*. Halifax: Nimbus Publishing, 2002.

Tinkham, Jennifer. "Lasting Impressions: The Volunteers of Pier 21." Canadian Museum of Immigration. https://www.pier21.ca/sites/default/files/uploads/files/research_lasting_impressions.pdf.

Vancouver Holocaust Education Centre. "Open Hearts, Closed Doors: Welcome to Canada." http://www.virtualmuseum.ca/sgc-cms/expositions-exhibitions/orphelins-orphans/english/themes/welcome/page1.html.

Vineberg, Robert. "Healthy Enough to Get In: The Evolution of Canadian Immigration Policy Related to Immigrant Health." *Journal of International Migration and Integration* 16.2 (2015): 279–97.

Weinfeld, Morton. "Jews." In *Encyclopedia of Canada's Peoples*, edited by Paul Robert Magocsi, 860–81. Toronto: University of Toronto Press, 1999.

Whitaker, Reginald. *Canadian Immigration Policy since Confederation*. Ottawa: Canadian Historical Association, 1991.

Wyman, Mark. *DPs: Europe's Displaced Persons, 1945–1951*. Utica, NY: Cornell University Press, 1989.

Znaimer, Moses. "D.P. with a Future." In *Passages: Welcome Home to Canada*, edited by Michael Ignatieff, 181–99. Toronto: Doubleday Canada, 2011.

———. "Our Remnant of a Family." In *The Land Newly Found: Eyewitness Accounts of the Canadian Immigrant Experience*, edited by Norman Hillmer and J.L. Granatstein, 233–39. Toronto: Thomas Allen, 2006.

INDEX